MARY WEIR was born in Yorkshire and Educated at the University of Hull where she gained a B.Sc. (Econ.) degree. Subsequently she undertook research posts in British Rail (1965-66); Department of Sociology, University of Manchester (1966-67); and the Board of Trade (1967-69), and since 1969 she has been a Research Fellow at Manchester Business School. She is working on studies of the relationship between job satisfaction and technology, particularly computer systems, and has lectured widely and published many articles on this subject.

48

Job Satisfaction

Challenge and Response
in Modern Britain

Edited by Mary Weir

Fontana/Collins

First published in Fontana 1976
Copyright © in the introduction and original material
Mary Weir 1976

This book is published in association with the Fontana
Modern Britain Series

Set in 9pt Monotype Times
Made and printed in Great Britain by
William Collins Sons & Co. Ltd Glasgow

Contents

Acknowledgements

I would like to thank all those people who have helped me in the preparation of this book, with ideas, encouragement and more practical help. In particular, I wish to thank Enid Mumford and my colleagues in the Computer and Work Design Research Unit at Manchester Business School, whose enthusiasm for the subject has been a constant source of inspiration; the secretarial assistance of Emily Stephenson and Kay Ansbro was especially valuable.

My greatest debt is to David whose help, both as editor of the Modern Britain Series and as my husband, has been that of a real partner.

December 1974   MARY WEIR

1 Introduction

For millions of people work is the least rewarding aspect of life. The hours spent at the work bench or in the office are more likely to be hours of endurance than enjoyment, when people do jobs which provide few opportunities to use their skills and abilities. A sense of personal satisfaction and achievement is more likely to be associated with their lives outside work than within it.

The aim of this book is to look at the efforts which are being made in Britain to seek ways of increasing the level of job satisfaction. Of course, a major problem is to define precisely what is meant by 'job satisfaction'. Most people, and indeed most research workers, use their own definition of job satisfaction, in terms of the particular aspects which they regard as most important. Unfortunately, this makes it difficult to compare the various studies which have been made, and to relate the views of different people, though they are all dealing with the same basic concepts.

The definitions and concepts used by social scientists for over twenty-five years were drawn together in 1964 by Vroom in his study, *Work and Motivation*. He found that the terms job satisfaction and job attitudes were often used interchangeably, but both referred to 'affective orientations on the part of individuals toward work roles which they are presently occupying'. The outcome of the research he reviewed was a general picture of a 'satisfying work role' which appeared to be one which provides high pay, substantial promotional opportunities, considerate and participative supervision, an opportunity to interact with one's colleagues, varied duties and a high degree of control over work methods and work pace. It seems reasonable to assume that these things are also likely to be conducive to job satisfaction at the present time, and that this definition will be valid for most of the material in this book.

Concern with job satisfaction is nothing new, though it has taken rather different directions over the last ten years. Since the Industrial Revolution, writers have been decrying the use of fragmented, meaningless tasks brought about by the division of labour and specialization, as being basically alienating and dehumanizing. The craftsmanship of earlier generations has been replaced by machines with human appendages, there to serve the technology rather than control it. For many people, work is no longer a creative activity, providing its own satisfactions, but a monotonous necessity in which there is no choice and no autonomy. Marx expressed this clearly when he wrote:

> What constitutes the alienation of labour? First, that the work is *external* to the worker, that it is not part of his nature; and that, consequently, he does not fulfil himself in his work but denies himself, has a feeling of misery rather than well-being, does not develop freely his mental and physical energies but is physically exhausted and mentally debased. The worker, therefore, feels himself at home only during his leisure time, whereas at work he feels homeless. His work is not voluntary but imposed, *forced labour*. It is not satisfying other needs. (*Karl Marx: Selected Writings in Sociology and Social Philosophy*, edited by T. B. Bottomore and M. Rubel, C. A. Watts & Co., 1963, pp. 169–70.)

Marx saw the source of this alienation as being in the existing conditions of production which dehumanize the worker, by reducing his specifically human qualities to the quantitative, interchangeable value of money. He concluded that alienation cannot be overcome while productive relations reduce social relationships to the level of a relationship between objects, and economists forget the essentially human element in production.

This analysis has been developed by Blauner in *Alienation and Freedom*, in which he sought to determine under what conditions the alienating tendencies identified by Marx are intensified in modern industry and what situations give rise to different forms of alienation. He showed that the particular industry in which a person worked 'greatly influences the extent to which he is free in his work life and the extent to which he is controlled by technology or supervision. It also influences his opportunity for personal growth and development – to learn, to advance, to take on responsibility.'

Blauner identifies four aspects of alienation – powerlessness, meaninglessness, isolation and self-estrangement – which vary in form and intensity, according to the specific conditions of industrial technology and the division of labour. He suggests that alienation is at its lowest level and the worker's freedom at a maximum in craft industry but that with the introduction of machine-based industry and in particular the assembly line, the level of alienation rises sharply and freedom declines. However, with the increase of automated industry, especially continuous process technology, the worker's control over his work process actually increases, with a resulting decline in his degree of alienation, as his work becomes more meaningful and respon-sible, giving him a sense of individual function.

Blauner's findings are borne out by other research studies which highlight the importance of technology in determining working behaviour. For instance, Woodward examined the relationship between the production system and other aspects of organizational structure such as the degree of specialization of functions, the span of control, the number of hierarchical levels and staff–worker ratios. She classified production systems broadly into three categories: unit and small batch; large batch, assembly and mass production; and process production. These broadly correspond to the categories which Blauner used. Woodward also found a considerable degree of similarity between the extremes of the scale, with the middle category being distinct on most of the variables she studied. It seems that in unit production systems there may be considerable latitude in the way the tech-nical operations are performed, while under process production, the manufacturing process itself largely dictates the operating procedures which are necessary. Both these types of production systems are likely to provide pleasanter and more satisfying working situations than those in the middle of the technical scale, where 'production control procedures were most elaborate and sanctions most rigorously applied'.

The middle range of the technical scale identified by Woodward, has been the main area of interest of, and in its contemporary form has been largely created by, the philosophy generally called Scientific Management. This was the term used by Fred-erick Taylor in 1911 to describe the methods of work measure-ment which he advocated to identify the 'quickest and best movements as well as the best implements' for doing each job. This one new method was then to be substituted for the ten or fifteen inferior series of movements which were previously used, and was to become standard and remain standard. Taylor's methods were widely adopted in industry, but unfortunately not always with the results which he intended. He hoped that rather than reducing a person to 'a mere automaton, a wooden man', his methods would enable him 'to do a much higher, more interesting, and finally more developing and more profitable kind of work than he was before able to do'. Perhaps Taylor's followers did not heed his own warning that the 'mechanism of management must not be mistaken for its essence or underlying philosophy. Precisely the same mechanism will in one case produce disastrous results and in another the most beneficient.' Nearly fifty years later, one of the main conclusions of the South Essex studies conducted by Woodward, was that 'the same principles can produce different results in different circumstances', thus restoring a more realistic perspective to the application of classical management principles and to the area of their validity.

During those fifty years, of course, a great deal of research work had been undertaken and many practical approaches tried out, to offset the worst consequences of rationalized and fragmented work, and to reduce the resulting alienation.

The Hawthorne studies, done at the Western Electric plants in Chicago by Mayo and his colleagues, highlighted the inadequacy of Scientific Management in treating the worker as an isolated individual and ignoring his relationship with his fellow workers. In a series of experiments, the physical conditions and working environment were altered and the effects on productivity were monitored. It was found that output increased, even when the changes in fact made conditions worse. The researchers concluded that the social relations at work, and in particular the influence of the immediate work group, played a greater part in determining behaviour than the physical environment or the control systems set up by management. In particular, they argued that workers gain meaning from their work through their relationships with others and derive their standards of behaviour from the work group, which exerts pressure on its members to conform.

As a result of these studies came the 'human relations'

policies for improving the lot of the worker. They advocated the development of a supportive environment in which inter-personal relationships could develop and provide meaningful social contacts to offset the detrimental effects of their work. Open communication and awareness of the feelings of the workers as people, were encouraged among supervision and management. They were to adopt, in McGregor's terms, a Theory Y approach, in which their main task was to encourage rather than push their subordinates, and to develop their capacities rather than to merely provide financial rewards.

There was interest too in another approach, which concentrated on the psychology of the individual, and looked at the motivation of the individual and the pattern of individual differences. The focus of many of these studies was to develop methods of 'fitting the worker to the job', that is to select those people whose skills, abilities and personalities made them particularly suited to the jobs for which they were applying. The National Institute of Industrial Psychology, in particular, is well-known for its early work in this field, especially in the development of work in selection and placement, and the use of counselling techniques. The underlying assumption, of course, is that there are people in the labour market whose skills and expectations are well suited to the jobs available. But, considering the mindless nature of many industrial and clerical jobs, it seems far more likely that people tailor their expectations to suit the jobs available to them, and even then they may be seriously under-using their potential.

In neither the human relations approach nor the development of selection methods were changes to the actual tasks considered. The jobs to be done were taken as given and little thought was directed towards ways in which the jobs themselves might be altered, to make them better suited to the needs and abilities of the workers. Indeed, there are those who would argue that there is such a gap between the jobs which industry has to offer and the needs of the people doing those jobs, that they cannot hope to fulfil their needs at work. They have learned that they can only expect to get financial rewards from work and these become the means to enable them to meet their needs in leisure activities.

The research work done by Goldthorpe and his colleagues at

Vauxhall in Luton tends to support this view. They found that the car workers there seemed to derive little intrinsic satisfaction from their work. In fact, in performing their work tasks they tended to experience monotony and physical tiredness and had to work at too fast a pace. These conditions were directly related to the characteristic features of assembly-line jobs, in particular the minute sub-division of tasks, repetitiveness and mechanically paced work. Consequently, the car workers stayed in their jobs chiefly through the extrinsic economic rewards which it afforded them. A third of them said that the level of pay was the *only* reason that they remained in their present work and three quarters gave this as the main reason. Work was for them primarily a means to ends outside the work situation. They were prepared to put up with a generally unsatisfying and stressful work situation, in order to enjoy a high standard of living outside.

However, Goldthorpe stressed that this instrumental view of their jobs should not primarily be seen as a consequence of the work they were doing. In fact, most of the men had become car assemblers because of a desire on their part to achieve high economic returns from work. They were prepared to forego satisfactions from work of an intrinsic kind, in order to achieve the extrinsic rewards which they desired. In other words, their instrumental orientation had led them to their present jobs rather than *vice versa*.

Of course the car assembly line is generally regarded as the extreme case of fragmented, repetitive work, and has become the classic symbol of the subjection of men to machines. The car industry has suffered extensively from strikes, disorders, and open conflict between management and workers, and many would see this as an inevitable result of the privations suffered by those doing this type of work. It is suggested that the only solution to the problem is to follow policies which will reduce the likely sources of conflict to a minimum. Careful attention to grievance procedures and wage-payment systems and acceptance of the inevitable uncertainty of the situation are the usual responses to such situations.

However, though many work situations have some of the unpleasant features of the car assembly line, there is often scope for a more constructive approach than merely a policy of avoidance. A movement has been gradually emerging which advocates a positive and creative approach to the problems resulting from work environments in which workers lose their sense of identity and have few opportunities for control or self expression. The movement may be broadly described as a concern for workers to have a much greater degree of participation in decisions which affect their work.

In the last ten years or so, there has been an extensive discussion on the need for people to participate more in the running of society and the institutions which affect them, for example, students participate in the running of their colleges and local groups have a greater say in planning decisions which affect them. The question of workers' participation in management is just one aspect of this wide-ranging move towards greater participation, but it seems to offer more hope of improving the 'quality of working life' than some of the other approaches tried in the past.

There are four broad arguments usually put forward in support of greater participation by workers. Clarke, Fatchett and Roberts have suggested that

'greater participation is desirable
1. as a means of promoting the satisfaction and personal development of the individual worker;
2. on the ground that workers should have a greater say in decision-making at work, as a means of extending democracy from the political to the industrial sphere;
3. as a means of improving industrial relations;
4. as a means of increasing efficiency.'

Clearly, great things are expected of 'participation', but as these authors point out, the discussion rarely makes clear what form of participation is envisaged, in what type of decision, and at what level. They distinguish between two main approaches to participation, which they characterize as power-centred and task-centred. It may be helpful to quote their definitions of these two approaches to participation.

Participation that is power-centred aims at extending the bargaining power of the workers within the enterprise and at making managerial decision-makers more accountable either to the unions or directly to the workers. The ultimate objective of some supporters of power-centred participation is to change the fundamental authority relationship in industry as a means of changing the character of society.

The task-centred approach emphasizes participation as a device likely to increase job satisfaction, and with it productivity, and also to improve industrial relations, thereby facilitating the attainment of managerially set goals for the enterprise . . . An increasing body of management literature has been concerned with the creation of an organizational pattern in which workers are permitted to exercise a greater degree of control over their work environment and performance.

There are, then, many different methods and levels of participation, and it is beyond the scope of this book to consider them all. The main concern of the book is the task-centred approach to participation, and the way this is being adopted in Britain.

The two main theoretical bases of this approach to increasing job satisfaction stem mainly from psychology and industrial engineering:

1. The development of ideas of 'job enrichment' by Herzberg and his colleagues from the early work on human needs by Maslow.
2. The job design studies, done in the United States under the name of job design, largely by Louis Davis; and in Britain, the research done on socio-technical systems mainly at the Tavistock Institute.

On the basis of interviews to discuss the events which led to a marked improvement, or a marked reduction, in job satisfaction, Herzberg developed the theory, which has become known as the Motivation–Hygiene theory. He showed that job satisfaction and job dissatisfaction are not, as is often assumed, opposite ends of a single continuum but do in fact result from entirely different factors in the work situation. The major factors associated with job satisfaction, which he called 'Motivators', describe the relationship with what the worker does in his job: his job content, achievement of a task, recognition for achieving a task, responsibility for a task, and professional advancement or improvement in ability to do a task. On the other hand, the major factors associated with job dissatisfaction describe the work environment: the kind of administration and supervision, the nature of interpersonal relationships, working conditions and salary. Herzberg called these the 'Hygiene' factors, and concluded that they could prevent job dissatisfaction but could not, in fact, contribute positively towards increased job satisfaction. He advocated that, where possible, jobs should be restructured to include a high proportion of those factors which he identified as motivators, so long as attention had also been paid to reducing the dissatisfying effects of the hygiene factors. This approach has come to be known as 'job enrichment or vertical job enlargement'. For instance, jobs can be 'enriched' by making either the individual or the group responsible for tasks dealing with the planning, control and inspection of the work. In addition, the care and maintenance of machinery may be done by the worker, who may also be given more control over the methods and pace of work. Of course, every situation is different and these changes may not always be possible, and some people may not wish to take on these additional responsibilities. However, the improvements can contribute a great deal to giving people more control over their own work and a higher level of satisfaction.

The other main basis of the task-centred approach to participation is derived from the work of Louis Davis in the USA, and the Tavistock Institute in Britain. Davis has attacked the conventional concept of job satisfaction because he says 'it is almost exclusively concerned with adaptation to jobs that, in the post-industrial context, begin to seem fundamentally unsuited for man. The study of job satisfaction has come to be the study of the minimal gratifications possible under deprived conditions.' He suggests that new technology is bringing in a new system of social and organizational values. Machines are gradually taking over a greater part of work and in the future people will be needed to undertake the 'non-programmable' activities, which cannot be done by the machines. They will be called on to deal with situations where there are many exceptions or variations, with which they can cope better than machines. Davis suggests that such jobs will require skills, job contents, and organizational structures quite different from the ones seen at present. Advanced technology removes man's conventional work role and requires him to make 'self-directed decisions' to deal with unexpected variations.

The concept of the 'socio-technical system' is valuable in

considering how to adapt to these changing circumstances. The socio-technical approach was developed by research workers at the Tavistock Institute in London, led by Trist, and is now widely used in industrial and business organizations as well as by social scientists. In essence, the theory sees an organization as consisting of independent technological and social systems operating jointly to achieve the purposes of the organization. This leads to the idea of joint optimization, which is central to the approach. When two independent but closely connected systems, such as the technical and social systems, must work together to achieve a particular objective, then it is impossible to achieve the best overall performance, without trying to optimize these connected systems jointly.

The theories of job design and socio-technical systems have highlighted three main categories of job requirements. Firstly, jobs must be designed so that the people doing them have some autonomy and are allowed to regulate and control their own work. In particular, some preparatory and control activities must be incorporated into the total work process, along with the accomplishment of the main task. Secondly, the job must encourage the individual to adapt, by enabling him to learn from what is going on around him, so he can grow and develop. He should be able to set his own standards of quantity and quality of performance, and get information of his performance over time. Lastly, there should be a wide range of tasks to provide variety in the job. In addition, the tasks within a job should form an overall pattern, reflecting the interdependence of the individual job and the wider production system. The tasks should also help to build and maintain the interdependence between the organization and the individual, who should be able to feel that his job is sufficiently meaningful to give him status within the community.

The application of these ideas is sometimes associated with another main theme of the research of the Tavistock Institute which deals with autonomous work groups. Where these are established, a group of workers is given responsibility for a complete area of work. The group is usually responsible for planning and organizing the work, problem-solving and quality control. The members of the group are interdependent and often some form of job rotation is operated, where they move round between the different tasks. The autonomous work group system has the advantage that the group itself has considerable control over its own work, is flexible enough to meet unexpected variations, and increases the job interest of the individual members.

A system of working which is very similar to that suggested by the Tavistock Institute is often created by the introduction of group technology into engineering workshops. In these cases, the machines themselves are grouped together into 'families' of machines dealing with components which require similar operations. The 'cells' formed in this way may each be manned by a group of ten to twelve men who are responsible for all the operations performed by that group of machines. They may be given responsibility for the planning and control of all the tasks carried out within the cell, as well as some responsibility for the maintenance of the machines. The system encourages flexibility and rotation of tasks between the men, as well as creating a group identity closely associated with a well-defined product.

The general term 'task-based participation' clearly covers a wide range of different methods of working, which must be adapted to the particular circumstances of each group of workers and each organization. Already, many experiments and projects have been carried out using these ideas, particularly in the USA and Europe, especially Scandinavia. For example, in the USA such companies as IBM, American Telephone and Telegraph, Texas Instruments and Bell Telephone have undertaken such projects; in Europe Philips, Volkswagen, Fiat and Olivetti are well known for their experiments; but perhaps the experiments which are most widely known are those undertaken in the Scandinavian countries, especially at Volvo and Saab.

Of all the companies which have introduced ways of increasing job satisfaction through greater task-based participation, Volvo's work has perhaps been the most far reaching. In response to a high rate of turnover and increasing difficulty in recruiting new employees, Volvo embarked on an ambitious programme to increase their employees' motivation and job satisfaction, by giving them greater responsibility, and involving them in decisions affecting their work, as well as improving the physical surroundings. An important part of improving the jobs at Volvo was the creation of small work groups which are responsible for the assembly of a complete section of the vehicle, such as the truck cab or the brakes and wheels. The size of each work group varies between three and twelve members, depending on the particular tasks involved. The group's tasks are allocated a few days in advance and the group members are responsible for organizing production, dividing the work between themselves and controlling the overall work pattern. The group elects a leader who becomes the spokesman for the group, to liaise with the foreman. A monthly meeting is held, consisting of the spokesman, some other members of the group, the production engineer and the foreman, to discuss questions about work patterns, equipment and tools as well as problems which have arisen, and general information. Job rotation has been introduced in many areas so that an individual may do several different work tasks, from assembly work up to inspection, and this introduces some variety into the jobs; a training programme has been introduced to give people the necessary additional skills. Some job enlargement schemes have also been used in Volvo, where the number of tasks completed by each operator is increased, to lengthen the cycle time of the task performed. Of course, neither job rotation nor job enlargement add planning and control tasks to the main task to be performed, since they only involve moving round tasks which are similar, or performing several similar tasks together. However, they do provide some relief from the highly specialized and repetitive tasks often associated with car assembly.

Volvo's most ambitious project is the building of two new plants with work systems designed to maximize the work group concept. The assembly line has been abolished, and the plants have been designed so that each work team has its own working area or 'bay' with rest room, changing rooms and buffer stocks separating them from other teams, to allow them to vary their pace of work. Of course, the construction of a plant along these lines has cost considerably more than a conventional assembly line layout would. However, the Volvo management feel that this additional investment will be well worthwhile in its contribution to improvements in job satisfaction.

But, exciting as these developments are, many question marks remain. For instance, a question which is often raised in discussions is how relevant are such ideas to the situation in Britain. Experiments have given encouraging results in the USA, Europe and Scandinavia, and indeed in Britain, too, some of the major companies such as ICI, Shell, and BOC are adopting ideas and policies similar to those of Volvo. As yet though, the proportion of workers affected by such projects is very small. Naturally, managers, trade unionists and workers alike are hesitant to embark on something as far reaching as the new philosophy and new methods of working suggested by some of the advocates of task-centred participation, and their caution is understandable. No philosophy or set of principles can be a complete panacea, particularly when circumstances and technologies change so rapidly. Nevertheless, it seems from the studies done so far, that such ideas can contribute to increasing job satisfaction, and the quality of working life, especially where fragmented, meaningless work has created boredom and alienation.

The aim of this book is to present an overview of the various ideas and methods on which task-centred participation is based, and to look at some of the ways these ideas are being applied in Britain. A wide range of different ideas and cases are included so that the reader can decide for himself whether these ideas are in fact of value for British industry, and perhaps for his own particular situation. An outline of the structure of the rest of the book may be helpful in enabling the reader to cope with the material easily. Chapter Two looks at the case for trying to improve 'the quality of working life'. In particular, the changing expectations of people and the need for some new philosophy as a basis for responding to such changes are considered; Chapter Three traces the development of some of the theoretical ideas on which the current studies are based; in Chapter Four the work experiences of people doing various different jobs are considered; some of the work being done by British research workers in this area is outlined in Chapter Five; Chapter Six looks at several case studies projects to improve jobs which have been undertaken in British of organizations; finally, Chapter Seven attempts to put these ideas into perspective, by considering how relevant they are, particularly to the British situation. Each chapter is followed by a further reading list, so that when the reader has considered which, if any, of the approaches are particularly interesting and relevant to his own situation, he may explore them more deeply than is possible in the overview presented in this book.

Further Reading: Introduction

D. BIRCHALL AND R. WILD, 'Job Restructuring Amongst Blue-collar Workers', *Personnel Review*, Vol. 2, No. 2, 1973.*

R. BLAUNER, *Alienation and Freedom: the factory worker and his industry*, Chicago, University of Chicago Press, 1964.

R. O. CLARKE, D. J. FATCHETT AND B. C. ROBERTS, *Workers' Participation in Management in Britain*, London, Heinemann, 1972.

L. E. DAVIS AND J. C. TAYLOR (Eds.) *Design of Jobs*, London, Penguin, 1972.

J. W. DICKSON, 'What's in a job', *Personnel Management*, June 1971, Vol. 3, No. 6, pp. 38–40.*

J. H. GOLDTHORPE, D. LOCKWOOD, F. BECHOFER AND J. PLATT, *The Affluent Worker: Industrial Attitudes and Behaviour*, Cambridge, Cambridge University Press, 1968.

F. HERZBERG, *Work and the Nature of Man*, London, Staples Press, 1968.

V. H. VROOM, *Work and Motivation*, New York, Wiley, 1964.

J. WOODWARD, *Industrial Organisation: Theory and Practice*, Oxford, Oxford University Press, 1965.

* These two references include useful definitions of terms used in this subject area.

2 The Quality of Working Life

During the past decade, there has been a gradually increasing
awareness of the importance of job satisfaction, and of the
possibility of taking positive steps to improve jobs. One manifestation of this trend was the publication of a report commis-
sioned by the Department of Employment from N. A. B.
Wilson, entitled *On the Quality of Working Life*. The occasion
was marked by the announcement by the then Secretary of
State for Employment, Maurice Macmillan, of the setting up
of a tripartite steering group on job satisfaction made up of
representatives from the Government, the CBI and the TUC.
He asked the group to 'consider ideas for improving satisfaction which people derive from their work', and if possible
to initiate work which would draw on current experience and
stimulate a wider understanding of what can and should be
done to improve the quality of working life. The chairman
of the steering group was **Robin Chichester-Clark**, at that time
Minister of State for Employment. He is the author of the
first article, in which he outlines the reasons for the setting up
of the tripartite steering group and some of their early work
and conclusions.

He suggests that 'the most compelling argument for asking
British industry and commerce to take job satisfaction seriously
. . . is to be found in the forty or fifty well-documented cases
of change in work or work organization . . . which have
shown that job satisfaction can be increased'. This present
book may help to bring these ideas to a wider audience, and
therefore assist in Chichester Clark's call for an effort to speed
up the dissemination of knowledge about what is being
achieved.

The initiative to improve jobs has also been taken up within
the Civil Service itself, and the author of the second reading,
Keith Robertson, has been closely concerned following his
earlier work on experiments carried out in ICI (see Chapter Six).
In this article, he traces the social and economic changes in

Britain over the last twenty years and argues that we are now in the early stages of a revolution in our outlook on the employment of people in industry. The need for this change in attitudes is felt among management and workers alike. 'No longer is it only humanitarians and radicals who wish to change the industrial system, it is managers.' Theoretical ideas are being applied in practical situations more and more, and a new approach to the management of people is being developed.

Many of the ideas being used by managers are derived from industrial psychology and the third reading discusses the role of the psychologist in the movement towards creating better working lives. **Albert Cherns** is himself closely involved with the International Council for the Quality of Working Life, which is dedicated to the cause of promoting the values of Life in Work. Cherns challenges the conventional measures of productivity and methods of costing as being far too arbitrary. He argues that the costs and burdens of under-using people's capacities are borne not by the organizations employing them, but by the community as a whole. The community has invested in education for its members, and might expect a return in the form of income, and participation in its activities. Instead it may be involved in providing support or retraining for those who cannot cope with or are unwanted by the industrial system. Cherns suggests that the psychologist's concern with job satisfaction is as valid as the accountant's concern with productivity. Yet even among accountants the subject of job satisfaction is being taken seriously. In an article in *The Accountant* entitled 'Industrial Democracy and Job Satisfaction' (6 September 1973) the author says 'It is the huge industrial combines where division of labour has reduced the job to boringly repetitive activities . . . that our energies need to be harnessed to finding ways and means of creating an atmosphere in which workers can find an interest in the work itself.' No doubt accountants will continue to use economic measures of job satisfaction, but it is valuable that they are using the concept in their work.

Finally, **Frank Heller** continues the discussion on the under-use and misuse of people's skills and abilities. He argues that there are technical, social and psychological barriers which prevent these skills from being used to the fullest extent. He gives examples of these barriers from all levels of the organization, and suggests that this concept may be valuable in understanding important current problems resulting from ineffective utilization of skilled manpower such as the so-called 'technological gap'.

On the Quality of Working Life

Robin Chichester-Clark

Reprinted with permission from *Personnel Management*, Vol. 5, No. 11, November 1973, pp. 26–9.

Like any other aspect of human activity, industrial relations is susceptible to changes of fashion – or, as some would say, fads. The current preoccupation is probably employee participation. But coming up hard on the rails is, if not its half brother, a fairly close relative. This is the area covered by such terms as job satisfaction, job enrichment or job enlargement. And those who are taking a close interest in this development, tend to think that what they are broadly concerned with is the quality of working life.

The trouble with all fashions in all walks of life is that they spawn a jargon of their own. This is frequently off-putting. It certainly – and understandably – breeds scepticism. It also tends to be confusing. The resultant fog can often obscure from public view what, to prolong the racing metaphor, is a genuine stayer.

Even the most common terms may be used by different people to mean rather different things. It is therefore, perhaps, important that at the outset I should give some indication of the sense or senses in which the more common terms are used.

The obvious starting point is job satisfaction. This term is concerned with the job from the point of view of the individual doing it. But to speak of a job as 'satisfying', or one that 'gives satisfaction', can only mean at the most that it appears to satisfy the generality of people doing it. The term has, in fact, traditionally been used in a general way to convey the extent to which people are content with their overall work situation – for example, with such aspects of the job as pay, relations with managers and supervisors, physical conditions and the convenience of its location as well as with the job itself.

More recently, however, it has been given an extra dimension relating specifically to the satisfactions (or dissatisfactions) which flow from the job itself and the way in which it is organized.

Moreover, the more common terms currently in use relate to job satisfaction in this sense.

Let us take, first, 'job enrichment'. This term has come to be closely associated with Professor Frederick Herzberg. As I understand it, Professor Herzberg sees a basic difference between the effect on the individual of the content of his actual job and of aspects of the context in which the job is performed. Poor pay, lack of expected fringe benefits and uncongenial physical conditions are examples of the context in which a job is done and which may contribute to dissatisfaction. Improvements in the context are essential if feelings of irritation and dissatisfaction are to be dispelled. But these measures cannot alter the job as a source of positive satisfaction. To do this, the nature of the work people do, and the way in which it is organized, must be changed.

There are a number of ways in which this has been tackled. The job may be 'enriched' by giving an individual a greater responsibility previously discharged by, say, supervisors – for organizing his work, for example; by ancillary staff – doing inspection, or by involving him in group decisions concerning the planning and organization of the work of his unit.

This is my understanding of the term, though I freely recognize that it is used in at least two senses – one, to cover any changes in the content or organization of a job which may lead to greater satisfaction; and the other, covering even more ground, to embrace measures aimed at increasing the employee's involvement in his firm through various forms of employee participation without necessarily affecting the content of his job.

It follows from this that 'job enlargement' can have a different and fairly precise meaning. This term is normally used to describe changes which increase the variety of tasks to be done by the individual without requiring the exercise of any greater level of skill or responsibility.

'Job rotation' is simply a special form of job enlargement under which workers move between jobs, usually at regular intervals ranging from a few hours to several weeks but sometimes on a more informal basis within a work group.

To recap: my concern in using the term job satisfaction is with the satisfaction to be derived from the *content and organization* of a particular job; job enrichment with *extending the responsibility* of the individual doing the particular job; job enlargement with *increasing the variety of tasks* to be performed; and job rotation with individuals *moving between jobs*.

The need to produce a glossary of the more common terms clearly demonstrates that concern for the satisfaction which people derive from their work is no new phenomenon. Social scientists, have been looking at behaviour at work for most of this century. Consistent evidence has been built up from studies of both work and workers which demonstrates the complexity of the association between satisfaction and performance. This means that there is clearly no single formula or universal panacea for making jobs more satisfying by improving their content.

Why, then, should we have seen a quickening of interest in job satisfaction, leading up to the formation of a tripartite steering group which the TUC and CBI have joined to study the subject?

At one extreme there are, no doubt, those who regard it as common British form – a sort of tribal ritual – to set up a committee to look at any idea, however harebrained. At the other, there may be cynics who see mixed motives in the formation of a tripartite body to examine any facet of human activity at work. Both, of course, overlook, if not ignore, two factors:

1. The right of individual workers to be treated as human beings with feelings and personalities rather than as inanimate units of production.

2. The manifest pressures in advanced industrial societies which arise from basic incompatibilities between social and technological change.

Therefore, I see our new-found national concern with job satisfaction as a genuine and intelligent response to the needs of a dynamic but basically sensitive industrial society. It shows that we recognize the need to explore the possibilities of making work more satisfying for the mass of people if we are to have a better chance of coping with social and technological change.

The need exists for a complex of reasons. We cannot hope – even if it were reasonable to do so – to run industry and commerce indefinitely on the basis of individuals doing repetitive, boring and even soul-destroying tasks. For one thing, men and women coming into workshops and offices are increasingly better educated. Longer full-time education, a quarter of a century of steady economic advance and virtual security from the dispiriting uncertainties of life between the wars have produced a new type of industrial and commercial worker. His – and her – horizons have extended in many directions. They are fuller, more rounded, personalities. Just as their expectations have increased, so have their demands. And these are continuing to grow.

Many people are still prepared to regard work as a means to an end which inevitably has to be borne. Others, armed with enough money to give them a satisfactory life-style, are not prepared to bear it for five days a week. Some may be less inclined to inflict overtime on themselves in spite of the higher reward. And others rebel in a variety of ways which can be expensive. In extreme cases some almost literally drop a spanner in the works.

It is a matter for argument how far this disaffection with the more mindless of modern industrial and commercial processes has gone. It is also difficult to measure it, for we do not know, for example, how far labour turnover reflects dissatisfaction with the content of particular jobs. Equally, we do not know the extent to which different circumstances such as the sex of the workforce, the economic pressures upon workers or their range of industrial choice may cloak or exacerbate genuine dissatisfaction. But what we do know is that the content of jobs is an important facet in determining what people feel about their work and what they do day-by-day at work.

People's willingness to go to work and to work hard and carefully when they are there depends, of course, on a large number of things which are of concern to personnel specialists and which it is their job to attend to. But there is a limit to the contribution which good selection, training, pay scales or sensible disciplinary practices can make.

It is worth, therefore, looking at the other side of the coin and inquiring whether something can be done with the tasks people are expected to perform and the way that these are organized so that the tasks are not entirely determined by the needs of technology, by historical precedents or by commercial necessity.

There is a strong case for regarding some facets of modern methods of working as stressful and a consensus of opinion among experts that these stresses lead to absence, labour turnover and problems in the use of manpower resources. Wilson cites forced, uniform pacing, especially if the pace is high;

repetitiveness and a very short time cycle leading to monotony, triviality and lack of meaning in work; large, impersonal structures of organization, working arrangements and relations; and objectives which seem distant and unreal to the worker.

But it is not merely evidence of dissatisfaction which is accumulating; so are examples of what can be done, at least in the short-term, to remedy the situation. For my part, the most compelling argument for asking British industry and commerce to take job satisfaction seriously is not such theoretical considerations as the incompatibilities between modern technology and workers' expectations, or even of alienation from work in the shape of such things as turnover and reject rates. It is to be found in the forty or fifty well-documented cases of change in work or work organization introduced in this country and abroad which have shown that job satisfaction can be increased – in the sense that the workers concerned at least prefer the new methods and would not revert to the old – while, at the same time, productive efficiency can be maintained or improved.

Changes of this kind have usually taken a long time – often some years – to introduce and have involved hard work on the part of management. Innovations so far have not been on a major scale in terms of the number of workers affected and certainly no one can yet be dogmatic about the best way to tackle these problems. But there is enough hard evidence to warrant an effort to speed up the dissemination of knowledge about what has been – and is being – done and achieved.

Obviously we know of Saab-Scania who claim to be the first modern automobile company to have replaced the straight line in final assembly by teams based on autonomous assembly groups. Similarly, Philips has been experimenting at Eindhoven, Holland, with autonomous production groups instead of television set assembly lines.

ICI and Volvo are other familiar examples in large organizations. But job satisfaction measures have been successfully introduced in Britain by small organizations as well. At one factory employing a few hundred people on assembly of electrical components several straightforward measures have been introduced which have led to reduced labour turnover and absenteeism and an apparent increase in individual job satisfaction.

The changes have included a reorganization of work enabling

some of the more skilful workers to assemble the whole of an item themselves, instead of doing just a small bit of a job on a production line, and the very simple one of re-designing production lines so that employees doing short-cycle repetitive work are able to chat to each other.

Already it is clear that:

1. Successful projects have been characterized by lengthy, careful consideration and open discussion at all levels; by an examination of the effects of changes which are contemplated in other parts of the organization; and by equitable distribution of what benefits eventually accrue.

2. There is agreement in the written evidence that there is little use trying to improve the content and organization of jobs in isolation from other sources of satisfaction including pay. This point, like the one above, is directly relevant to the charge sometimes made that measures to increase job satisfaction are suspect because they may be used as a substitute for collective bargaining.

3. We need to recognize that not everyone wants more responsibility – there have been cases where jobs which have been enlarged have become more stressful and have caused more dissatisfaction.

4. As a corollary of (3) there is the importance of managers analysing the situation which confronts them, recognizing that people are complex beings possessing different sources of motivation and orientation to work and different needs and expectations which may vary for each individual at different periods of his working life.

It may be that broad general principles will emerge for dealing with the repetition, boredom and seeming pointlessness which characterizes some facets of life in workplaces and offices. But it is virtually certain that there are no tailor-made solutions.

Managing People and Jobs

Keith Robertson

Reprinted with permission from *Personnel Management*, Vol. 1, No. 5, September 1969, pp. 20–4.

British industry is in the initial stages of a profound revolution, in which personnel managers have a key role to play at the very centre of events. For what is changing, and will change further, is our whole outlook on the employment of people in industry.

As in any revolution, human values and philosophy, politics and practice are all embroiled; basic assumptions are challenged before alternatives are fully defined; tensions arise between practitioners and theoreticians, between the *avante-garde* and those who have to look after reality. The process is important; we are involved in it, and should understand it as best we can. Nothing is more difficult or more necessary to manage than revolution – if its outcome is to be beneficial. The outcome in this particular case is likely to take some getting used to, but it promises (unless we shirk the issue) to give industry a new role and a new importance in the shaping of our society.

In the nineteenth century, Great Britain's natural resources and domestic markets could sustain strong and successful enterprises; labour was cheap, its bargaining power limited; mechanization provided simple and prescribed tasks for poorly educated people. There was no need for management to concern itself with the issues and the problems of human motivation. Like slaves and peasants in other more distant societies, factory workers were clearly shaped by nature to fulfil their allotted function. Humanitarians and radicals might quibble, but the manager's job was to manage.

These conditions of stability apply less and less in the UK today. While in North America wage-price inflation is only just beginning to threaten the sense of security and permanence which comes from vast natural resources and huge domestic markets, we in Britain have had twenty years in which to adjust ourselves, slowly and painfully, to the realization that our enterprises are no longer automatically strong and successful. To be a wealthy country is not necessarily to be a wealth-producing country.

Statistics may lie, but there comes a time when they can no longer be ignored. For twenty years now, international comparisons have continued to tell the same unpalatable story: gross national product per head already lower than in most other industrial economies, and rising more slowly; wages rising more slowly than elsewhere, but wage cost per unit of output rising faster – due perhaps to our idiosyncrasy of employing between one-and-a-half and four times as many people to do the same work; export prices, in between devaluations, rising faster than our competitors'; and, not surprisingly, our share of world trade inexorably declining. Far from our being second only to the United States among the developed nations of the world – as many still believe – increasingly one has to look to countries like Spain, Greece and Turkey to find a single indicator of economic performance which provides a comparison favourable to the UK.

Mercifully there are other factors in the situation which economic statistics don't reveal, but the message is clear: it is time we came to terms with the realities of our industrial life. What are some of these realities?

First, labour has stopped being cheap and will become ever more expensive. During those same twenty years of inadequate economic performance, the cost of employing people has typically risen by something over 6 per cent per annum compound. When an essential raw material becomes expensive, it makes sense to explore all possible ways in which its yield might be increased, even at the price of changing the organization or modifying the technology. It does not make sense to go on using it as though it were cheap and then to complain about its cost.

Secondly, labour's bargaining power has become immense: not only by virtue of its having become organized, which we are more or less used to now, but also because technological development has been such that small groups are now in a position to disrupt whole industries, and larger groups can hold the country's economy to ransom. Haunted by the spectre of industrial anarchy, it is all too easy to be stampeded into the blind alley of demands for law and order. It is no solution to a problem to pass a law saying that it does not exist. Sooner or later we have to tackle the problem at its root, dealing with causes rather than with symptoms. Those with experience of industrial relations, on both management and union sides, know that the causes of industrial strife are rarely what they appear to be on the surface. People may not be very coherent in their demands, but more often than not it would seem that what is really at issue is not just a specific wage increase or demarcation dispute, but rather the whole industrial mess of poor communication, inadequate human consideration, meaningless procedures, neglected conditions and soul-destroying jobs.

Thirdly, and most important, labour has stopped being labour. The modern industrial workforce is a complex structure in which staff and technicians of various kinds often outnumber the older-style manual workers, and in which unskilled labour may be a relatively unimportant element. It is the classic case of the tail wagging the dog, not only in the matter of strikes, but much more deeply than that, in management thinking.

It is no longer adequate today to take the traditional economist's or industrial engineer's view of labour. In the past, as we noted, mechanization provided simple and prescribed tasks for poorly-educated people. This was a fortunate accident which enabled illiterate peasants to adapt to factory life with the minimum of fuss. Later, when scientific management engineered yet more specialization of labour and simplification of tasks, the accidental became enshrined as the purposeful. But what was accepted by illiterate peasants last century, and put up with by hungry men this century, is not necessarily tolerable today. Nor even necessarily efficient. It no longer provides a model upon which to base our whole approach to the management of people and jobs.

Our experience with productivity agreements is a case in point. So long as we merely deal in the enclosed area of so-called restrictive practices, productivity bargaining in the end becomes counter-productive. It certainly results in more expensive labour, it may well result in labour that is even more resistant to future change. But, if we are lucky, we discover in the process that it is in our management structure where much of the inefficiency lies, that it is management demarcations which restrict initiative and management attitudes which form a barrier to change. If we want flexibility and a sense of responsibility from our workforce, we must create the climate in which such things flourish.

If this is the message from within industry, it is even more urgently the message from outside. It is sensible occasionally to look at what is happening in the wider environment of our society, the society from which we recruit, and which ultimately we serve.

People today enjoy a higher standard of living than their fathers did. A higher standard of living is not just a statistic, it is an experience. People with a different experience have different standards, different aspirations and different values. The point is not that 1969 working-class incomes lead to the adoption of 1939 middle-class attitudes; that is too comfortable an interpretation of what is happening. The situation is more explosive than that. In 1969, economic emancipation clashes with psychological slavery.

Emancipation is not only economic, it is educational. A higher proportion of young people today are educated to a higher standard than ever before; during the last twenty years average standards of educational attainment have steadily risen. There is no comparable evidence that the challenge of industrial jobs has increased to keep pace. It is not only in numbers that we waste labour.

But even this is not the most important thing that is happening. Most readers of this article will have shared with its author one common and formative experience, namely that of school. School in which one sat in large classes, – graded by ability – adhering rigidly to a set timetable; not daring to speak to one's neighbour, much less to seek his help with a problem; classes in which the teacher stood at the front, omniscient, imparting information; a school with fixed boundaries, strict rules and competitive tests. This experience gave us our norms and taught us most of what we know about management. It is strange to think that if we went back the chances are that we would scarcely recognize where we were. In more and more schools we would find classes more mixed, the timetable more flexible, individual learning programmes and group discussion work both freely employed and encouraged. To get help from one's neighbour is no longer cheating, it is sensible use of resources. The teacher, we would find, no longer claims to know all the answers, only to be able to help us find them – he has become more of a consultant. Projects would take us outside the school, into the town and the community; we would be encouraged to find our own medium in which to work, at our own pace, to build on our own ideas. This is what we would be assessed on, over the long term, with the object of helping us further as individuals rather than in order to categorize us amongst our fellows. Such is the modern experience of pre-industrial management.

Dangers for industry

The contrast between this kind of experience and that of industry itself must be traumatic. And yet this, or some aspect of it at least, is the experience of those whom we are currently recruiting into our employment. The fact that it is only at the universities so far that tension between young people and the establishment has flared into open struggle does not mean that much the same tension is not smouldering beneath the surface in industry, ready to complicate our industrial relations in ways as yet unforseen.

The 'good old days' have passed for good. The age we live in is at once more complex, more dangerous and more hopeful. The manager's job is still to manage – more so than ever before – but no longer can we assume that the industrial system is divinely ordered. It would be nice to patch it up and make it work, but too much has changed. The sands of society have shifted: our assumptions, premises and landmarks no longer safely guide us. Harder work, more efficient methods, greater self-discipline – none of these is the answer to our economic crisis, for they are mere exhortations to do better, to work the system more competently. This is why backing Britain was doomed: not only because of its anachronistic appeal to patriotism, but because it offered no solution to the problem. Our challenge is not to do the same things better, but to do something different. No longer is it only humanitarians and radicals who wish to change the industrial system, it is managers.

We are fortunate in having a body of knowledge to guide us. Previous generations of managers had to rely on hunch and intuition, the very process which has brought us to where we are now. They had no choice – we have. For a great deal is now understood about the phenomenon of people at work. The science is young, its evidence tends to be of a different kind from that of the natural sciences, its conclusions probabilistic rather than arithmetic. But faced with the reality of change in our society, we cannot afford to be snobbish or obscurantist. The manager whose factory is closed by an intractable strike, but who rejects industrial psychology as a pseudo-science, is like the drowning Englishman who refuses a stranger's hand on the grounds that he has not been introduced. In evolutionary terms, it is the kind of behaviour which leads to extinction.

The resource of knowledge

What knowledge do we, in fact, have? We know that people do indeed differ, but that the differences between them are much less important than the similarities.

We know that man is a complex organism with various kinds of needs or drives. These may form a hierarchy, starting with the most basic or instinctual needs (such as to breathe, to eat and not to be lonely) and progressing through intermediate social and ego needs (such as that of being respected) to the ultimate individual need for self-fulfilment. If so, the more the lower level needs are satisfied – which they tend to be in our society – the more important, relatively, do the higher order needs become. Or it may be that there are two distinct dimensions to man's psychology: that which he shares with his fellow animals, the need to avoid pain (and therefore, in human terms, to have money, security, comfort and status), and that which is unique to man as a human being – the need to achieve, to learn, to demonstrate competence, to 'grow' psychologically. If so, then to restrict our consideration to one dimension would not seem to be the best way of getting results on the other dimension.

We know that when people's higher order needs are frustrated, or when the specifically human dimension of their psychology is ignored, they are able in practice to adapt all right. But we have learned not to confuse symptoms of adaptation with demonstrations of basic nature.

If people are treated as child-like for long enough, they become child-like; if they are assumed at every turn to be irresponsible, they become irresponsible. A vicious circle is set up in which people respond as the system expects them to respond, which in turn reinforces the system. One common form of adaptation is withdrawal: people become lazy, disinterested, resistant to change. Another kind of adaptation is to seek compensation in other ways, to which money is the all important gateway.

We know that people are not always able to recognize these things for themselves, which is why – from a research point of view – it is more important to analyse people's experiences than it is to collect their opinions. People may be quite incoherent in their demands; they commonly believe themselves that the last thing they want is more responsibility and that all that matters is the pay packet. But the fact that we have succeeded so well in fooling the people we employ is no reason to fool ourselves.

All this is understood nowadays, in much greater depth than this simple summary can indicate. And much more is known as well: about the behaviour of people in groups, for example, and the effects of different managerial styles. But enough may have been said to illustrate that the implications of this knowledge – if only we have the courage to admit it – are profound.

In practice we concern ourselves almost exclusively with man's lower level needs: we still think of labour as labour. We work, argue, negotiate and act almost entirely on the animal dimension of man's psychology, though we hanker after and sermonize about commitment, responsibility, initiative and achievement. We rely on money, threats and bargains – and would like to rely on the law as well – to provide the 'incentive' and the 'control' we feel to be so important. We will not admit, though the facts stare us in the face, that our old-fashioned principles of military leadership – or the paternalistic, 'human relations' approach of keeping people happy so that they produce more – both look pretty sick in an age when educated, competent, imaginative and rebellious young people form an ever increasing proportion of the working population.

Not only is our industrial system anachronistic in terms of economic and social reality, it no longer even accords with our knowledge.

While writers of articles – none more than this one – make points by rhetoric, progress in industry is, in fact, made by patient, practical experimentation. The significant development which has taken place over the last few years in this country is that the kind of knowledge we have been discussing is no longer merely theoretical. We are beginning to have considerable practical experience of applying the concepts of behavioural science to 'real life' situations; we are beginning, as a result, to understand at first hand what is involved in doing so. Experiences differ in detail, but they have a lot of common ground.

New approach to managing people

In practice, what seems to be emerging is that there are three main planks in any viable new approach to the management of people and jobs in industry. First, more attention should be paid to the objectives of work, rather than the mere duties of a job; secondly, there should be a greater concern for individual job enrichment rather than the mere parcelling out of tasks; thirdly, a more participative style of management, rather than the mere direction and control of the people, needs to be developed. These three things are so closely interrelated that, so long as each is pursued firmly in the context of behavioural understanding and not as a quick-return gimmick, it does not seem to matter very much which one starts with – it is bound to overlap with and lead naturally into the other two.

To focus attention on the need for and the purpose of each piece of work, the basic approach of management by objectives, reflects the understanding that unnecessary or pointless work was never satisfying to anyone, nor ever helpful to an organization. So mesmerized have we become with the forms of our organizations and the duties of our jobs, that it is nothing like so easy as it sounds to define the objectives of the enterprise as a whole or any unit of it. Typically, even in a small unit, the process takes many months and more than one attempt.

Nor is it the sort of thing that can ever be more than half done without genuine participation. The real value and point of the exercise is not to set objectives, but mutually to define and to agree objectives on a continuing basis. It is to provide a framework within which progress may be sensibly reviewed, not in order to apportion blame for failure but rather jointly to examine ways in which obstacles can best be surmounted, or objectives modified. It is an exercise in communication, not in its old-fashioned sense of passing information up and down the line, but in its fuller and proper sense of achieving mutual understanding and as much commitment as is reasonable to the achievement of common purposes. If it is implemented as a subtle management control system (a 'do-it-yourself hangman's kit', as it has been described), then management by objectives gets, and deserves, a backlash of cynicism and it founders in gamesmanship. But if it is approached as a discipline within which gradually to achieve an alignment between the organization's needs and the individual's needs respecting the validity of both, then the evidence suggests that it produces valuable and continuing gains in both productivity and flexibility.

Job enrichment

A greater concern for individual job enrichment is the necessary complement of attention to operational objectives. While management by objectives concentrates on what tasks have to be done, ensuring that jobs are authentic in their contribution to business objectives, job enrichment concentrates on how tasks are done and who does them, ensuring that jobs are motivational to the individual.

Job enrichment is not just delegation. Delegation is looking at the job from the point of view of the manager: it leads, in practice, to the passing down of the easy, the routine, the safe, the easily checkable. Job enrichment, on the other hand, is a discipline within which to ensure that the specifically human dimension of man's psychology is not overlooked. It requires that people have the opportunity for achievement in their jobs, that their achievement is acknowledged, that tasks are interesting and challenging and responsible, providing scope for advancement and growth. It is more likely, as a result, to lead to the passing down of the difficult, the non-routine, the ambiguous and the important. Unlike any mere mechanism of consultation, job enrichment does not seek to give people a 'sense of involvement', nor does it ask from people a 'sense of responsibility': it goes ahead and actually involves people in the act of management, no matter at what level it takes place; it demands responsible action from people, for it puts a bit of the business firmly in their hands.

There is the rub, and that is what so many of us shy away

from – managers and university dons alike. It reveals our very natural fear, that we shall lose control, lose authority, lose prestige: it is not our job to allow mistakes to be made, to preside over the lowering of standards. But the truth is we are not all that firmly in control as it is, and the standards of which we are the guardians are not all that high. Those managers who have had the courage to act within the context of our behavioural understanding have discovered that their fear was illusory. Not once, in any reported application of job enrichment, has any kind of disaster been experienced. People respond cautiously to new responsibility; they are more than willing to use the manager as a resource person (which is exactly what a good management by objectives framework provides for). There is a gain, not a loss, of authority on the manager's part. Not only is the same work carried out at a lower level in the organization, with all the resulting benefit that that brings, but in practice job enrichment results in better work being done and higher standards being achieved.

The dynamic which sustains both management by objectives and job enrichment, enabling them to be developed to greater strength, is the parallel development of genuinely participative management. This has nothing to do with being nice to people, being consultative, democratic or soft: those are the tired old ploys of appeasement. Participative management is the discipline whereby an organization learns how to tap something of the latent potential of its members. It involves entirely new skills of behaviour; it requires from managers a whole new understanding of the processes that happen both within and between groups of people. It is, in fact, the gradual, stressful, risk-taking process of experience by which management matures from its outmoded role of directing, controlling and governing to its new role of enabling, encouraging, assisting and reinforcing achievement by others.

It is not the kind of thing that is learned from books, though the managers who practice it are the ones who realize how important it is to read the books. It is not the kind of thing that is achieved by new year resolutions. It is only through action that one discovers that the 10 per cent of one's time spent worrying about what the job really is, how it should be set up and how others can best be helped to do it is a more profitable activity than the 90 per cent spent fire-fighting or doing the job oneself. The next step is to worry about how others can be encouraged to go through the same 10 per cent process, for that is where the real profit lies. The results are a re-ordering of priorities, a new view on what is possible and practicable, and ultimately a new confidence, which is the most impressive result of all.

In ways such as these we are gradually learning what the management of people and jobs in industry might look like against the background of our changing society. The decision whether or not to go down this road (whatever its exact route) is not really a decision at all: if we don't go willingly, in the end we shall be pushed. In the meantime, the cost of delay will be immense, in terms of both increasing inefficiency and mounting ill-will. The UK is in no position to bear that kind of cost.

The point is that none of this happens of its own accord. It has to be pioneered, organized and managed. The time when a few bold managers experimented single-handed in these areas while everyone waited to see them come a cropper is, or should be, past. If it is not, it is up to personnel managers, as the custodians of industry's conscience and expertise in this area, to make sure it passes soon.

What is required is nothing less than a change of culture. The starting point is education – but this is no platitude. What it means is a patient effort at all levels, to examine the issues honestly, to explore the knowledge and experience available to us. The effort must be persistent and increasing. Also, it must get tougher. While in the early days it may be politic to provide potted versions of behavioural science thinking, ultimately the subject must be explored in depth; in the early days it may be necessary to apologize for the fact that much of the work is American – in the end, the 'not invented here' complex must be shown up for what it is.

But change was never engineered only on training courses. Experimentation is required as well, and it must be both bold and on different fronts simultaneously. The results of this experimental work must be measured, however difficult and foreign this may seem. Gradually what must be built up within the organization is a bank of practical experience, data and enthusiasm. Gradually the culture changes, shifting from being 5 per cent innovative to being more like 50 per cent innovative. As results are achieved, so authenticity is gained.

As experience and practice increases, the need becomes ever more urgent to legitimize it, to integrate it into a conscious framework of managerial strategy, and finally to define it and declare it as company policy.

Better Working Lives – a Social Scientist's View
Albert Cherns

Reprinted with permission from *Occupational Psychology*, Vol. 47, 1973, pp. 23–8.

Psychologists have been extraordinarily slow to concern themselves with the quality of people's working lives as a whole. Yet this has been one of two objectives underlying the application of psychological concepts and methods to the study of people at work. The other objective has been the increased efficiency of work organizations. Usually the two objectives have been reconciled by the tacit assumptions that better quality of working life means better jobs; that better jobs mean greater job satisfaction; that greater job satisfaction means better job performance, and that better job performance means improved functioning of the organization. Partly because this chain of reasoning has some very weak links, the topic of 'job satisfaction' has become a new *pons asinorum*. The psychologist has been all too prone to accept the conventional assessments of organizational efficiency and its associated concept of 'productivity' provided by accountants, and the design of job systems provided by industrial engineers, systems analysts and the other experts such as management information systems designers and operational researchers.

The achievements of industrial or occupational psychology have thus been patchy. On the one hand substantial contributions have been made to 'fitting the worker to the job and fitting the job to the worker'. Psychological work in the fields of selection, training and counselling, environmental psychology and ergonomics have become highly sophisticated and received considerable application. On the other hand, the knowledge and concepts of social psychology have also received wide application, with human relations training, sensitivity training, morale and job satisfaction studies, job enlargement, job enrichment, all enthusiastically embraced if often with the ardour more appropriate to a 'cause' than to a serious scientific endeavour.

But the obstinate fact has remained that the one purely psychological measure – job satisfaction – bears no clear relationship to measures of productivity. One might take this as justification for adopting a behaviourist standpoint, and regarding job satisfaction as an epi-phenomenon. But without some access to the individual's view of what is happening to him, all is subordinated to the organizational perspective, the stated goals of the organization. Occupational behaviourism is frankly exploitative.

The psychological horizon was broadened by the socio-technical approach that draws attention to group processes in relation to the task performed. The technology that an organization adopts to achieve its goals is the source of the variances which its social system has to control. But technology has been selected and designed on the basis of assumptions about people and groups. Ergonomists showed years ago that some machines were apparently designed for workers with a stature of 4′ 6″ and a reach of 8′. The designers' assumptions about motivation and behavioural characteristics were hardly less bizarre. Unlike those concerning stature and reach, they are largely self-fulfilling prophecies – motivation and behaviour being comparatively easily constrained by the system of reinforcement allied to task design.

The more sophisticated the production system, the more important the assumptions of its designers. With a comparatively simple system, the ingenuity of its operators can find a way to correct the designers' worst mistakes. Unauthorized modifications are easy to make to looms; but intolerable, if not impossible to make, to radar control systems. With large areas of organization design under the effective control of systems analysts and computer programmers the workers are impotent to alter their situation. And since the aim of industrial engineers, systems analysts and most management consultants is to eliminate as far as possible the effects of man's innate unpredictableness, all their products are designed to control and constrain human behaviour.

The importance of all this is often denied on two grounds. The first is that the picture I have drawn is true only for manufacturing industry, that manufacturing industry employs year by year a declining proportion of the workforce and will in any case solve all these problems by automation. The second ground is that work is not for everyone the most significant part of life; that for the man or woman with a low degree of self investment in work, the low demands work makes on self-regarding functions leaves the greater freedom to pursue self expression outside work.

The first objection is easier to answer than the second. Some of the most awful jobs are to be found in the non-manufacturing sector, even in white-collar jobs. Worse still, in a misguided attempt to promote 'efficiency' and 'productivity' in these sectors, some of the worst aspects of 'scientific management' are being imported.

The second point is harder to argue. If some jobs are irremediably lousy, it is probably better that their performers should not obtain their self concepts and social identity from them, but that they should adopt a purely instrumental attitude. But the hypothesis that a low self investment in one's job is associated with higher self investments in other parts of life is so far only weakly demonstrated. Indeed support is forth-coming for the opposite view. At least two 'experiments' show that people whose jobs have become more rewarding have tended to increase their participation in local affairs. Thus the problem of the irremediable job should be examined in three steps. First is the job absolutely essential and irremediable? Secondly, can it be broken into tasks which can be rostered or can it be rostered as a job? Thirdly, if it has to be filled by one person full-time, can it form part of a career moving on to other better jobs?

Thus far I have been concerned to show that bad jobs will not disappear as a result of automation or the growth of tertiary (service) and quaternary (education, government administration) employment sectors, and that owners of bad jobs may not be adversely affected if they invest little of themselves in their work lives. I now want to turn attention away from the design of the job itself and touch on other aspects of working lives.

Jobs and their environment

For very many, perhaps most, people in advanced industrial countries the job determines within fairly narrow limits where they will live and how. Where we live, of course, also affects the choice of job, and workers in many industries accept the conditions of their work and the size of their pay packets because it is near 'home'. The interactions of job availability, local amenity, the geographical mobility of work people, local community traditions, local social structure and educational infrastructures are among the complex of problems faced by employers selecting sites for new ventures or expanding or moving old ones.

In the relationship of plant and locality, however, I want to draw out two strands, one concerning the individual worker and the other concerning the community. First, the individual: partly because psychological studies of work have been conducted predominantly within the 'plant' and have been concerned with the nature of relationships at work and to work, the boundary separating work from non-work has tended to be drawn congruently with the work site, the 'plant'. By contrast, studies of workers whose workplace is not geographically defined, such as long distance lorry drivers, have adopted a totally different perspective which is not solely determined by the necessarily different methodology employed. We all know, however, that our working life includes our journeys to and from work and the way in which the demands of work structure the day and the week. We have tended to argue that industrialization brought about a separation of work from non-work through detaching work from its setting in the household and transferring it to a physically separate location. But this did not separate working life from non-working life to anything like the same extent. Indeed early factory life, like peasant agriculture, occupied virtually all of people's working hours, and they mixed at work with their neighbours, indeed their own wives and children. Working lives are not confined to what goes on in the place of work.

Employer and the community

The second aspect of the relationship between plant and locality concerns the community as a whole. The employer provides jobs, pays local rates as well as national taxes, provides business for local suppliers and brings certain categories of people into the district. He receives service of all kinds, consumes part of the output of the educational system, avails himself for his employees of the health and welfare services and so on. An input-output analysis of the relationship in economic terms would be immensely difficult; in social costs and benefits it is far beyond our present capacities to estimate. Put in this way such analysis may be virtually meaningless in that the plant forms an integral part of the locality – community. If we consider a non-manufacturing employing organization, such as a transport undertaking, a laundry, a hotel, a hospital or local government, we realize that the distinction between community and employing organization is indeed tenuous.

As a result we have adopted arbitrary ways of balancing the financial transactions of organizations and community. Appropriate enough to the comparatively small impacts of industry in the early stages of industrialization and to the limited knowledge about these impacts, they are grossly inadequate and inappropriate today. We have come to recognize this in relation to the physical environment. Until recently it has paid firms to develop and utilize technologies which placed heavy burdens on the community for which the firms did not have to pay. If a polluting technology was cheaper to install and run it made commercial sense from the firm's point of view. But the direct and indirect costs to the community probably far outweighed the extra cost of avoiding pollution in the first place.

It has become clear that the law must insist on firms' paying the costs of their own clearing up; when choosing new technologies firms will now find it commercial sense to select those which do not involve them in this endless commitment. Something of the same pressure operates in relation to industrial injuries. Not only are there safety regulations with sanctions but again the potential cost of a dangerous technology is made higher by the requirement that an injured employee must be compensated. With changing social views about the value to the individual of the amenities of life, the corresponding value placed by the courts on compensation for injury and disablement is rising, making dangerous technologies less profitable.

But there is no corresponding requirement that employers compensate the community for avoidable loads on its services or the misuse of its outputs. The policies of firms which result in heavily peaked traffic loads impose unrequited costs on the community as a whole. Likewise, the under-use of people's capacities and the failure to maintain their skills imposes costs and burdens on the community. The community's expenditure on educational institutions creates in each of the students graduating from them a capital investment. If adequately used this investment returns to the community both money in the form of expended income and contributions in kind – participation in the community's activities. The worker whose skills are inadequately or inappropriately used receives less to spend. He is also likely to be less creative in his community. If he suffers psychologically, the burden falls on his family and on community institutions. If his skills are not maintained and updated, he may require retraining at the community's expense. Thus it may still make commercial sense for a work organization to misuse its human investment because somebody else pays the difference in the same way that it paid firms to adopt polluting technologies.

Productivity v. *job satisfaction*

Now because the 'productivity' of a worker is a ratio of 'output' measured in arbitrary ways divided by an equally arbitrary selection of 'inputs' and because its calculation ignores undesirable outputs and inputs provided at someone else's expense, it is a pretty faulty economic index, although it may be a useful accounting method for an organization. Psychologists have, however, accepted this indicator as if it had legitimacy as a hard datum which could be used as a criterion measure for the effects of psychologically oriented changes. I would like to offer the challenge: 'job satisfaction', with all its faults as a concept, is as much a social and economic good as 'productivity' which is an even more arbitrary and shaky concept. For years psychologists have agonized about the ambiguous relationship between 'job satisfaction' and 'productivity' and with undue humility have regarded this as evidence against the validity of the former, not noticing that the latter is just as invalid. Unfortunately, this has encouraged organizations in the service and public administration sectors to introduce system-aids to 'productivity' at the expense of the satisfactions which formerly accrued to such humble people as teachers, civil servants, hospital workers, engine drivers and gas workers, whose dissatisfactions, expressed as ever in terms of pay, are currently headline news.

Lest it appear that I regard psychologists as the only professionals or scientists possessing answers to the problems of working lives, let me make it clear that psychologists, along with industrial engineers, accountants, economists and lawyers, are all prisoners of perspectives which have provided in their time notable services to improving work and working lives; that each of these perspectives was appropriate to tackling circumscribed problems which perhaps interacted less than they do today; and that without mutual comprehension and parallel approaches the contributions of each discipline separately are today not only partial but sub-optimal.

The basic assumptions of accountants derive from a time when firms were small and when their operations affected comparatively few, when community and government provided few services and it made reasonable sense to treat each firm as a separate self-contained unit. Likewise, most psychological work in industry and in other organizations has adopted the boundaries of the organization as its own boundary and the goals of the enterprise as beyond question. The outcome has been described in some quarters as 'plant psychology' and 'plant sociology' with the implied slur that it is boss-serving. Although this may be unjustified it is true that psychologists have misled themselves in believing that their approach was value free and objective, and so they have done less to advance the cause of human values in work than they might have done had they accepted the inevitability of a value-laden approach. On the other hand, we must admit that the 'human relators' were crusaders and that their work suffered in consequence, but more from the limitations of their perspective than from their enthusiasm.

The 'open socio-technical system' approach, for all its scientific methodology and language, is also frankly ideological; its two value judgements are that autonomy and interdependence are not only adaptive values in most work situations, but are social goods in their own right; and that self involvement in work is not only (as a result of open system characteristics) related positively to self investment in other life activities, but is a positive human value.

The more the psychologist aims to promote human values in his work the more responsive he must be to the value changes in society. The phrase 'human values' has a reassuringly permanent ring to it. But they are constantly changing and take meaning from the concrete situations to which they have to be applied, and which themselves change with technological, economic and demographic developments. Psychologists concerned with work and with better working lives must be aware of the changing social definitions of work and changes in the work ethic. The Hippy, fallen angel in so many ways appears to share the post-Adam view of work as vicarious punishment: the medieval view transposed to a period when all may eat without the sweat of many brows – a period brought about by the success of an ethic which saw work as the high road to Grace, not as evidence of the loss of it. But psychologists responsive to changes in social values and social ethics tend to be interested in the poor or the oppressed or those who appropriate the rhetoric of poverty and oppression; they tend to leave the study of industry and other work organizations to the conventional.

In our present state of psychological knowledge, we can probably not do better than maintain *in work* Emery's and Thorsrud's six criteria: need for variety; for continued learning; for some area of decision; for recognition; for relevance; and for a future; and in the relationship between work and non-work the single criterion that work organizations be obliged to account to the community for their custodianship of its resources, not least its people.

On the Misuse of Human Skill

Frank Heller

Reprinted with permission from Tavistock Institute of Human Relations Document HRC 318, 1970.

One day it will seem strange, in retrospect, that we spent much more thought and effort on developing human ability than on making good use of it once we had it.

There are innumerable examples. We hear them in casual conversation and occasionally they attract a journalist's attention. Doctors provide a good source of complaints: they have to undergo a particularly protracted and detailed training and – at the end of it – many of them spend a substantial part of their working day in relatively routine or clerical operations. Has anybody ever estimated how much money could be saved by splitting up these two aspects of a GP's job? Nurses have recently reiterated their age-old complaint that their scarce and skilled womanpower is frittered away in quite unskilled work. The educational world is full of examples of highly paid specialists typing their own letters with two fingers. We promote top research academics to headships of departments and give them inadequate support services. Even in business, the provision of secretarial help tends to go by seniority and not by the volume of routine work that has to be done.

Many people will shrug their shoulders; after all, life is not, and should not be, a precision machine. Nobody would want us to be constantly productive; it would in any case be impracticable to deal with all these fiddling complaints. Only the egghead economist is supposed to be worried about *alternative* uses of our scarce resources.

Oddly enough, even the economists have not been worried about the misuse of skills along the lines to be discussed in this article. Like the rest of us they have concentrated their energies on assessing the cost of *developing* skills and on the relationship between economic progress and the *need* for more *skilled manpower*. Other social scientists have followed the same line and have worked on perfecting training methods and selection procedures. The emphasis has always been on creating more skills and making sure that only the best, or the most suitable, get the jobs. Few people get worked up about what happens after that – except in casual conversation.

And so we have no theoretical framework and almost no research which investigates the effective utilization of skilled manpower.

Previously, I put forward a simple schema for drawing attention to the relation between available skills and good intentions (motives) on the one hand, and their lack of use on the other. This was done by means of a 'reservoir model' in the shape of a funnel. The funnel operates like a hopper used by industrial engineers. All our hard-won abilities, skills and talents, plus the necessary motivations are put into the hopper and stored there ready for use. Gravity alone wouuld normally allow these human resources to slide into the operating system, unless there were barriers that prevent the skills from being used. One can identify three major barriers: 1. technical; 2. social; and 3. psychological. In practice these three sources of ineffective skill utilization are often intertwined. This can be illustrated by describing some examples.

It has not been easy to collect good evidence to illustrate the reservoir model because, as inferred, past thinking was not directed along these lines. However, we have assembled a number of examples from the highest level of skill down to quite routine levels to make a case for applying something like our model to important current problems, such as the alleged 'technological gap'.

We will start off at the top of the skill pyramid by using the example of decision-making behaviour of directors of public companies, based on a recent investigation. The work was carried out in South America and may have no exact counterpart elsewhere, but this is not important. We are concerned with evidence for the relationship between the various labels in our reservoir model. Trained manpower is by definition very scarce in developing countries; in this case, the directors as a group were more highly educated and experienced than 99 per cent of the population from which they came. Even a slight loss of effectiveness of such a scarce resource would be serious. The board room work of two groups of companies was examined in detail. In one group of five companies, directors received minutes of each meeting describing the decisions taken and how they were to be implemented. In the other group of six companies, the minutes were not pre-circulated. They were available in a folder in the board room as each meeting assembled, but there was no time to give them more than a superficial glance. Five measurable criteria of decision-making productivity were devised; the directors with pre-circulated information were significantly more effective on all of them. Since the two groups were identical in experience and training, it seems that the technique of communication was probably responsible for the different results. The available highly developed skills could clearly be used more effectively when the directors had time to study and prepare their contribution to the board meetings. Failure to pre-circulate minutes was a technical obstacle in the hopper and may also have reduced the motivation of directors in the more unproductive group.

The second example is based on an investigation of the shorthand skills of fifty-two secretaries and the 260 managers for whom they worked. The secretaries had all passed a very careful selection procedure which was designed to measure shorthand speed and accuracy of reproduction. Girls with very high shorthand speeds started at the top of the salary scale. This procedure and the incentives had been devised to speed up the work-flow in the offices. Careful statistical investigations and interviews revealed that only twelve out of 260 managers dictated letters or reports, while the others used longhand. As a consequence, the girls' shorthand skill was converted into a wasting asset; it was at its peak when they were taken on and deteriorated with every month they spent in the firm. The problem was investigated because of the large number of girls who left the company to avoid becoming entirely unskilled.

One important area of *skill loss* is due to clashes of attitudes and values between different groups or levels of staff. It is important to realize that attitudes can inhibit the use of skills as effectively as technical or structural barriers.

Our third example describes the measurement of dissatisfaction of a group of scientists. It was found that in a large sample of British chemists, the greatest dissatisfaction was caused by obstacles due to the work organization and the controls imposed on them. They complained of red tape, delays, secrecy and pettiness in administration, an unnecessary emphasis on paper output rather than on results and of inadequate organization in general. They were also dissatisfied with the responsibility they were given and their lack of freedom to make even small decisions relating to their scientific work. In a similar investigation with mechanical engineers, over 50 per cent disliked their jobs because they were not required to use their full abilities.

Again and again, two priorities emerge from investigations into skilled work. One is for a certain amount of autonomy, or more specifically, for the chance to exert reasonable influence over the decisions that affect one's work. The second persistent need is for the fullest possible opportunity to use one's skill rather than to waste it. When people oppose these findings they usually claim that such requests are unworkable, that there is a limited amount of influence to be divided up, that discussions waste time and that organizations are set up to get specific jobs done rather than to allow people to show off their own skills. This rebuttal sounds plausible, at least until it is checked against actual examples. Work can nearly always be arranged so that major needs are integrated with organizational objectives. This is true even where highly qualified scientists are expected to produce commercial results. Extensive investigation in eleven research organizations has demonstrated that the highest research productivity was achieved when decisions were made by a number of people and not just by the researcher himself. Moreover, the poorest results were associated with departments whose heads made most of the decisions themselves.

Three further sources of the misuse of available skills will be mentioned, each with brief examples. Firstly, the problem of haphazard and isolated training. It seems that we have not yet absorbed the evidence of extensive experience and research, which has again and again shown how inefficient it is to take a small group of people out of their natural habitat – foremen for instance – submit them to intensive training and then re-insert them into their former environment. The environment is nearly always dominant and the new skills atrophy. Since we know that people are as devoted to their competence and talents as to other assets, the struggle to give up what has been won is usually frustrating. Although all the 'experts' know about this, somehow we carry on regardless. The alternative – integrated manpower development – is a long way off. This problem can be illustrated with an example of a manual skill, although at that level the difficulties are usually much less apparent than with intangible abilities. A trade school had been set up for building construction workers. They had recruited very competent instructors and excellent and expensive equipment. The apprentices were taught the latest methods, including certain ways of mixing cement, constructing scaffolding and using a new and super-efficient trowel. The effort was almost completely wasted, since the apprentices went out to normal building sites and an investigation showed that the site foremen refused to let the new boys do things their own 'new-fangled' way.

Then there is the problem of immobility. In this country it is traditional to regard labour turnover as an unmitigated evil, rather than an alternative to immobility. Of course, one can have too much even of a good thing and, by normal accounting procedures, labour turnover seems expensive. But we may pay a hidden price, particularly at the management level, where we tend to encourage loyalty above initiative. 'Some of the very worst employers, as well as some of the best, excel in the art of making subordinates afraid to seek an outside appointment, for fear of letting the side down.' In a recent comparison of six European countries, Britain had by far the largest percentage of senior managers who had worked in one company all their lives (46 per cent). By contrast, in a similar sample of senior German managers under 10 per cent had worked in only one firm, and 41 per cent in more than three. In Britain, only 19 per cent had worked in more than three companies. The penalties of immobility are manifold. For the successful company, in-breeding could mean that, when the existing staff have spent their best talents (which often happens early in life), the company is cut off from a renewal of energy and ideas. For the unsuccessful or average company, the consequences of immobility are much more serious, since they prevent the needed infusion of ability and flair. In terms of our reservoir model we can say that a man frequently has many more talents than he customarily uses, even more than he may be aware of. The chances that a man's first job produces a perfect fit between what he has to offer and what the firm needs, are probably remote, selection procedures notwithstanding. The extreme case can be exemplified by what can be called the 'Truman effect'. Here was a man who had stayed in an obscure and relatively unimportant job for a long time and who, unlike some of his successors, was not conscious that his skill endowment might be sufficient for the highest position in the land. When circumstances precipitated him into the Presidency of the United States the world howled with astonished commiseration and saw nothing but catastrophe ahead. It is quite likely, however, that Truman will take his place in history in the upper half of any distribution curve of presidential achievements. Without a change of jobs this particular reservoir would never have been adequately tapped. Events like this, which are not as rare as we are inclined to think, should serve as a constant reminder of the substantial unharnessed resources we fail to use.

Another advantage of mobility is illustrated by the popular saying 'No man is a prophet in his own company'. We have substituted the word 'company' for the more usual 'country' to draw attention to the possibility that the man whose skill hopper is subjected to too many obstacles in one firm, may find his unused skills more highly appreciated elsewhere. Some recent research suggests that this could well be so.

Our final example relates to age. We know that many of the important human accomplishments were created by young people. Inventiveness, intelligence and probably a host of other facilities reach their peak well before mid-career. This certainly does not mean that from then on everything has to go downhill; far from it. There are important experiences and talents which often develop late or do not diminish rapidly. Nevertheless it seems almost inevitable that if we do not give people substantial responsibilities and opportunities before mid-career, we deprive ourselves of abundant sources of capability that we can ill afford to waste. The greatest skill loss due to age is our capacity to change. It seems that we are probably most conservative up to adolescence and again after middle age. A society, or an industry, which needs to adapt itself to a very rapidly changing environment should find ways of putting people into senior positions before they have exhausted themselves, and before they have reverted back to the conservatism of childhood. The evidence is not reassuring. In a sample of the largest European companies, Britain had only 5 per cent of its top executives under forty-five years; France had 26 per cent, Germany 12 per cent, Italy 14 per cent, Belgium 25 per cent and only the Netherlands had a smaller percentage than Britain. There is an obvious link here with immobility. Given the universality of a pyramidal organization, if staff are encouraged to stay in one firm all their working lives, it becomes extremely difficult for young people to show their worth and find a short cut to the top before mid-career.

The examples that have been given cover a considerable amount of ground, even if they lack depth. They suggest that the full utilization of available skills is a complex business. Technical, social and psychological factors intervene. These include a company's policy, the practices of senior and subordinate managers, outside talent scouts, communication procedures and a host of other circumstances. It is important to recognize that, in the absence of a new framework of analysis, these people and circumstances are not identified as being *facilitators* or *obstacles in* our *manpower policy*. We bring them in, if at all, by chance.

It may be worth speculating, for instance, about the real nature of the so-called technological gap. The OECD has recently investigated the difference between the USA in technological innovation and the exploitation of available know-how. It was found that the British research effort was very considerable and in many ways substantially ahead of other European countries. In relation to R & D, Britain spends a higher proportion of GNP, employs more scientists, engineers and technicians and has the highest rate of innovation in Europe. Given this great investment, the economic outcome is very disappointing. The problem has not been fully investigated, but it may be worth exploring the under-utilization of R & D skills in terms of the reservoir model.

When we think of manpower resources, either at the national level or in a business, we think in terms of education and training, selection and retirement. We assume that some *invisible hand* will guide our statistical manpower units through all the many obstacles we have described above. The hard evidence suggests that the invisible hand has not done its job at all well.

Further Reading: The Quality of Working Life

A. B. CHERNS, *Work or Life*, Presidential address, Section N, 'Quality of Working Life', British Association for the Advancement of Science, Canterbury, August 1973.

S. COTGROVE, 'Technology at Work', *Technology and Society*, Vol. 8, No. 2, July 1973, pp. 70–74.

L. E. DAVIS, 'Job Satisfaction research: the post-industrial view', *Industrial Relations*, Vol. 10, 1971, pp. 176–93.

P. B. WARR, A. B. CHERNS, P. JACKSON AND D. PYM, 'Better Working Lives – a symposium', *Occupational Psychology*, 1973, Vol. 47, Nos. 1–2, pp. 15–36.

N. A. B. WILSON, *On the Quality of Working Life*, London, HMSO, Manpower Papers No. 7, 1973.

3   The History and Theory of Job Satisfaction

The publication in 1911 of the *The Principles of Scientific Management* by Frederick Taylor marked the beginning of a vast movement concerned with work measurement which has typified much advanced industrial production in this century. The atomization and close control of work were based on the assumption that individuals would be motivated to perform well if rewards were related directly to the performance of carefully planned tasks. Taylor's concepts were refined by engineers, work-study men and managers into a battery of incentive schemes and 'rationalized work', creating fortunes for a few and boredom for many. Unfortunately, his ideas were often applied in a piecemeal fashion and 'in the wrong spirit'. The most extensive application of Taylor's ideas was made by Henry Ford in the car assembly lines in his Detroit factories, which have since become synonymous with alienating and fragmented work. Our first extract is abridged from Taylor's writing.

It soon became clear, not least through Charlie Chaplin's portrayal in *Modern Times*, that something was amiss with the application of Taylor's ideas. The Hawthorne studies undertaken at the Western Electric plant by Elton Mayo and his colleagues contributed a great deal to the understanding of the problem in their 'discovery' of groups of people within the plant, who surprisingly preferred being treated as people, and often acted as a group with their own norms. Their findings resulted in the development of the human relations movement from the 1930s with its concern for worker satisfaction and emphasis on leadership and personal relations. At about the same time, the work of Lewin and his colleagues on studies of democratic leadership and group dynamics gave added force to this new movement. Later developments in understanding the relation between the individual and the organization emphasized the need to release the potential of the individual by creating an environment in which participation and identification are encouraged. The organizational controls and procedures, and the style of management are important factors in the creation of this environment. The work of McGregor, Argyris and Likert contributed greatly to the development of these theories and to the programmes for action associated with them.

In 1943, the work of American psychologist **Abraham Maslow** shed new light on the motivation of people at work. He suggested that human needs form a five-level hierarchy ranging from basic physiological needs to higher order needs for 'self-actualization' or achieving one's creative potential. As one need is satisfied, the higher order need gradually emerges and becomes the motivator of behaviour. Our second piece by Maslow describes his theory of human motivation.

Although his theory has never been rigorously tested, it has been widely used by behavioural scientists, and formed a basis for the development of ideas about job enrichment by **Herzberg** and others around 1960. From a study of the job attitudes of a group of 200 accountants and engineers, he concluded that the factors which alleviated job dissatisfaction were different from those which resulted in positive job satisfaction, and therefore these are not opposite ends of a single continuum but are in fact two separate traits. Herzberg called the two groups of factors he had identified the Hygienes and Motivators and showed that the former group are mainly concerned with the context of work or things extrinsic to the actual job while the latter group of factors concentrate on the content of work and those things intrinsic to the work itself. The third reading in this chapter outlines Herzberg's Motivation–Hygiene theory.

However, Herzberg's work has met with considerable criticism, for example from those who claim that his results are dependent on the method of interviewing used. He has also been criticized for making the assumption that all workers want intrinsically satisfying work and for not taking account of the fact that people vary a great deal in their expectations of work. For instance, in their study of Vauxhall workers at Luton, Goldthorpe and his research team, showed that car-workers chose their jobs largely for the extrinsic reasons of pay and security rather than for intrinsic reasons. Their main satisfactions in life were outside and work merely provided the money to enable them to seek these satisfactions.

The influence of expectations on performance has also been the subject of work by Lawler and others in the USA. They emphasize that people will only try to perform well if they think their efforts will achieve a goal which they value. Unless they feel they have a reasonable amount of control over the outcome of their work they are unlikely to be highly motivated towards it.

Meanwhile, a different line of approach had been growing from around 1950 with the development of theories of socio-technical systems and job design by the Tavistock Institute in London and Louis E. Davis and his colleagues in America. Both these theories stressed the need to consider the social system as well as the technical system in the design of work. The aim was that an optimum balance should be reached between the people and the technology, so that neither would have to be adapted to the other in ways which would be unduly detrimental. The studies by the Tavistock researchers also emphasized the use of autonomous groups, working together to complete their task, rather than being directed by a foreman or supervisor. Experiments were set up in the coal industry using these ideas; the results demonstrated their value in the work situation. The research in the area has continued partly in Norway, and the fourth article is by Eric Trist who was closely involved with his work, describing the development of the socio-technical theories up to the late 1960s.

The parallel development of job design theories in America from about 1955 concentrated more on the relationship between technology, organizational and personal needs. Davis defines job design as the 'specification of the contents, methods and relationships of jobs in order to satisfy technological and organizational requirements as well as the social and personal requirements of the job holder'. In their early work, Davis and his colleagues highlighted the contradiction between the prevalent use of scientific management practices which sought to minimize the contribution of the individual to the work of the organization, and the human relations policies which emphasized his importance and value to the organization. They argued that no programme aimed at increasing motivation or productivity could hope to succeed unless it began with 'soundly conceived job designs based upon efficient criteria'. In our final extract in this chapter, Louis Davis discusses the state of job design research in 1966 and the conclusions from studies done up to that time.

The readings in this chapter give a broad outline of the main developments in job satisfaction theories over the last forty years, concentrating on those which form the basis of the current interest in making work more satisfying for the majority of people.

The Principles of Scientific Management
Frederick Taylor

Reprinted with permission from *Scientific Management*, Harper & Row Publishers Inc., 1911, pp. 82–3, 100–1, 114–18, 125–9.

Before starting to illustrate the principles of scientific management, or 'task management' as it is briefly called, it seems desirable to outline what the writer believes will be recognized as the best type of management which is in common use. This is done so that the great difference between the best of the ordinary management and scientific management may be fully appreciated.

In an industrial establishment which employs say from 500 to 1000 workmen, there will be found in many cases at least twenty to thirty different trades. The workmen in each of these trades have had their knowledge handed down to them by word of mouth, through the many years in which their trade has been developed from the primitive condition, in which our far-distant ancestors each one practised the rudiments of many different trades, to the present state of great and growing subdivision of labour, in which each man specializes upon some comparatively small class of work.

The ingenuity of each generation has developed quicker and better methods for doing every element of the work in every trade. Thus the methods which are now in use may in a broad sense be said to be an evolution representing the survival of the fittest and best of the ideas which have been developed since starting of each trade. However, while this is true in a broad sense, only those who are intimately acquainted with each of these trades are fully aware of the fact that in hardly any element of any trade is there uniformity in the methods which are used. Instead of having only one way which is generally accepted as a standard, there are in daily use, say, fifty or a hundred different ways of doing each element of the work. And a little thought will make it clear that this must inevitably be the case, since our methods have been handed down from man to man by word of mouth, or have, in most cases, been almost unconsciously learned through personal observation. Practically in no instances have they been codified or systematically analysed or described. The ingenuity and experience of each generation – of each decade, even, have without doubt handed over better methods to the next. This mass of rule-of-thumb or traditional knowledge may be said to be the principal asset or possession of every tradesman.

The most experienced managers therefore frankly place before their workmen the problem of doing the work in the best and most economical way. They recognize the task before them as that of inducing each workman to use his best endeavours, his hardest work, all his traditional knowledge, his skill, his ingenuity, and his good-will – in a word, his 'initiative', so as to yield the largest possible return to his employer. The problem before the management, then, may be briefly said to be that of obtaining the best *initiative* of every workman.

In order to have any hope of obtaining the initiative of his workmen the manager must give some *special incentive* to his men beyond that which is given to the average of the trade. This incentive can be given in several different ways, as, for example, the hope of rapid promotion or advancement; higher wages, either in the form of generous piece-work prices or of a premium or bonus of some kind for good and rapid work; shorter hours of labour; better surroundings and working conditions than are ordinarily given, etc., and, above all, this special incentive should be accompanied by that personal consideration for, and friendly contact with, his workmen which comes only from a genuine and kindly interest in the welfare of those under him.

Broadly speaking, then, the best type of management in ordinary use may be defined as management in which the workmen give their best *initiative* and in return receive some *special incentive* from their employers. This type of management will be referred to as the management of '*initiative and incentive*' in contra-distinction to scientific management, or task management, with which it is to be compared.

Under the old type of management success depends almost entirely upon getting the 'initiative' of the workmen, and it is indeed a rare case in which this initiative is really attained. Under scientific management the 'initiative' of the workmen (that is, their hard work, their good-will, and their ingenuity) is obtained with absolute uniformity and to a greater extent than is possible under the old system; and in addition to this improvement on the part of the men, the managers assume new burdens, new duties, and responsibilities never dreamed of in the past. The managers assume, for instance, the burden of gathering together all of the traditional knowledge which in the past has been possessed by the workmen and then of classifying, tabulating, and reducing this knowledge to rules, laws, and formulae which are immensely helpful to the workmen in doing their daily work. In addition to developing a *science* in this way, the management take on other types of duties which involve new and heavy burdens for themselves.

These new duties are grouped under four heads:

1. They develop a science for each element of a man's work, which replaces the old rule-of-thumb method.

2. They scientifically select and then train, teach, and develop the workman, whereas in the past he chose his own work and trained himself as best he could.

3. They heartily cooperate with the men so as to insure all of the work being done in accordance with the principles of the science which has been developed.

4. There is an almost equal division of the work and the responsibility between the management and the workmen. The management take over all work for which they are better fitted than the workmen, while in the past almost all of the work and the greater part of the responsibility were thrown upon the men.

It is this combination of the initiative of the workmen, coupled with the new types of work done by the management, that makes scientific management so much more efficient than the old plan.

Perhaps the most prominent single element in modern scientific management is the task idea. The work of every workman is fully planned out by the management at least one day in advance, and each man receives in most cases complete written instructions, describing in detail the task which he is to accomplish, as well as the means to be used in doing the work. And the work planned in advance in this way constitutes a task which is to be solved, as explained above, not by the workman alone, but in almost all cases by the joint effort of the workman and the management. This task specifies not only what is to be done but how it is to be done and the exact time allowed for doing it. And whenever the workman succeeds in doing his task right, and within the time limit specified, he receives an addition of from 30 per cent to 100 per cent to his ordinary wages. These tasks are carefully planned, so that both good and careful work are called for in their performance, but it should be distinctly understood that in no case is the workman called upon to work at a pace which would be injurious to his health. The task is always so regulated that the man who is well suited to his job will thrive while working at this rate during a long term of years and grow happier and more prosperous, instead of being overworked. Scientific management consists very largely in preparing for and carrying out these tasks.

No one bricklayer can work much faster than the one next to him. Nor has any one workman the authority to make other men cooperate with him to do faster work. It is only through *enforced* standardization of methods, *enforced* adoption of the best implements and working conditions, and *enforced* cooperation that this faster work can be assured. And the duty of enforcing the adoption of standards and of enforcing this co-operation rests with the *management* alone. The *management* must supply continually one or more teachers to show each new man the new and simpler motions, and the slower men must be constantly watched and helped until they have risen to their proper speed. All of those who, after proper teaching, either will not or cannot work in accordance with the new methods and at the higher speed must be discharged by the *management*. The *management* must also recognize the broad fact that workmen will not submit to this more rigid standardization and will not work extra hard, unless they receive extra pay for doing it.

The change from rule-of-thumb management to scientific management involves, however, not only a study of what is the proper speed for doing the work and a remodelling of the tools and the implements in the shop, but also a complete change in the mental attitude of all the men in the shop toward their work and toward their employers. The physical improvements in the machines necessary to insure large gains, and the motion study followed by minute study with a stop-watch of the time in which each workman should do his work, can be made comparatively quickly. But the change in the mental attitude and in the habits of the three hundred or more workmen can be brought about only slowly and through a long series of object-lessons, which finally demonstrates to each man the great advantage which he will gain by heartily cooperating in his every-day work with the men in the management.

It will be seen that the useful results have hinged mainly upon 1. the substitution of a science for the individual judgement of the workman; 2. the scientific selection and development of the workman, after each man has been studied, taught, and trained, and one may say experimented with, instead of allowing the workmen to select themselves and develop in a haphazard way; and 3. the intimate cooperation of the management with the workmen, so that they together do the work in accordance with the scientific laws which have been developed, instead of leaving the solution of each problem in the hands of the individual workman. In applying these new principles, in place of the old individual effort of each workman, both sides share almost equally in the daily performance of each task, the management doing that part of the work for which they are best fitted, and the workmen the balance.

The development of a science sounds like a formidable undertaking. In almost all cases, in fact, the laws or rules which are developed are so simple that the average man would hardly dignify them with the name of a science. In most trades, the science is developed through a comparatively simple analysis and time study of the movements required by the workmen to do some small part of his work, and this study is usually made by a man equipped merely with a stop-watch and a properly ruled notebook.

The general steps to be taken in developing a simple law of this class are as follows:

1. Find, say, ten or fifteen different men (preferably in as many separate establishments and different parts of the country) who are especially skilful in doing the particular work to be analysed.

2. Study the exact series of elementary operations or motions which each of these men uses in doing the work which is being investigated, as well as the implements each man uses.

3. Study with a stop-watch the time required to make each of these elementary movements and then select the quickest way of doing each element of the work.

4. Eliminate all false movements, slow movements, and useless movements.

5. After doing away with all unnecessary movements, collect into one series the quickest and best movements as well as the best implements.

This one new method, involving that series of motions which can be made quickest and best, is then substituted in place of the ten or fifteen inferior series which were formerly in use. This best method becomes standard, and remains standard, to be taught first to the teachers (or functional foremen) and by them to every workman in the establishment until it is superseded by a quicker and better series of movements. In this simple way one element after another of the science is developed.

Now, when through all of this teaching and this minute instruction the work is apparently made so smooth and easy for the workman, the first impression is that this all tends to make him a mere automaton, a wooden man. As the workmen frequently say when they first come under this system, 'Why, I am not allowed to think or move without someone interfering or doing it for me!' The same criticism and objection, however, can be raised against all other modern subdivision of labour.

What really happens is that, with the aid of the science which is invariably developed, and through the instructions from his teachers, each workman of a given intellectual capacity is enabled to do a much higher, more interesting, and finally more developing and more profitable kind of work than he was before able to do. The labourer who before was unable to do anything beyond, perhaps, shovelling and wheeling dirt from place to place, or carrying the work from one part of the shop to another, is in many cases taught to do the more elementary machinist's work, accompanied by the agreeable surroundings and the interesting variety and higher wages which go with the machinist's trade. The cheap machinist or helper, who before was able to run perhaps merely a drill press, is taught to do the more intricate and higher priced lathe and planer work, while the highly skilled and more intelligent machinists become functional foremen and teachers. And so on, right up the line.

The history of the development of scientific management up to date, however, calls for a word of warning. The mechanism of management must not be mistaken for its essence, or underlying philosophy. Precisely the same mechanism will in one case produce disastrous results and in another the most beneficent.

The same mechanism which will produce the finest results when made to serve the underlying principles of scientific management will lead to failure and disaster if accompanied by the wrong spirit in those who are using it.

A Theory of Human Motivation
Abraham Maslow

Reprinted with permission from *Motivation and Personality*, Harper & Row Publishers Inc., 1970, pp. 35–47, 53–4.

The Physiological Needs

The needs that are usually taken as the starting point for motivation theory are the so-called physiological drives.

Undoubtedly these physiological needs are the most prepotent of all needs. What this means specifically is that in the human being who is missing everything in life in an extreme fashion, it is most likely that the major motivation would be the physiological needs rather than any others. A person who is lacking food, safety, love, and esteem would most probably hunger for food more strongly than for anything else.

If all the needs are unsatisfied, and the organism is then dominated by the physiological needs, all other needs may become simply non-existent or be pushed into the background. It is then fair to characterize the whole organism by saying simply that it is hungry, for consciousness is almost completely pre-empted by hunger. All capacities are put into the service of hunger-satisfaction, and the organization of these capacities is almost entirely determined by the one purpose of satisfying hunger.

Anything else will be defined as unimportant. Freedom, love, community feeling, respect, philosophy, may all be waved aside as fripperies that are useless, since they fail to fill the stomach. Such a man may fairly be said to live by bread alone.

It cannot possibly be denied that such things are true, but their *generality* can be denied. Emergency conditions are, almost by definition, rare in the normally functioning peaceful society.

In most of the known societies, chronic extreme hunger of the emergency type is rare, rather than common. In any case, this is still true in the United States. The average American citizen is experiencing appetite rather than hunger when he says, 'I am hungry.' He is apt to experience sheer life-and-death hunger only by accident and then only a few times through his entire life.

Obviously a good way to obscure the higher motivations, and to get a lopsided view of human capacities and human nature, is to make the organism extremely and chronically hungry or thirsty. Anyone who attempts to make an emergency picture into a typical one, and who will measure all of man's goals and desires by his behaviour during extreme physiological deprivation is certainly being blind to many things. It is quite true that man lives by bread alone – when there is no bread. But what happens to man's desires when there *is* plenty of bread and when his belly is chronically filled?

At once other (and higher) needs emerge and these, rather than physiological hungers, dominate the organism. And when these in turn are satisfied, again new (and still higher) needs emerge, and so on. This is what we mean by saying that the basic human needs are organized into a hierarchy of relative prepotency.

One main implication of this phrasing is that gratification becomes as important a concept as deprivation in motivation theory, for it releases the organism from the domination of a relatively more physiological need, permitting thereby the emergence of other more social goals. The physiological needs, along with their partial goals, when chronically gratified cease to exist as active determinants or organizers of behaviour. They now exist only in a potential fashion in the sense that they may emerge again to dominate the organism if they are thwarted. But a want that is satisfied is no longer a want. The organism is dominated and its behaviour organized only by unsatisfied needs. If hunger is satisfied, it becomes unimportant in the current dynamics of the individual.

The Safety Needs

If the physiological needs are relatively well gratified, there then emerges a new set of needs, which we may categorize roughly as the safety needs. All that has been said of the physiological needs is equally true, although in less degree, of these desires. The organism may equally well be wholly dominated by them. They may serve as the almost exclusive organizers of behaviour, recruiting all the capacities of the organism in their service, and we may then fairly describe the whole organism as a safety-seeking mechanism. Again, as in the hungry man, we find that the dominating goal is a strong determinant not only of his current world outlook and philosophy but also of his philosophy of the future. Practically everything looks less important than safety (even sometimes the physiological needs, which being satisfied are now underestimated). A man in this state, if it is extreme enough and chronic enough, may be characterized as living almost for safety alone.

Although we are interested primarily in the needs of the adult, we can approach an understanding of his safety needs perhaps more efficiently by observation of infants and children, in whom these needs are much more simple and obvious. One reason for the clearer appearance of the threat or danger reaction in infants is that they do not inhibit this reaction at all, whereas adults in our society have been taught to inhibit it at all costs. Thus even when adults do feel their safety to be threatened, we may not be able to see this on the surface. Infants will react in a total fashion and as if they were endangered, if they are disturbed or dropped suddenly, startled by loud noises, flashing light, or other unusual sensory stimulation, by rough handling, by general loss of support in the mother's arms, or by inadequate support.

Another indication of the child's need for safety is his preference for some kind of undisrupted routine or rhythm. He seems to want a predictable, orderly world. For instance, injustice, unfairness, or inconsistency in the parents seems to make a child feel anxious and unsafe. This attitude may be not so much because of the injustice *per se* or any particular pains involved, but rather because this treatment threatens to make the world look unreliable, or unsafe, or unpredictable. Perhaps one could express this more accurately by saying that the child needs an organized world rather than an unorganized or unstructured one.

The healthy, normal, fortunate adult in our culture is largely satisfied in his safety needs. The peaceful, smoothly running, good society ordinarily makes its members feel safe enough from wild animals, extremes of temperature, criminal assault, murder, tyranny, etc. Therefore, in a very real sense, he no longer has any safety needs as active motivators. Just as a sated man no longer feels hungry, a safe man no longer feels endangered. If we wish to see these needs directly and clearly we must turn to neurotic or near-neurotic individuals, and to the economic and social underdogs. In between these extremes, we can perceive the expressions of safety needs only in such phenomena as, for instance, the common preference for a job with tenure and protection, the desire for a savings account, and for insurance of various kinds.

Other broader aspects of the attempt to seek safety and stability in the world are seen in the very common preference for familiar rather than unfamiliar things, or for the known rather than the unknown. The tendency to have some religion or world philosophy that organizes the universe and the men in it into some sort of satisfactorily coherent, meaningful whole is also in part motivated by safety seeking. Here too we may list science and philosophy in general as partially motivated by the safety needs.

Otherwise the need for safety is seen as an active and dominant mobilizer of the organism's resources only in emergencies, e.g., war, disease, natural catastrophes, crime waves, societal disorganization, neurosis, brain injury, chronically bad situations.

The Belongingness and Love Needs

If both the physiological and the safety needs are fairly well gratified, there will emerge the love and affection and belongingness needs, and the whole cycle already described will repeat itself with this new centre. Now the person will feel keenly, as never before, the absence of friends, or a sweetheart, or a wife or children. He will hunger for affectionate relations with people in general, namely, for a place in his group, and he will strive with great intensity to achieve this goal. He will want to attain such a place more than anything else in the world and may even forget that once, when he was hungry, he sneered at love as unreal or unnecessary or unimportant.

In our society the thwarting of these needs is the most commonly found core in cases of maladjustment and more severe psychopathology. Love and affection, as well as their possible expression in sexuality, are generally looked upon with ambivalence and are customarily hedged about with many restrictions and inhibitions. Practically all theorists of psychopathology have stressed thwarting of the love needs as basic in the picture of maladjustment.

One thing that must be stressed at this point is that love is not synonymous with sex. Sex may be studied as a purely physiological need. Ordinarily sexual behaviour is multi-determined, that is to say, determined not only by sexual but also by other needs, chief among which are the love and affection needs. Also not to be overlooked is the fact that the love needs involve both giving *and* receiving love.

The Esteem Needs

All people in our society (with a few pathological exceptions) have a need or desire for a stable, firmly based, usually high evaluation of themselves, for self-respect, or self-esteem, and for the esteem of others. These needs may therefore be classified into two subsidiary sets. These are, first, the desire for strength, for achievement, for adequacy, for mastery and competence, for confidence in the face of the world, and for independence and freedom. Second, we have what we may call the desire for reputation or prestige (defining it as respect or esteem from other people), status, dominance, recognition, attention, importance, or appreciation.

Satisfaction of the self-esteem need leads to feelings of self-confidence, worth, strength, capability, and adequacy, of being useful and necessary in the world. But thwarting of these needs produces feelings of inferiority, of weakness, and of helplessness. These feelings in turn give rise to either basic discouragement or else compensatory or neurotic trends.

We have been learning more and more of the dangers of basing self-esteem on the opinions of others rather than on real capacity, competence, and adequacy to the task. The most stable and therefore most healthy self-esteem is based on *deserved* respect from others rather than on external fame or celebrity and unwarranted adulation.

The Need for Self-Actualization

Even if all these needs are satisfied, we may still often (if not always) expect that a new discontent and restlessness will soon develop, unless the individual is doing what he is fitted for. A musician must make music, an artist must paint, a poet must write, if he is to be ultimately at peace with himself. What a man *can* be, he *must* be. This need we may call self-actualization.

This term refers to man's desire for self-fulfilment, namely, to the tendency for him to become actualized in what he is potentially. This tendency might be phrased as the desire to become more and more what one is, to become everything that one is capable of becoming.

The specific form that these needs will take will of course vary greatly from person to person. In one individual it may take the form of the desire to be an ideal mother, in another it may be expressed athletically, and in still another it may be expressed in painting pictures or in inventions.

The clear emergence of these needs usually rests upon prior satisfaction of the physiological, safety, love, and esteem needs.

Degrees of Relative Satisfaction

So far, our theoretical discussion may have given the impression that these five sets of needs are somehow in such terms as the following: If one need is satisfied, then another emerges. This statement might give the false impression that a need must be satisfied 100 per cent before the next need emerges. In actual fact, most members of our society who are normal are partially satisfied in all their basic needs and partially unsatisfied in all their basic needs at the same time. A more realistic description of the hierarchy would be in terms of decreasing percentages of satisfaction as we go up the hierarchy of prepotency. For instance, if I may assign arbitrary figures for the sake of illustration, it is as if the average citizen is satisfied perhaps 85 per cent in his physiological needs, 70 per cent in his safety needs, 50 per cent in his love needs, 40 per cent in his self-esteem needs, and 10 per cent in his self-actualization needs.

As for the concept of emergence of a new need after satisfaction of the prepotent need, this emergence is not a sudden, saltatory phenomenon, but rather a gradual emergence by slow degrees from nothingness. For instance, if prepotent need A is satisfied only 10 per cent, then need B may not be visible at all. However, as this need A becomes satisfied 25 per cent, need B may emerge 5 per cent, as need A becomes satisfied 75 per cent, need B may emerge 50 per cent, and so on.

The Motivation – Hygiene Theory
Frederick Herzberg

Reprinted with permission from *Work and the Nature of Man*, Staples Press, 1968, pp. 71–80.

The motivation–hygiene concept of job attitudes was reported in *The Motivation to Work*. This study was designed to test the concept that man has two sets of needs: his need as an animal to avoid pain and his need as a human to grow psychologically.

For those who have not read *The Motivation to Work*, I will summarize the highlights of that study. Two hundred engineers and accountants, who represented a cross-section of Pittsburgh industry, were interviewed. They were asked about events they had experienced at work which either had resulted in a marked improvement in their job satisfaction or had led to a marked reduction in job satisfaction.

The interviewers began by asking the engineers and accountants to recall a time when they had felt exceptionally good about their jobs. Keeping in mind the time that had brought about the good feelings, the interviewers proceeded to probe for the reasons why the engineers and accountants felt as they did. The workers were asked also if the feelings of satisfaction in regard to their work had affected their performance, their personal relationships and their well-being.

Finally, the nature of the sequence of events that served to return the workers' attitudes to 'normal' was elicited. Following the narration of a sequence of events, the interview was repeated, but this time the subjects were asked to describe a sequence of events that resulted in negative feelings about their jobs. As many sequences as the respondents were able to give were recorded within the criteria of an acceptable sequence. These were the criteria:

First, the sequence must revolve around an event or series of events; that is, there must be some objective happening. The report cannot be concerned entirely with the respondent's psychological reactions or feelings.

Second, the sequence of events must be bound by time; it should have a beginning that can be identified, a middle and, unless the events are still in process, some sort of identifiable ending (although the cessation of events does not have to be dramatic or abrupt).

Third, the sequence of events must have taken place during a period in which feelings about the job were either exceptionally good or exceptionally bad.

Fourth, the story must be centred on a period in the respondent's life when he held a position that fell within the limits of our sample. However, there were a few exceptions. Stories involving aspirations to professional work or transitions from sub-professional to professional levels were included.

Fifth, the story must be about a situation in which the respondent's feelings about his job were directly affected, not about a sequence of events unrelated to the job that caused high or low spirits.

Figure 1, reproduced from *The Motivation to Work*, shows the major findings of this study. The factors listed are a kind of shorthand for summarizing the 'objective' events that each respondent described. The length of each box represents the frequency with which the factor appeared in the events presented. The width of the box indicates the period in which the good or bad job attitude lasted, in terms of a classification of short duration and long duration. A short duration of attitude change did not last longer than two weeks, while a long duration of attitude change may have lasted for years.

Five factors stand out as strong determiners of job satisfaction

– *achievement, recognition, work itself, responsibility* and *advancement* – the last three being of greater importance for lasting change of attitudes. These five factors appeared very infrequently when the respondents described events that paralleled job dissatisfaction feelings. A further word on *recognition:* when it appeared in a 'high' sequence of events, it referred to recognition for achievement rather than to recognition as a human-relations

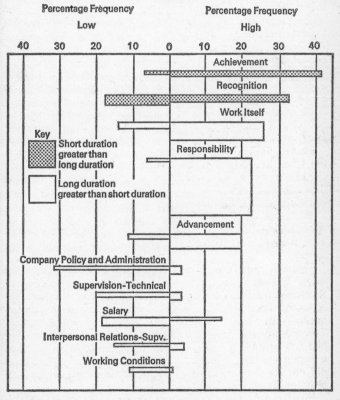

Figure 1. Comparison of Satisfiers and Dissatisfiers.

tool divorced from any accomplishment. The latter type of recognition does not serve as a 'satisfier'.

When the factors involved in the job dissatisfaction events were coded, an entirely different set of factors evolved. These factors were similar to the satisfiers in their unidimensional effect. This time, however, they served only to bring about job dissatisfaction and were rarely involved in events that led to positive job attitudes. Also, unlike the 'satisfiers', the 'dissatisfiers' consistently produced short-term changes in job attitudes. The major dissatisfiers were *company policy and administration, supervision, salary, interpersonal relations* and *working conditions*.

What is the explanation of such results? Do the two sets of factors have two separate themes? It appears so, for the factors on the right of Figure 1 all seem to describe man's relationship to what he does: his job content, achievement on a task, recognition for task achievement, the nature of the task, responsibility for a task and professional advancement or growth in task capability.

What is the central theme for the dissatisfiers? Restating the factors as the kind of administration and supervision received in doing the job, the nature of interpersonal relationships and working conditions that surround the job and the effect of salary suggest the distinction from the 'satisfier' factors. Rather than describe man's relationship to what he does, the 'dissatisfier' factors describe his relationship to the context or environment in which he does his job. One cluster of factors relates to what the person does and the other to the situation in which he does it.

Since the dissatisfier factors essentially describe the environment and serve primarily to prevent job dissatisfaction, while having little effect on positive job attitudes, they have been named the *hygiene* factors. This is an analogy to the medical use of the term meaning 'preventative and environmental'. Another term for these factors in current use is *maintenance* factors. The 'satisfier' factors were named the *motivators*, since other findings of the study suggest that they are effective in motivating the individual to superior performance and effort.

So far, I have described that part of the interview that was restricted to determining the actual objective events as reported by the respondents (first level of analysis). They were also asked to interpret the events, to tell why the particular event led to a change in their feelings about their jobs (second level of analysis). The principal result of the analysis of this data was to suggest that the hygiene or maintenance events led to job dissatisfaction because of a need to *avoid* unpleasantness; the motivator events led to job satisfaction because of a need for growth or self-actualization. At the psychological level, the two dimensions of job attitudes reflected a two-dimensional need structure: one need system for the avoidance of unpleasantness and a parallel need system for personal growth.

The discussion so far has paved the way for the explanation of the duality of job-attitude results. Why do the hygiene factors serve as dissatisfiers? They represent the environment to which man the animal is constantly trying to adjust. The hygiene factors listed are the major environmental aspects of work.

Why do the motivators affect motivation in the positive direction? An analogy drawn from a familiar example of psychological growth in children may be useful. When a child learns to ride a bicycle, he is becoming more competent, increasing the repertory of his behaviour, expanding his skills – psychologically growing. In the process of the child's learning to master a bicycle, the parents can love him with all the zeal and compassion of the most devoted mother and father. They can safeguard the child from injury by providing the safest and most hygienic area in which to practise; they can offer all kinds of incentives and rewards, and they can provide the most expert instructions. But the child will never, never learn to ride the bicycle – unless he is given a bicycle! The hygiene factors are not a valid contributor to psychological growth. The substance of a task is required to achieve growth goals. Similarly, you cannot love an engineer into creativity, although by this approach you can avoid his dissatisfactions with the way you treat him. Creativity will require a potentially creative task to do.

In summary, two essential findings were derived from this study. First, the factors involved in producing job satisfaction were *separate* and *distinct* from the factors that led to job dissatisfaction. Since separate factors needed to be considered, depending on whether job satisfaction or job dissatisfaction was involved, it followed that these two feelings were not the obverse of each other. Thus, the opposite of job satisfaction would not be job dissatisfaction, but rather *no* job satisfaction; similarly, the opposite of job dissatisfaction is *no* job dissatisfaction, not satisfaction with one's job. The fact that job satisfaction is made up of two unipolar traits is not unique, but it remains a difficult concept to grasp.

Thus, the hypothesis with which the study of motivation began appears to be verified. The factors on the right of Figure 1 that led to satisfaction (*achievement, recognition, work itself, responsibility* and *advancement*) are mainly unipolar; that is, they contribute very little to job dissatisfaction. Conversely, the dissatisfiers (*company policy and administration, supervision, interpersonal relations, working conditions* and *salary*) contribute very little to job satisfaction.

For the job-dissatisfied situation the subjects reported that they were made unhappy mostly because they felt they were being treated unfairly or that they found the situation unpleasant or painful. On the other hand, the common denominator for the reasons for positive job attitudes seemed to be variations on the theme of feelings of psychological growth, the fulfilment of self-actualizing needs. There was an approach-avoidance dichotomy with respect to job adjustment. A need to avoid unpleasant job environments led to job dissatisfaction; the need for self-realization led to job satisfaction when the opportunity for self-realization was afforded.

A 'hygienic' environment prevents discontent with a job, but such an environment cannot lead the individual beyond a minimal adjustment consisting of the absence of dissatisfaction. A positive 'happiness' seems to require some attainment of psychological growth.

It is clear why the hygiene factors fail to provide for positive satisfactions: they do not possess the characteristics necessary for giving an individual a sense of growth. To feel that one has grown depends on achievement in tasks that have meaning to the individual, and since the hygiene factors do not relate to the task, they are powerless to give such meaning to the individual. Growth is dependent on some achievements, but achievement requires a task. The motivators are task factors and thus are necessary for growth; they provide the psychological stimulation by which the individual can be activated toward his self-realization needs.

While the incidents in which job satisfaction were reported almost always contained the factors that related to the job task – the motivators – there were some individuals who reported receiving job satisfaction solely from hygiene factors, that is, from some aspect of the job environment. Commenting on this reversal, the authors of *The Motivation to Work* suggest that 'there may be individuals who because of their training and because of the things that have happened to them have learned to react positively to the factors associated with the *context* of their jobs'. The hygiene seekers are primarily attracted to things that usually serve only to prevent dissatisfaction, not to be a source of positive feelings. The hygiene seekers have not reached a stage of personality development at which self-actualizing needs are active. From this point of view, they are fixated at a less mature level of personal adjustment.

Critique of Scientific Management in Terms of Socio-Technical Theory

Eric Trist

Reprinted with permission from *Prakseologia*, Vol. 39–40, 1971, pp. 159–74.

The term 'scientific management' begs two questions – what is 'science' and what is 'management'. If, philosophically, the answers are plural and ambiguous, historically, the answer is singular and clear. Scientific management refers to the movement concerned with work measurement, inaugurated by Frederick Taylor at the end of the first century of the first industrial revolution. Since then it has become the vast enterprise known as production or industrial engineering. Since then has also begun the second industrial revolution based on an information technology rather than simply an energy technology. With this second industrial revolution 'management science' growing out of operational research is becoming as intimately associated as scientific management has been with the first.

Along with a number of others, the writer holds the view that the more complex, fast-changing, interdependent but uncertain world growing up in the wake of the second industrial revolution is rapidly rendering obsolete and maladaptive many of the values, organizational structures and work practices brought about by the first. In fact, something like their opposite seems to be required. This is nowhere more apparent than in the efforts of some of the most sophisticated firms in the advanced science-based industries to decentralize their operations, to debureaucratize their organizational form and to secure the involvement and commitment of their personnel at all levels by developing forms of participatory democracy.

Nevertheless, the classic efficiency cult, which Taylorism has come to symbolize, remains the prevailing value of contemporary industry. The majority of those pursuing the second industrial revolution are as much obsessed with it as those who pursued the first, including many operational research workers who treat systems in much the same way as most industrial engineers treat jobs. It will take some time before the minority who have already learnt to think in much wider terms secure an extensive hearing. By then much will have happened in the way of violence, alienation and poor performance that could have been avoided – if the world were a more rational place.

There is less need in the present context to elaborate on the extent to which the concentration, atomization and control of work was carried than to point to the nature of the penalty paid for the benefits gained. If the latter brought more productivity at less cost in the short run within the enterprise itself, the former brought more alienation in the longer run which spread into the larger society only to react back on the more immediate economic sphere. For some time this was masked in the classic forms of industrial struggle as organized labour sought better conditions for the mass of semi-skilled and unskilled workers – more pay, shorter hours, improved amenities, etc. After a period of initial resistance unions began to learn how to use work-study as a bargaining method in their own interest. Nor was the question inherently related to ownership of the means of production. Lenin entertained high hopes of what Taylor's scientific management might do for industry in the Soviet Union.

But as the first of the affluent society began to appear, as the Great Depression faded into the background and a new level of economic well-being established itself after World War II, it became evident that something of another kind was wrong whatever the amount of take-home pay or even security of employment. A first glimpse of what this might be had been obtained in the Hawthorne Experiments carried out by Elton Mayo and his followers in Western Electric's plants in the Chicago area at the height of the scientific management wave. These were the first extensive studies made in industry by social scientists as distinct from psychologists concerned with more limited psychophysical problems. They led to the curious and belated discovery that the worker was human even in the workplace and that he responded to being treated as such. This led to the rise of the human relations movement which in sophistication of theory and method has reached a degree of elaboration as great as scientific management though it has never matched it in extensiveness of application.

Quite early in the post World War II period, 1948–51, the Tavistock Institute undertook an intensive action research study at the London factories of the Glacier Metal Company. Concerned with group relations at all levels, it led to the establishment of a new type of representative structure. Enlightened personnel policies and wage practices were implemented with usual thoroughness. Yet the underlying alienation of the ordinary worker persisted. The 'split at the bottom of the executive chain' remained. The only major factor which had not undergone change was the task or work organization deriving from the technology. This has remained in the old modality. What would happen if this modality itself were changed?

An opportunity to begin finding out arose at this same time in the then recently nationalized coal industry where strikes, labour turnover and absenteeism were persisting unabated despite the change over to public ownership and the introduction of many improvements in pay and working conditions. In the first of what turned out to be a very long series of researches the writer and a colleague who had been a former miner were able to observe at a pit in the Yorkshire coal field what happened when the method of work organization was changed from the traditional form of job-breakdown to one in which autonomous groups interchanged tasks and took responsibility for the production cycle as a whole. The new groups were formed by the men themselves. More extensive experiments using what became known as the composite method were made in East Midland Division between 1951 and

1953, initiated by V. W. Sheppard, who was later to become NCB's Director General for Production. The gains in productivity and job satisfaction were both substantial, the former being up between 20 and 10 per cent for less cost and the latter, apart from expressions of opinion, manifesting itself in decreased absenteeism, negligible labour turnover and an improved health record. During further studies in Durham Division, 1954–8, an opportunity arose to carry out a crucial experiment in which the performance of two identical coal faces using an identical longwall technology, one organized in the conventional the other in the composite way, were monitored over a period of two years. The composite face was superior in all respects.

Meanwhile another Tavistock research worker, A. K. Rice, had applied composite principles in another industry in another country – the textile industry in Ahmedabad, India. As soon as the idea of a group of workers becoming responsible for a group of looms was mentioned in discussing the experimental reorganization of an automatic loomshed, the workers spontaneously took up the idea, returning next day with a scheme which was accepted and immediately tried out. Early success was followed by vicissitudes due to many factors which were investigated, but thereafter, a steady state of significantly improved performance was attained. Higher wages were earned and the internally led loom groups, which carried out their own maintenance, offered 'careers' from less to more skilled roles, while Hindus and Moslems worked together. The system spread to ordinary looms.

While their own change experiments were proceeding, the Tavistock workers were able to ascertain that sporadic developments along the same lines had taken place in the telephone industry in Sweden, in the building industry in Holland and in appliance manufacture and chemicals in the United States. There was another way to organizing productive work than the prevailing way. There was *organizational choice*.

In the United States recognition grew that quantified external control and job fractionation had been carried too far and job enlargement received extensive trial. A distinction was made between extrinsic job satisfaction (which included the pay packet) and intrinsic satisfaction deriving from the quality of the job itself. This was recognized as a major factor affecting motivation. But such recognition implied altering the way jobs were *designed*.

This meant changing the technological organization, the system which the human relations school had left intact and which the scientific management school had continued to design according to the atomistic ideology that had characterized 19th-century science.

From the beginning the Tavistock workers had felt that a new unit of analysis was required. This led the writer to introduce the concept of the *socio-technical system*. The problem was neither that of simply 'adjusting' people to technology nor technology to people but organizing the interface so that the best match could be obtained between both. Only the socio-technical whole could be effectively 'optimized'. In the limit the socio-technical whole comprised the enterprise as a whole – in relation to its environment – as well as its primary work groups and intervening sub-systems. It was necessary to change the basic model in which organization theory had been conceived.

Emery has formulated the matching process in terms of *joint optimization*.

Putting together the findings of a number of investigations, he has offered a set of general socio-technical principles for job-design.

These requirements are obviously not confined to any one level of employment. Nor is it possible to meet these requirements in the same way in all work settings or for all kinds of people. Complicating matters further is the fact that these needs cannot always be judged from conscious expression. Like *any* general psychological requirements they are subject to a wide range of vicissitudes. Thus, where there is no expectation that any of the jobs open to a person will offer much chance of learning, that person will soon learn to 'forget' such requirements.

These requirements, however true they may be, are too general to serve as principles for job redesign. For this purpose they need to be linked to the objective characteristics of industrial jobs. Since these principles were formulated a good deal of experience has been gained with more advanced technologies which depend on processes of continuous production and a high level of auto-mation and computerization. As a result, a nine step analytical model for socio-technical inquiry has been gradually taking shape.

This analytical model, which uses an open systems approach is not intended as a procedure for the sole use of research workers.

It is intended also for operating people in plants where management and workers together have decided to undertake change in which explicit use will be made of socio-technical principles.

Though towards the end of the fifties the Tavistock research group had extended its inquiries to examples of the more advanced technologies, these had remained descriptive studies. No further opportunities to conduct operational field experiments arose in a British setting. The next major developments took place in Norway in conjunction with what has become known as the Norwegian Industrial Democracy Project. This has given a new dimension to socio-technical studies relating them to central questions of value change as the era of the post-industrial society is brought nearer by the technologies of the second industrial revolution.

The project began in 1961 and is still proceeding. It grew out of a crisis between the Norwegian Confederation of Employers and the Norwegian Confederation of Labour over a sudden increase in the demand for workers' representation on boards of management proposed as a way of reducing alienation and increasing productivity.

The first phase of the project consisted of a field study of what actually happened in the five major concerns where workers were represented on the boards. These were either government owned or part-owned enterprises obliged by law to have workers' representatives. The results showed that very little happened except at the symbolic and ceremonial level. There was no increase in participation by the rank and file, no decrease in work alienation, no increase in productivity. The overall state of industrial relations being stable within a stable framework of political democracy, little was added simply by adding a workers' representative to the board of directors. The second phase of the project, which was to search out ways for securing improved conditions for personal participation in a man's immediate setting as constituting 'a different and perhaps more important basis for the democratization of the work place than the formal systems of representation'. This led to the idea of socio-technical experiments in selected plants in key industries, which, if successful, could serve as demonstration models for diffusion purposes.

The first experiment was carried out in the metal-working industry, a sector regarded as critical but requiring considerable rehabilitation. A rather dilapidated wire drawing plant in a large engineering concern was chosen on the grounds that if improvements could be brought about here they could be brought about anywhere. Productivity increased so much that the experiment was suspended; the workers concerned had begun to take home pay packets in excess of the most skilled workers in the plant; a very large problem had now to be sorted. If this experiment confirmed earlier findings regarding what could be accomplished when alienation is reduced, it showed up for the first time the magnitude of the constraining forces lying in wage structures and agreements negotiated according to the norms of the prevailing work culture and accumulating historically. The difficulty of changing such structures accounted in considerable measure for the failure to spread of earlier pilot experiments.

The second experiment was in the pulp and paper industry, also regarded as a critical sector, but where the problem was not so much to upgrade performance with old technologies as to gain control over new. A sophisticated chemical plant was selected, where the basic work was information handling -- the core task in the technologies of the second industrial revolution. The requisite skills are perceptual and conceptual; the requisite work organization is one capable of handling the complex information flows on which controlling the process depends. To do this requires immense flexibility and capability for self-regulation.

The model was established of an 'action group' consisting of the operators concerned actively using supervisors, specialists and managers as resources, rather than passively responding to them simply as bosses – in order to fashion an optimum work organization for a new technology – as they were learning the know-how of its operation. This model was now taken up by Norskhydro, the largest enterprise in Norway, which manufactures fertilizers and other chemicals for the world market. The model was first used to refashion an old plant, then to develop the entire organization and operating procedures for a new one.

The success of the Norskhydro experiments has been widely publicized throughout Scandinavia. It marked the beginning of the third phase of the project concerned with the diffusion process itself. In Norway the Joint Committee which originally sponsored the project was transformed into a National Participation Council and a new Parliamentary Commission on Industrial Democracy was formed. In Sweden similar developments have recently taken place at the national level, but it will be some time before a critical mass of concrete experience with the new methods can build up. Similarly in Denmark. Meanwhile in Norway the most significant recent developments have taken place in the shipping industry in the manning of bulk carriers.

Undoubtedly there are features in the culture of the Scandinavian countries and in their situation, Norway most particularly, which have enabled them to act as the laboratory of the world in developing a new concept of industrial democracy based on socio-technical theory. In larger countries which are more authoritarian, where the first industrial revolution has left a deeper imprint, or where the culture is more fragmented, much greater difficulties are to be expected. In Britain there are signs of the trail being taken up again by specific but important firms. The refining side of Shell, for example, some five years ago invited the Tavistock Institute to assist it in developing a new management philosophy based on the principle of joint optimization. In Ireland, the national transport undertaking (CIE) undertook an extensive project. Sporadic developments continue here and there in the US.

The underlying change which has taken place is that in the science-based industries of the second industrial revolution the worker is not a worker in the sense of the first industrial revolution. He is no longer embedded in the technology, contributing his energy to it, or even his manipulative skill, but outside it, handling information from it and himself becoming a source of information critical for its management. This change of position and role makes him in fact a manager, different in degree but not in kind from those who traditionally have carried this title. For the task of management is the regulation of systems and the function of managerial intervention (decision) to establish control over the boundary conditions. Such is the type of activity in which the worker now primarily engages, as fact-finder, interpreter, diagnostician, judge, adjuster, and change agent; whatever else he does is secondary. In Jaques' terms the *prescribed* part of his role has become minimal, for the 'programme' is in the machine; the *discretionary* part has become maximal – for the reason for his presence is to assess the performance of the programme and, if necessary, to change it, either himself or in conjunction with others at higher levels. No longer is there 'a split at the bottom of the executive chain' which separates managers and managed. Everyone is now on the same side of the 'great divide' and whatever fences there may still be on the common side would seem best kept low. A general change is in consequence taking place in all role-relations in the enterprise. This is the underlying reason for the bureaucratic model being experienced as obsolete and maladaptive, and also for a possible new role beginning to emerge for trade unions.

To maintain in a steady state the intricate interdependencies on which the science-based industries depend requires commitment to and involvement in their work from the men on the shop floor (those who are left) as much as from anyone higher up (and there are fewer of these at intermediate levels). External supervision may correct errors that have been made but only internal super-vision can prevent their occurrence. The amount of error which capital-intensive continuous production plants can tolerate is small compared with plants based on technologies which are labour-intensive and discontinuous. There is a straight economic reason for this; work-stoppages have become too costly, whether they result from machine breakdowns due to incompetence or carelessness, or from labour trouble due to bad internal relations or external pressures. But if anything at all has become clear about automated plants it is that they do not work automatically. They are the creation of those who man them as much as of those who build them; design continues as operation commences and operational experience informs further design, which from the beginning has to be developed as a socio-technical process. Moreover, this socio-technical creativeness must be maintained because the change-rate is both rapid and continuous. The autonomous work group setting out on an expedition of learning and innovation from which there is no return would appear to be the organizational paradigm which matches and which is 'directively correlated' with the information technology. The advance of technology itself has reversed the world of Frederick Taylor.

Though a great deal of industry does not yet belong to the in-formation technology and though some of it will never belong, the part that does has already become the 'leading part'. Its influence on the rest may be expected to increase. Moreover, in all contexts there is organizational choice. This is likely to be more frequently exercised in the direction of the new paradigm now that the old paradigm is no longer taken to be a law of nature. Marshal McLuhan seems to be right in thinking that automation means 'learning a living'.

The transition to a new concept of the world of work may be slow, unpleasant and difficult, but intolerance (whether in the form of rebellion or dropping out) of narrow and overprescribed jobs is mounting. The contemporary malaise deplored by the 'silent majority' may itself be a main force which will hasten beneficial change, for the technological excuse is rapidly diminishing for any job to be inhuman rather than human. Those who wish to be human will have more of a chance in the future than many have had in the past. It is disconcerting, however, to think of industry as being the place where one will find out who one is.

The Design of Jobs
Louis E. Davis

Reprinted with permission from *Industrial Relations*, Vol. 6, 1966, pp. 21–45

Job design means specification of the contents, methods, and relationships of jobs in order to satisfy technological and organizational requirements as well as the social and personal requirements of the job-holder.

For the purposes of discussion only, specification of job contents can be divided into two categories: 1. physical-environment and physiological requirements, and 2. organization, social, and personal requirements. An extensive body of knowledge exists on the first category and is assiduously applied in designing plant environment, work methods, equipment, and tools, and in fitting the physical work demand to the capabilities of workers. No conflict exists over the application of this physiological and ergonomic knowledge for it does not require any models of human behaviour in complex organizations. Man's responses to the physical environments and work tasks are studied at the microscopic level with man taken as a machine element, albeit a human one, in the system. The objectives are either adjustment of man, as by training, or adjustment of environment or technology, as by design of tools, equipment, and dials and machine controls for rapid and error-free operation or to suit particular human capabilities, such as those of older workers.

On the side of organizational, social, and personal requirements, what is the state of job design today? There is a large discrepancy between available knowledge and practice, although – paradoxically, perhaps – there is much evidence that management faithfully keeps abreast of developments in job and organization design research. The thinking of many a management today appears to be not unlike that of an old farmer who went to a lecture delivered by a county agent to a group of small farmers in a remote rural area about a new development in farming that would increase crop yield. When asked by the county agent whether he would use the new development, the old-timer said, 'I won't – I already know how to farm better than I am doing.'

Managements are well aware that there now exists a considerable body of evidence which challenges accepted organizational and job design practices. Experimental and empirical findings, for instance, indicate that imposed pacing of work is detrimental to output and to quality, yet paced work is common and is considered to be desirable. There is extensive evidence concerning the positive effects of group reward systems in achieving an organization's primary objectives. There is also considerable evidence of the effects of variety of job content and of task assignments that permit social relationships and communication patterns to develop, all of which enhance performance and personal satisfaction on the job. Yet in a very few instances do we find application of such findings to job designs.

The incentive to apply job design knowledge must be presumed to be strong, for the very simple reason that there are gains to be made all round – for the organization in productivity, quality, and costs of performance, and for workers in personal satisfactions. On the other hand, inhibitions against application are formidable. The *status quo* bristles with institutional barriers in the form of established personnel policies, job evaluation plans, union relationships and contracts, supervisory practices at all levels, and, not least, managerial practices. All of these barriers are perpetually present, prompting the manager to choose the path of least resistance and to do as little as the situation compels, that is, to satisfy the obvious needs of technology. At a deeper level, the *status quo* is reinforced by more basic and pervasive inhibitions which again and again lead the manager to fall back on time-honoured, but inappropriate and unrealistic models which are based on unsupported dogma or on popular clichés regarding human behaviour in productive organizations.

The practical consequences are inconsistent and incompatible job designs, as well as *ad hoc* use of piecemeal research results. With minor modifications, there is still a strong commitment to the proposition that meeting the requirements of the technology (process, equipment) will yield superior job performance, measured by organizationally relevant criteria, and a deep-seated conviction that the same performance will *not* be achieved if technological requirements are not given exclusive consideration. Requirements such as communication, group formation, personality development, decision-making, and control are seen as marginal at best, and at worst as opposed to the satisfaction of technological requirements. This fictitious conflict reveals the poverty of present conceptualization of human behaviour in productive organizations and helps to maintain the dominance of technological requirements as exclusive determinants of job contents and relationships.

Models of Human Behaviour

Models and concepts of individual-organization relationships and of human behaviour in productive organizations have a history almost as long as that of Western civilization. However, only two have been historically influential in their contribution to purposeful job design. Both were handed down to us by late-eighteenth-century economists – the ubiquitous model of man as an economic animal and the concept of the division of labour. The former has provided the rationale for our present reward systems, as well as for our concentration on monetary rewards as the only ones suitable for consideration. The division-of-labour concept provided the basis for specialization and, as a result, for our existing job and organization structures. Based on these approaches, organizations were able to make immediate use of an untutored and unskilled work force. To the extent that lack of education and skill are still the main characteristics of a work force, the concept has utility, even if there are secondary costs in the form of reduced contribution on the part of individuals and the need for a coordination apparatus.

During the late nineteenth century, a series of models were developed; all of them derived from the mechanistic model of human behaviour in which man's role was conceived to be that of an element or cog in a complex production system dominated by costly equipment. In mechanical systems, elements must be completely designed if they are to function. When transposed to human effort, this requirement states that initiative and self-organization are not acceptable, for they may increase system variability and the risk of failure. (Incidentally, the question raised today of whether workers are responsible or irresponsible appears not to have entered into consideration.) The result was rigidly specified task assignments and complete job descriptions indicating the specific behaviours desired and their organizational and temporal bounds. The drive to achieve reduced sources of variability encouraged the development of the concept of minimum skill requirements for task performance. Given highly specialized or fractionated jobs consisting of few minimally skilled tasks, skills could be rapidly acquired with short training. That man might engage in behaviour other than that specifically required by the system was never part of the conceptual framework of the mechanistic model. To insure successful outcomes, reward systems were designed that provided reinforcement only for the precisely specified behaviours desired. To be sure, many of these principles were applied without conscious design and in the euphoric atmosphere of applying science to complex organizations.

The more recent models of individual-organization relationships which have undergirded the evolution of job design can be classified into four groups. The oldest of these is the minimum interaction model, under which there is a minimal connection between the individual and the organization in terms of skill, training, involvement, and complexity of his contribution, in return for maximum flexibility and independence on the part of the organization in using its manpower. In other words, the organization strives for maximum interchangeability of personnel (with minimum training) to reduce its dependence on availability, ability, or motivation of individuals. This model has been the basis for the development of twentieth-century industrial relations practices and for modern personnel management. In application, it frequently takes the form of the work-flow or process-flow model of job design. In this model the material or information processes are in themselves the job content, or determine it.

Evolving from and tied to the minimum interaction model is the welfare model, which gives nodding recognition to the inadequacy of the 'economic man' theory. Without disturbing job and organization structures, it attempts to build extra-role and extra-job associations and, hopefully, loyalties to the organization. It places great faith in the prospect that meaningful social relationships can be built with fellow workers and supervisors outside the immediate production framework, which continues to operate on the basis of the restricted role of the individual and of minimum organizational interaction. In applying the model, organizations bubble with programmes that provide fun and games for workers after hours, company newspapers that jolly workers along to make them feel part of the organization, extra-job rewards, profit shares, etc.

The third group of models grew out of the shock of the Hawthorne studies and is characterized by emphasis on leadership and personal relations. Growth of awareness that there are informal leaders and groups, and that groups have social standards and norms, led to the development of the human relations movement. If informal leaders and groups exist, no matter what the formal organization description indicates, then management had better get busy, either to capture these or provide leadership patterns and personal relations that go some way toward reconciling the informal and formal structures. Having been built on these objectives, the human relations movement is now seriously hampered by restricting itself to them. Its narrow approach, which completely overlooks job content and the interaction between social, organizational, and technological requirements, was bound to produce the limited success it has achieved thus far.

The last and most recent group of models grew directly out of the impact of social and behavioural science research. Results of various studies provide information on self-selected aspects of the whole man at work in an organization. In most instances, the studies are piecemeal approaches which nibble at the edges of the central problems of job design, the role of the individual in a productive organization, and his control over the functions performed. Most of these approaches unfortunately assume that job content is not a significant variable or is so fixed by the needs of technology that it is not worth examining, since it cannot be altered in any event. Only ignorance of technology can lead to such a conclusion. Within this group are such approaches as sensitivity development; group-member participation, and status and personality development; communication; and even job enlargement, whatever that may be. The unfortunate consequence is a series of competing fads, one continually replacing the other as offering the true answer.

Recent Job Design Studies

Job design research is relatively new, having originated only in the last decade. More recently, a few industrial firms have begun to manipulate some job contents and configurations. The first such experiment that was reported took place in the late forties in a large US electronics firm which undertook a series of job changes in the form of job enlargement. The changes were instituted as a part of management industrial relations policy.

What characterizes the difference between job design research and personnel, industrial psychological, and sociological studies? Job design studies take technology as an operant variable and, as a consequence, are concerned with the interaction between personal, social, and organization needs and technology as manifested in jobs. The other studies take technology as given and therefore do not consider it as a variable to be examined. Job design studies can be classified into two groups, both based on field experiments: those carried out in the United States under the name of job design and those carried out in England, where they are known as socio-technical systems studies. The former studies have sought to manipulate the configuration of technology, as interpreted in task designs and assignments making up jobs, and to determine what variations are possible and what the effects of these are on personal, social, and organization variables. The latter studies have approached jobs and organization configurations from the direction of social psychology, modifying technological configurations of tasks to permit the development of social structure in support of functions and objectives of work groups. Both types of studies are concerned with jobs and organizations as socio-technical systems.

The studies undertaken lend support to the general model of responsible autonomous job behaviour as a key facet of individual-organizational-technological relationships in productive organizations. Responsible behaviour as defined here implies 1. acceptance of responsibility by the individual or group for the cycle of activities required to complete the product or service, 2. acceptance of responsibility for rate, quantity, and quality of output, and 3. recognition of interdependence of the individual or group on others for effective progress of a cycle of activities. Similarly, autonomous behaviour encompasses 1. self-regulation of work content and structure within the job, where the job is an assignment having inputs, facilities, and outputs, 2. self-evaluation of performance, 3. self-adjustment to changes required by technological variability, and 4. participation in setting up of goals or objectives for job outputs.

Furthermore, the studies provide a partial demonstration of the positive effects on total performance of job and organization designs which lead to responsible autonomous job behaviour, i.e., positive effects on objective organization performance, as well as on the attitudes, perceptions, and satisfactions of members of the organization. Such designs also tend to maintain a production system in an on-going state of relative equilibrium. For example, in many of the studies total performance was found to have been enhanced substantially by job designs which provided compatibility among technological, organizational, and personal requirements. This suggests that here, as elsewhere, the system approach leads to more effective designs of organizations and jobs. The component or piecemeal approach (so prevalent at present), which concentrates on job designs exclusively tailored to one component of the system, namely technology, tends to result in less than optimal total performance. While failing to achieve the output and quality levels possible, it imposes higher direct costs on management and workers alike, reflected in increased inspection, supervision, and absenteeism, coupled with reduced satisfactions, negative attitudes, and hostility.

That some processes or activities may be automated does not alter the fact that for the organization as a whole people are the prime agents for the utilization of technology in the interests of achievement of an organization's objectives. The model of responsible autonomous job behaviour makes it both permissible and imperative to view personal requirements in the focus of job design activity. But if the model is to be used as a basis for job (and organization) design, then these non-modifiable personal requirements and the characteristics of their interactions with technology and the organization will have to be specified as design criteria aimed at achieving compatibility. Variations in design may result from interpretations of non-modifiable criteria and from the introduction of others.

Some of the job characteristics of importance to job and organization design have asserted their dominance in the studies. They can be classified into two types: 1. job content and structure characteristics, which reflect the interaction between personal and technological requirements, and 2. job environment characteristics, which reflect the interaction between personal and organizational requirements. Job content characteristics are concerned with the number and kinds of tasks and their inter-relationships. Many of these are specific illustrations of the need for the development of a work role which provides comprehensiveness, i.e., the opportunity to perform all tasks required for product or process completion and at the same time imposes the responsibility and confers the authority for self-direction and self-regulation.

Improvement in total performance was thus frequently obtained when the scope of jobs included all tasks required to complete a part, product, or service, when the job content included all four types of tasks inherent in productive work: auxiliary or service (supply, tooling), preparatory (set-up), processing or transformation, and control (inspection); when the tasks included in the job content permitted closure of the activity, if not product completion, permitting development of identity with product or process. Tangible gains in performance were also obtained by the introduction of task variety in the form of larger numbers and kinds of tasks and skills as well as more complex tasks. The

J.S.   D characteristics of processing tasks which led to improved performance were self-regulation of speed of work and self-determination of work methods and sequence. Total performance also improved when control tasks were included in jobs, permitting outputs to be evaluated by self-inspection, and when product quality acceptance was within the authority of the jobholder.

The job environment characteristics that contributed to improvement in total performance were again those that supported the development of responsible autonomous job behaviour. They indicate a job structure that permits social interaction among jobholders and communication with peers and supervisors, particularly when the maintenance of continuity of operation is required. A reward system that supports responsible autonomy was shown to provide gains beyond those of simple increases in task output.

Appropriate management behaviour is, of course, required for jobs having these characteristics. The behaviours called for are supportive in providing service, general planning of activities, and evaluation of results on the basis of organizationally meaningful objectives. They stand in contrast to present overly specific task planning and work measurement, obtrusive supervision, coercive external control, imposed external integration of specialized tasks, and external coordination of fractionated activities.

Certain important aspects of organizational design were also brought to light by the studies. Where small organizational units, or work groups, are required, group structures having the following features appeared to lead to improved performance: 1. group composition that permits self-regulation of the group's functioning, 2. group composition that deliberately provides for the full range of skills required to carry out all the tasks in an activity cycle, 3. delegation of authority, formal or informal, to the group for self-assignment of tasks and roles to group members, 4. group structure that permits internal communication, and 5. a group reward system for joint output. As regards the design requirements for larger organizational units with more complex interactions, it would be hazardous to draw any conclusions from the studies. Whether or not present extensive research will make a contribution to our understanding of the design requirements of large organizations is not yet clear.

Overall it is obvious that we are only beginning to identify relationships among technology, organization, and the individual which are capable of being translated into organization and job design recommendations. Nevertheless, it requires no very great powers of foresight to suggest that we are rapidly approaching the time when re-evaluation of management precepts and practices will have to take place. Many currently fashionable management programmes are mere palliatives, addressed to patching up essentially inappropriate organization and job structures. Among these, the so-called worker communications programmes, participation techniques directed at providing workers with 'feelings of importance', and human relations programmes dealing with personal relationships and supervision (often in the abstract, outside the industrial or business context) do not stand up under objective scrutiny. Almost without exception their achievements fall short even of their own stated objectives.

In summary, changes in organization and job design are indicated, as are associated changes in management behaviour. Whether and when they will take place cannot be forecast. Industrial and business history is replete with examples of the continuation of superannuated institutions and procedures.

Further Reading: The History and Theory of Job Satisfaction

C. ARGYRIS, *Integrating the Individual and the Organization*, London, Wiley, 1964.

L. E. DAVIS, R. R. CANTER AND J. HOFFMAN, 'Current Job Design Criteria', *Journal of Industrial Engineering*, Vol. 6, 1955, 5–11.

L. E. DAVIS AND J. C. TAYLOR (Eds.) *The Design of Jobs*, Harmondsworth, Penguin, 1972.

J. H. GOLDTHORPE, D. LOCKWOOD, F. BECHOFER AND J. PLATT, *The Affluent Worker: Industrial Attitudes and Behaviour*, Cambridge, Cambridge University Press, 1968.

P. G. HERBST, *Socio-Technical Design: Strategies in Multi-disciplinary Research*, London, Tavistock, 1974.

F. HERZBERG, B. MAUSNER AND B. SYNDERMAN, *The Motivation to Work*, New York, Wiley, 1959.

E. E. LAWLER, 'Job Design and Employee Motivation', *Journal of Applied Psychology*, Vol. 55, 1971, 259–86.

B. LIKERT, *New Patterns of Management*, New York, McGraw-Hill, 1961.

D. MCGREGOR, *The Human Side of Enterprise*, New York, McGraw-Hill, 1960.

F. J. ROETHLISBERGER AND W. J. DICKSON, *Management and the Worker*, Harvard, Harvard University Press, 1939.

E. TRIST, G. HIGGIN, H. MURRAY AND A. P. POLLOCK, *Organizational Choice*, London, Tavistock, 1963.

V. H. VROOM, *Work and Motivation*, New York, Wiley, 1964.

4 The Experience of Work

In this chapter we are taking a rather different approach to work. This chapter is concerned with the actual experience of people at work; what it feels like to do a boring, routine, meaningless job, regardless of whether that job is manual or white collar, and why some people who are able to, would prefer to opt out.

Obviously there are plenty of people who gain a great deal of satisfaction from their jobs, but just as good news does not often hit the newspaper headlines, so these jobs do not feature prominently in the literature in this subject area, since the main focus is the need to improve the multitude of unsatisfying jobs which exist.

Tony Lane describes the experience and feelings of a 'machine minder'; the lack of control which reduces him to an automaton serving an alien machine; the unpleasant conditions, and the irritants in the situation which to him symbolize oppression.

This theme is continued in the second extract which deals with that archetype of scientific management, the car assembly plant. In the study described here, Huw Beynon talked to some of the men about their 'ideal' job and their experiences in training and adapting to work on the line. Their comments portray well the problems and frustrations of this sort of work.

White-collar jobs can be just as routine and boring as manual jobs, particularly with the widespread use of computers. In many cases too the pay may be no higher than for manual jobs, though the conditions and surroundings are usually better. The third piece, by Philip Callow, is an account of the various clerical jobs which he has held and his description shows that his reactions to the jobs were very similar to those of the machine minder and car assemblers, even though the actual tasks he was performing were quite different.

Traditionally, there has been an assumption that the working class were mainly concerned with the financial rewards of work, while the middle classes placed greater emphasis on the interest and responsibility of work. Indeed Hulin and Blood have suggested that differences in response to job enlargement may be explained by these differences in work values. They argue that white-collar workers and manual workers in rural areas tend to identify with middle-class values and therefore to respond favourably to job enlargement, whereas manual workers in urban settings do not. Our fourth reading, by Roger Williams and David Guest suggests that the traditional assumptions may need to be questioned. They discern the beginnings of a change in the values of some middle-class people, who no longer regard their work as a 'central life interest' and may give priority to family and leisure interests. Another middle-class group, including doctors and teachers are becoming more concerned with the relative financial rewards of their work and no longer see the intrinsic rewards of their work as sufficient compensation.

Finally, Stanley Parker analyses the statements made by people in a wide range of jobs, published in the book *Work: Twenty Personal Accounts*. From this analysis he has drawn out the main themes about what makes work satisfying and dissatisfying for them and he suggests that there is a considerable gap between the most and least rewarding kinds of work, which cannot be entirely justified by the differences in the abilities of the people concerned. He also discusses the meaning which people attach to their work and the ways in which this varies, with type of occupation, industry and status of the individuals.

Throughout this chapter we will look at the ways in which people relate to their work and in particular to the monotonous jobs which characterize many other advanced industrial societies as well as Britain. The following chapters will consider efforts which have been and are being made at both theoretical and practical levels to alleviate the frustrations which come out so clearly in the readings in this chapter.

The Machine Minders

Tony Lane

Reprinted with permission from *New Society*, 30 January 1969, pp. 163–4.

Machine minders. Official euphemism: machine operators. Official classification: semi-skilled. Products of divided labour. Mill a bit here, drill a bit there. De-burr here, ream there. Spot-face here, countersink there. Mill 700 items a day; drill 900 a day; spot-face 2,700 a day. Seven and a half hour day – one half-hour meal break. Work like automatons, eat like pigs. Shifts. 7 am to 3 pm this week: 3 pm to 11 pm next.

Noise. Screaming air-drills. Whirring motors, roaring motors, clanking motors. Foreman's never heard of industrial deafness. Who cares about Concorde? We have got more than our share of decibels: all day.

Fifteen pounds a week basic. Fiddle your piece rate and work Sunday morning to make it twenty. The 'affluent society': private wealth and public squalor. Emphatically public squalor, but who is hiding the private wealth? Not us. Average wage – says Department of Employment and Productivity – twenty-two pounds ten. Where is my two pounds ten?

The machine. Grey, appropriately enough. Dominates the senses: ears overpowered, eyes hypnotized yet watchful of rhythms, hands geared to buttons, knobs, parts machined, parts not yet machined. Enslavement: total. For seven and a half hours a day. For half the waking hours. For three quarters of the average life-span.

First machine minder: 'I suppose someone must like working in a factory.'

Second machine minder (looking amazed): 'Don't be bloody daft. They just go on from day to day, week to week, year to year, and before they know where they are they're drawing their pension.'

Myopic – on the way to work. Resigned to another day of oppression we prepare ourselves by dulling our perceptions. Exchanges of taciturn greetings and ironic remarks of how great it is to be at work again.

'You have to be mad to work in this place.' Says a bloke who has exhausted the employment possibilities in every factory within a ten mile radius.

'You daren't think about it.' Says a bloke who has done nothing but mind machines since he left school twenty years ago.

Beaten – on the way home. The last seven and a half hours a blank. Overcome by inertia. Ears readjust to more subtle nuances of sound. Disconcerted – momentarily – to encounter clean air. A little surprised to find it is either light or dark outside. Artificial light of the factory gives little indication of the sun's progress. Morose for an hour afterwards. Wife and children learn to ignore me for a while as I re-absorb one of the saner interludes of my life.

'They look like zombies when they come out.' Says a bloke who is just going in.

It's a job – as we say when we are asked about it. We don't classify it as 'good' or 'bad'. In a bad week we can buy the essentials. In a good week there are a few extras.

'It's a good job here. We are expanding all the time.' Says the personnel supervisor with a personnel smile.

Management imbued with the Panglossian doctrine: 'Private misfortunes contribute to the general good, so that the more private misfortunes there are, the more we find that all is well.'

'You have to be mad to work here . . .'

What I mean is not that you have to be mad to work in this specific place, for the same fundamental conditions prevail elsewhere, but that you have to be mad to put up with this sort of work. Perhaps this is false consciousness. I project on to myself the insanity of a technological rationale which makes me an object.

'You daren't think about it . . .'

Daniel Bell states in *The End of Ideology*: 'Whatever the derogating effects, the men who use power-driven tools sense these instruments, almost as in driving an automobile, as an extension and enlargement of their own bodies, their machines responding, almost organically, to their commands and adding new dexterity and power to their own muscle skills.' This is plausible. But only to those seeking an apologia.

A machine does not do things that I cannot do myself. Machines

are creations of men and can therefore perform only those operations that men have done or can conceive of doing. Machines
are duplicators: they may be more accurate and consistent than
men but they remain duplicators.

I am to my machine what the eunuch was to the sultan: an
enslaved impotent. The machine is an alien dictator. To call me
an operator is to abuse the language. To operate on something
implies control. And to argue that I 'control' my machine is to
impose a very restricted meaning on the word. On a strictly
empirical basis I do of course control the machine for I push the
buttons and pull the levers that actuate and terminate the
machine's cycle. Yet here, as elsewhere, empiricism is apt to miss
the subtleties. It is of *no* importance that I start a process: it is
of *great* importance to consider the relationship in which I
stand to my machine.

The machine is alien. And not just because it minimizes and
ridicules one small part of my skills. Not just because it makes
an automaton of me by making no intellectual demands and
requiring only the most rudimentary muscular skills. The
machine is alien, not so much because of what it demands, but
because it *demands:* peremptorily. I am in the classical position
of the slave. It is not then surprising that when my machine
breaks down I have a feeling of elation. A temporary victory
has been secured. The master has fallen. But only symbolically:
he will rise again.

My machine demands rhythmically hundreds or thousands of
the same type of activity. Pause for a drink and a smoke. But
not too long or too often: the machine has human allies. No
escape into the alleged fantasy world of the factory worker. My
machine requires a sort of fitful concentration. Thought or
dream processes are constantly interrupted. The only continuity
is in the workings of the machine: its apparent endless demands
for the same specific motions. Bell might *think* that '. . . machines
respond, almost organically, to men's commands . . .' My
experience is different.

'They look like zombies when they come out . . .'

In ancient Greece, according to Hannah Arendt: 'To labour
meant to be enslaved by necessity, and this enslavement was
inherent in the conditions of human life. Because men were
dominated by the necessities of life, they could win their freedom

only through the domination of those whom they subjected to necessity by force.'

I labour primarily to escape the domination of an inadequate supply of necessities yet frequently, although not invariably, my labour is directed at the production of commodities that could not be described, at least in the classical sense, of being necessities. The *given* world yields up to those who work upon it the necessities of continued existence. But I do not work upon the world: I labour to produce commodities that will be exchanged for the products of those who do. I am alienated from the world for my labour in no transparent or direct sense is related to it.

Let Marx have the last word: 'The more the worker spends himself, the more powerful becomes the alien world of objects which he creates over and against himself, the poorer he himself – his inner world – becomes, the less belongs to him as his own.'

'It's a good job here. We are expanding all the time . . .'

It is implicit in this statement that management now accepts – or appears to accept – my criterion of a good job: security.

Capitalism has conferred certain benefits on mankind. Its justifying doctrine of *laissez-faire* gave to the exploited what they had lacked before: aspirations for realization in this world rather than in the next. Not least among these desires was one for security. And this means more than is implied in the legalistic phrase 'security of tenure' – that is to say guaranteed employment. It is doubtful that to pre-industrial man the idea of 'security' would have had any meaning for it derives its contemporary meaning from a money economy. No money: no food, no clothing, no shelter.

But men, in acquiring the notion of security, experienced a loss. A loss that was a result of the lost intimacy with the world.

When the sociologist asks me what I like most about this job I say: security. I give security top rating. Partly because I know this is intelligible to 'them', but mainly because I know it is useless to expect work demanding involvement. Because I know that it is an unattainable ideal to expect work that would use my actual or potential skills. Yet, although I say: 'The days of the craftsman have gone,' I still stubbornly resist the productive forces and relations that make me a thing. I do not ultimately accept defeat. From time to time, a complex of circumstances gives a transparency to my situation. My resistance, always latent, becomes overt. Over grievances apparently trivial I revolt. I 'go slow'. I work to rule. I sit down. I walk out without warning.

I don't like tea machines: the tea is lousy. I don't like it when the machine breaks down: I am thirsty. I don't like an oil mist over the machine shop: it makes me sweat and stink of Swarf and oil. I don't like mistakes in my pay packet: it means a protracted wait at the wages office after knock-off time. If I were a 'reasonable' man I would accept that these irritants, superficially seen as minor, are subject to remedy in the fullness of time. But for me these apparent trivia are symbolic of my oppression.

Contrary to some academic belief strikes *are* about what I, the striker, say they are about. Strikes are not reducible to personalities, to subversive and 'demented' left-wing groups, to the fact that x's wife won't sleep with him this week. The grievances are genuine enough. Any wider interpretation must take into account the total situation in which I appear as a slave. When commentators accuse me of sheer cussedness they are dead right. And anyone concerned with humanity should be delighted with the fact. I am not letting the country down for I am apart from it: I am its victim. And I don't like it.

'Human relations' and 'man management' types can manipulate all they like: they leave me unmoved or at most contemptuous. The assumption underpinning their theory is that harmony prevails – or ought to. They choose to ignore, or to lend no credence to the idea that I am in fundamental conflict with their system.

Theorists such as Ralf Dahrendorf (in his *Class and Conflict in Industrial Society*) add further confusion. He argues that since ownership and control of capital are now frequently divorced, the Marxist notion of class conflict is outdated and redundant. Industrial conflicts, he says, are the consequences of the authority structure of industry: 'Independent of the particular personnel of positions of authority, industrial enterprises remain imperatively coordinated associations the structure of which generates quasi-groups and conflicting latent interests.' In other words conflict only arises in the very narrow sense of authority as implied in discipline. It apparently has nothing to do with my sense, as a machine minder, of oppression of my whole being. On Dahrendorf's argument I am only chafing at the bit of discipline.

To me it is irrelevant that my employers are controllers rather than owners: to me they are 'them'. An analytical distinction between owning and controlling may have some relevance to some issues but it has no bearing on my perceptions. I am conscious of myself as a member of a class of slaves.

On the Line

Huw Beynon

Reprinted with permission from *Working for Ford*, Penguin Education, 1973, pp. 109–19.

Working in a car plant involves coming to terms with the assembly line. 'The line never stops', you are told. Why not ? ' . . . don't ask. It *never* stops.' The assembly plant itself is huge and on two levels, with the paint shop on the one floor and the trim and final assembly departments below. The car shell is painted in the paint shop and passed by lift and conveyor to the first station of the trim assembly department. From this point the body shell is carried up and down the 500-yard length of the plant until it is finally driven off, tested, and stored in the car park.

Few men see the cars being driven off the line. While an assembly worker is always dealing with a moving car it is never moving under its own steam. The line – or 'the track' as some managers who have been 'stateside' refer to it – stands two feet above floor level and moves the cars monotonously, easily along. Walking along the floor of the plant as a stranger you are deafened by the whine of the compressed air spanners, you step gingerly between and upon the knots of connecting air pipes which writhe like snakes in your path, and you stare at the moving cars on either side. This is the world of the operator. In and out of the cars, up and over the line, check the line speed and the model mix. Your mind restlessly alert, because there's no guarantee that the next car will be the same as the last, that a Thames van won't suddenly appear. But still a blank – you keep trying to blot out what's happening. 'When I'm here my mind's a blank. I *make* it go blank.' They all say that. They all tell the story about the man who left Ford to work in a sweet-factory where he had to divide up the reds from the blues, but left because he couldn't take the decision-making. Or the country lad who couldn't believe that he had to work on *every* car: 'Oh no. I've done my car. That one down there. A green one it was.' If you stand on the catwalk at the end of the plant you can look down over the whole assembly floor. Few people do, for to stand there and look at the endless, perpetual tedium of it all is to be threatened by the overwhelming insanity of it. The sheer audacious madness of a system based upon men like those wishing their lives away.

People, living their lives, develop a pretty accurate idea of their own life chances, of the odds they face and the hopes that they can realistically entertain. One of the more obvious criticisms of much that passes for social science is that it drastically underestimates people's intelligence. Working-class people are faced with a limited number of employment prospects all of which are pretty dreary. If you're young, with family responsibilities and want to move out of the house you know to be a slum you attempt to get as much money as you can by selling to the highest bidder. In a hard world you become a hard man. This doesn't mean that you are not aware of alternative things, better ways of living, but merely that these are unlikely to be open to you. If you work at Ford's, on the line, you let your mind go blank and look forward to pay day and the weekend. As one man put it:

I just adapt to it. I suppose you could adapt to anything really. It depends upon your circumstances. I'm married and I've taken out a mortgage. This affects your attitude to your work. I just close my eyes and stick it out. I think about the kids and the next premium being paid. That's about all there is with this job. It gets frustrating but that's it. What can you do?

I had previously talked to him about the notion of an 'ideal job'. This involved problems but he did say this:

Oh. You're talking about in my dreams, like. The sort of thing I'd *really* like to do if I had the chance. Oh yes . . . I'd like to work on a newspaper. I'd like to meet people. To do something like you're doing yourself. Find out the facts about people's problems. You know about social problems. I've a reasonable knowledge of English. I used to write in the school magazine. I've always had it in the back of my mind. My school teachers said I should do it. I often think about it. There's no possibility now, like.

Another man made the relationship between the real and the ideal more explicitly:

Your choice of job is governed too much by money. You've got to be a realist. What I'd like to do though would be a sports teacher – teach physical education to lads. That's my ideal job, it's important, it would give me a better outlook on life.

You don't achieve anything here. A robot could do it. The line here is made for morons. It doesn't need any thought. They tell you that. 'We don't pay you for thinking,' they say. Everyone comes to realize that they're not doing a worthwhile job. They're just on the line. For the money. Nobody likes to think that they're a failure. It's bad when you *know* that you're just a little cog. You just look at your pay packet – you look at what it does for your wife and kids. That's the only answer.

Most of the Ford workers that I talked to expressed sentiments broadly similar to those quoted above. There was a tendency for men working on sub-assembly operations, which involved them in preparing a batch of components for the line operator and enabled them to 'make their own time', to find the work less frustrating than the men who were actually on the line. The differences weren't all that great, all the men I talked to felt that their job was either 'completely dull and monotonous' or 'dull most of the time'. Similarly most of them had some idea of the sort of job that they would like to do if they had or had had the opportunity. The two quotations are unrepresentative in one sense however. While all the 'ideal jobs' mentioned were chosen for their intrinsic qualities, a majority of the sample of members opted for jobs which took them 'outside the system' where they were 'their own boss'. They talked of being back in the services or at sea or driving a lorry again.

In the absence of an 'ideal job' these men came to terms with working in a car plant; with working on or around the line. They arrived and were put straight on to a job. The Ford Motor Company doesn't have, or need, much of a training programme for its new operatives. The automobile industry is the domain of the new 'semi-skilled' worker. Less than one worker in a hundred in a car plant can call himself skilled in any real sense. As early as 1925, in fact, Henry Ford had estimated that 79 per cent of his workers could be made proficient in eight days and as many as 43 per cent of them required only one day's training. In the PTA plant at Halewood it would be difficult to claim, without doing severe damage to the meaning of words, that the production workers were trained at all.

> Oh they've got a *great* training programme here. A great training programme. I can't remember how long it is . . . two days I think. I'm not sure though. I didn't get any training at all when I came here, but I think they get two days now.

What does this training involve? Do men still go straight on to the line?

> Oh yes, they go straight on the line all right. You know the sort of thing 'this is Fred, he'll show you what to do.' 'Hello' says Fred 'you stick this in here and that in there – I'm not paid for this y'know.' You either do it or you don't. If you don't you're 'unsuitable' and you get your cards.

As a consequence of this the introduction to the line is often a harrowing experience. A mate of mine went to work on the assembly line in the Vauxhall plant at Ellesmere Port, over the water from Liverpool. He was six feet two, a bit dozey and not too agile. He was put on the night shift, fitting electric wiring through the dash board of the Viva. He lasted two shifts. While his mates were trying to do the job that bit faster so that they could work back up the line and create a few minutes break in every hour, he found himself working just that bit slower. He was ending up several stations down the line. Getting in the way of his mates; falling over; getting cursed. Tall, dozey men don't belong on an assembly line.

Most people survive their period of probation and become fully fledged assembly-line operatives. They all found the experience painful and had established means of coping with it. They 'blanked out their minds', perfected 'mental blackouts' or thought about crossword puzzles. Complete social isolation may be a 'solution' but many of the assemblers felt this to be unbearable. They make great efforts to communicate with their mates but there was the problem of the noise. 'You can talk but you can't have a conversation in this place.' They develop a system of handsigns, they gain minutes by working back up the line, all 'to have a laugh and a joke. That's about all that keeps you going.' If they're lucky they can get a change of job, and if they are very lucky they can get off the line.

A twenty-three year old fork lift driver put it like this:

When you're doing the same job, day in, day out, you'd rather do almost anything for a change. I'm used to it though. Sometimes you look around and ask when are you going to be anything other than a clock number. Now take you, you can pick, you know you'll do something worthwhile. With me it's just a case of asking 'is it ever going to change?'

And a twenty-one year old worker from the Final Assembly Department:

There's nothing interesting in the job. It's just boring. Whenever there's a vacancy I ask for a move just for a change. I moved from the Anglia to the Cortina engine dress because I was really fed up. It's not much of a change but it's a bit different – for a few shifts at least. I'd prefer to be on sub-assembly really. You can make your own time there.

And another thirty year old:

I place the car off the hoist, I've been doing that for three years now. With the line you've got to adapt yourself to the speed. Some rush and get a break. I used to try and do that but the job used to get out of hand. I just amble along now. Thirty seems a lot when you're working here. Some jobs you're on you can't talk or you'll lose concentration. When I came here first I couldn't talk at all. Now I can manage a few words with the man opposite me.

To be off the line is to experience an immense sense of relief. Those who have escaped or dodged the line dread the thought of being caught up in it again.

> It's a relief when you get off the moving line. It's such a tremendous relief. I can't put it into words. When you're on the line it's on top of you all the time. You may feel ill, not one hundred per cent but that line will be one hundred per cent. Being on sub-assembly is like getting off the roundabout. Y'know . . . day in day out . . . never stopping. I still have nightmares about it. I couldn't go back on that line. Not for anything.

They feel no moral involvement with the firm or any identification with the job. No one that I talked to thought that he'd feel too bad about leaving Ford's for a 'similar job in the area'; seven of the sample in fact thought that they'd be quite pleased. To quote a man on the cross feed:

> I bring books and crossword puzzles to work. This gives me something to think about when I'm doing the job. You walk out of here in a dream.
>
> I *will* leave soon. It's getting me down. It's so monotonous, tedious, boring. I was just going to make a convenience of Ford's for a few months but I'm still here. Not for much longer though. Yes: I'm leaving soon. I'm not happy here. I'm definitely not going to stay for much longer.

And another on the Trim:

> It's the most boring job in the world. It's the same thing over and over again. There's no change in it, it wears you out. It makes you awful tired. It slows your thinking right down. There's no need to think. It's just a formality. You just carry on. You just endure it for the money. That's what we're paid for – to endure the boredom of it.
>
> If I had the chance to move I'd leave right away. It's the conditions here. Ford class you more as machines than men. They're on top of you all the time. They expect you to work every minute of the day. The atmosphere you get in here is so completely false. Everyone is downcast and fed up. You can't

even talk about football. You end up doing stupid things. Childish things – playing tricks on each other.

The only regrets they'd have would be the mates they'd leave behind.

The Clerk
Philip Callow

Reprinted with permission from *Work: Twenty Personal Accounts*, ed. Ronald Fraser, Pelican Books, 1968, pp. 55–62.

Start at the beginning: Civil Service Clerk, Temporary, at the local Ministry of Works depot in my home town. Can't get any lower than that. At the base of the bureaucratic pyramid, buried alive in fact, the temporary clerk is the navvy of the Civil Service, without status or security. When I took the job I'd only worked in factories, and so was a bit in awe of the office world I was about to enter. As an apprentice, queuing in the spotless corridor on Thursdays outside the Wages window, peering in at the comparative purity of desks and paper and slick dandified staff, you got a queer, dizzy sensation – something like Alice in Wonderland. My brother was a clerk himself, at the Council House, but I never connected him with this Thursday vision.

On my first day as a clerk, going down the street with my brother, I confessed how nervous I was. 'Listen,' he said, 'you can write your name can't you? You can add up? Then you can be a clerk.'

It was true. The depot was a big old house near the city centre, with the offices upstairs. My boss had a room at the front to himself, and behind him was a door leading to my den, which contained three others. This boss, a big, bumbling embarrassed man addressed us all with the 'Mr' fixed firmly between, as if to maintain his distance. Everybody accepted his remoteness as inevitable, something which struck me as weird from the beginning, especially as you had to go to and fro behind his chair to the outer door every time you went to the lavatory, to the foreman downstairs, to interview Irish labourers, and so forth. The boss sat through it all encased in silence and dignity, like an Under Secretary.

Holed up in the back room it was snug and at first I liked it, till the novelty wore off and the chronic, stagnant boredom began to take over. An old man, the only other Temporary, made tea in a corner where he sat, and he did all the menial labouring jobs, stamping and numbering time sheets, sorting vouchers: so at first I helped him. The other two did the more skilled entering and balancing, working on wage sheets, PAYE tabulations and other mysteries I never penetrated. It seemed to culminate, their activity, in the grand climax of pay day, which was Friday. Then the boss, for an hour or so, came out of his fastness and was nearly human. He'd march in smiling with the box stuffed full of money, and together they would count and parcel it. Out went the box again, stuffed with pay envelopes.

I ought to mention another clerk, who worked out in the boss's sanctum, I presume because of lack of space. I don't think he was higher in grade than the other two. Between him and the two in my place there was a non-stop cold war going on – I never found out why. The old man was treated with amiable contempt by the established clerks, who asserted their superiority now and again, and, as the old man was deaf, kept up a running commentary, half fun and half malice, which they evidently found necessary to break the monotony. Before long I needed it as much as they did. The worst aspect of a clerk's existence was being rubbed into me: it's how prison must be. At first you don't even notice; then it starts to bite in. Because of the terrible limitation on your physical freedom – *chained to a desk* is right – you are soon forced to make your own amusements in order to make life bearable. You have to liven it up. And with the constriction comes inevitably an undertow of bitterness, and all kinds of petty behaviour arise out of the rubbing frustration, the enforced closeness. Plenty of it is malicious.

In a factory, which I used to think was a bad enough prison, it is at least big enough for you to wander about physically and visit your mates on other sections. If you can stray from your desk as a clerk you're lucky, though it's true that no two office jobs are alike. The very worst kind, and they ought to be abolished, are those that have you lined up in rows facing the front, with the eagle eye on you and no excuse for moving at all. I had one exactly like that in a vast ordnance depot, Civil Service again, and the place of work was nothing more than a huge draughty shed with girder work in the roof and no ceiling. It held about fifty clerks, men and women, spaced out equally on a concrete floor at trestle tables, and all facing the glass box which contained the administrative staff. The boss in this fantastic set-up was a woman, and contact with this dragon – not that anybody wanted it – was impossible, unless you were on the mat for some crime. The jobs being done by all of us out on the floor were identical, as far as I could see. We had a pile of stores vouchers, a register, an indelible pencil each. There were numbers in your register which tallied with the vouchers. You had to find the corresponding number, tick a space, turn the voucher from a pile on your right to one on your left. No talking, no contact, nothing – unless you counted trips to the bogs. I had to move my legs somehow, just to convince myself I was still alive, so my trips became more and more frequent. When I wasn't squeezing out a drop of water I was washing my hands. I think I stuck it a week, then was hauled up in front of the dragon one morning for being half an hour late. I have never stumbled on such a nightmare since, and began to wonder if I dreamt it. How long could those others have been there, and why did they stick it? Monsters they must have been. When you find yourself amongst it, one of the damned like that, you don't pity your fellow victims, you loathe them. Somehow they get the blame for being there, for trotting in like sheep every day, for letting it exist. No doubt though it is still rotting merrily away, the whole shed-full.

Another clerical job, at a builder's merchants, was redeemed to some extent by the fact that you were actually in the warehouse, among storemen, sales reps, and all the tangible, fascinating paraphernalia of the trade, racks and bins and lofts stacked with it: one occupational hazard facing a clerk is always the sense of futility he struggles against, or is more often just overwhelmed by. Unlike even the humblest worker on a production line, he doesn't produce *anything*. He battles with phantoms, abstracts: runs in a paper chase that goes on year after year, and seems utterly pointless. How can there be anything else other than boredom in it for him?

I admit that when I started in my first office job at the Ministry of Works, after years in a big factory, I liked it. For one thing it was much more human and relaxed, almost a family affair – even if the family got a bit testy now and then. I realize this was mainly a matter of size: working in a converted house with about twenty staff in it somewhere, as against 2,000 men in a great shed of machines and din, grinding in and out of the gates in herds, clocking in and out. Even the 'Mr' I enjoyed, though it made me feel daft. At least I was an individual again, not a number on a card.

But a really big office can be just as inhuman as a factory, you can punch a clock just the same, and the only real difference is your clean collar and alleged respectability. As for the idea that you're part of management, nobody is fobbed off with that guff any more. The only ones who want to believe it are the little bosses, the section heads on the climb up. The higher grade administrative staff, of course, *are* management in sympathy and aspiration, yet in my union, NALGO, they are members alongside the rank and file. Thus it is that a daily paper could refer to NALGO as a middle-class union. When a dispute blows up, and a work-to-rule is ordered it is laughable to see the predicament of those union members who are section heads aspiring to management. The whole issue is split down the middle by their 'division of loyalty': nobody knows who is friend or foe. Intimidation of timid waverers is an easy matter in these circumstances. No wonder we are called an 'association' rather than a trade union.

I work now in the engineering department of an Electricity Board. I am more or less given a free hand; as long as the routine stuff gets done and there are no complaints, nobody worries. It is an easy number, time to think and day-dream, congenial workmates, and I know from hard experience I'm not likely to find anything more pleasant. I'm not ungrateful. The basic fact remains though that, in common with the other jobs I've had, it has no value as work. It is drudgery done in congenial surroundings. You feel dispensable, interim: automation will take it over one day, the sooner the better. You are there for the money, no other reason. You begrudge the time. Incidentally, what makes this particular job congenial is not hard to understand: I gravitated to it via the Consumer Section and the Commercial Office. The first was a sweatshop in a basement, an atmosphere of browbeating in overcrowded conditions with next to no daylight. The second was not much better, pressure of work and nagging phone complaints from the public helping to generate a cynical, why-don't-you-drop-dead attitude. Both of these places were ruled by clerks, in the shadow of accountants and ever-tightening schedules of the machine billing. In the Consumer Section of those days, not long after Vesting Day (when it was normal to pick up a phone and hear an irate consumer snarling 'Nationalized? You mean paralysed!') my first job was to vet the meter reading books. I had a temporary clerk helping me, a slow-moving pensioner who was regarded humourously as a 'character'. We worked, elbows touching, at a big sloping desk which put me in mind of Dickens. So did the debtors arriving at the inquiry window with tales of woe, so did the boss delivering his homilies, threats and explanations. I half listened to all this and found it hard to concentrate on the endless flapped-back, dog-eared pages of the meter reading books, looking for missed readings, watching the clock, remembering the time the driver came to collect the next pile of books for the accountants. If a quarterly reading had been left blank I had to estimate it by turning back to the corresponding quarter the previous year, then insert my version, signed and dated in red ink. The other quarters of the year were also supposed to be taken into account and a rough estimate struck, but I never had time for more than an intelligent guess. In addition I had to use the reading cards left at houses because of no reply and returned within forty-eight hours. Some made no sense after you had deciphered them: more waste, and the clock was ticking, the van coming, and any minute now one of the two dreaded phones on top of the desk would ring. My colleague, nervous of problems, used to say he couldn't hear too well and leave these calls to me. No wonder: they were hardly ever straightforward. It could be a consumer changing his address, wanting the meters read at his old address and connected at the new one. This was called a Tenancy Ending, and meant calculations, forms, time. Or it was someone reporting a failure of supply: message to be delivered to Emergency Engineer. Or a person had just moved into a house, couldn't get electricity and wanted it connecting. After frantic rushes up and down, asking colleagues who were reluctant to be involved, you might find it was a slot meter and only needed feeding with a shilling. Back to the meter reading books – and one mistake any day in those hundreds of pages could put you 'on the mat'. 'What the hell made you write this – you *are* working out these estimates?' Yes, definitely, every one, every time! I used to stare down at the tremulous red-ink scratches on the grimy sheet, perpetrated weeks ago and back now in treacherous accusation. Had I committed that crime? I even hung my head, condemned. Things were at a low ebb; I touched bottom in that jangling office. Never again will I plead guilty or be made to feel guilty, when it is the administrators who are to blame, they and the dehumanized system they operate with such relish.

Paper work was the prime element, the fabric of life. Going from there to the engineers and their world was like entering paradise. Engineers as bosses are like no bosses at all to a clerk. Paper work to them is a necessary evil. Far from kow-towing to it, they want to have as little as possible to do with it. Consequently you are left to your own devices. The big headache, always, in the preparation of records and statistics, is how to drag the information out of them. They're too busy, on the way out, can't be bothered. Wonderful – yet when they want a vital bit of information they can't understand why it's not available.

The caste system in England is complex and still very much intact. In an industry where everybody is supposed to be working together, clerks and workers don't mix. The worker today, with his more powerful union, his feeling of importance, looks on the clerk with a mixture of incomprehension, contempt and distrust. He knows he makes it go, not the clerk, yet when he comes into the office he is intimidated by the clerk's clever-Dick air. He is convinced all the same that he's carrying the whole office staff on his back. The professional engineer, for his part, sees a clerk as a batman: useful, but definitely not an equal. These class differences in the Electricity Boards and I dare say everywhere, are gradually being undermined. There is steady pressure from below. The workers are now no longer 'manual workers' but industrial staff. They are salaried. They don't clock in any more. They have three weeks leave a year. Their hours are down to forty. Their pay gets better, and you have anomalies such as a foreman earning more than the engineer in charge of him. Faced with this, the clerk is finding it harder to see what privileges he has which compensate for his poor wage. The older engineer moans snobbishly about maintaining the 'differential', the young blood just wants more money. NALGO takes a ballot, goes into the TUC, then makes history by threatening a national strike.

By its very nature it seems impossible to make a clerk's daily life interesting, even if anybody in authority wanted it. The only strike I am really interested in is the one that aims at putting everything in new hands, to reorganize, redesign everything with man and his need for meaning at the very centre, and the work that can't be enjoyed, that sucks a man's juices and turns him sour before his time, chucked out, abolished. It will come to that one day: boredom will bring it about. If it doesn't kill us first. I remember a fellow in our office once (he's been a clerk for seventeen years, and before that he drove a lorry) standing at the window during a slack time and saying: 'Sometimes it's not so bad, I don't notice it, but today it's awful . . . Know what I feel like? I feel like painting the side of that house over there . . . painting the roof, anything, as long as I can see *something* for my work . . .'

Are the Middle Classes Becoming Work Shy?
Roger Williams and David Guest

Reprinted with permission from *New Society*, 1 July 1971, pp. 9–11.

The village milkman in a small hamlet in Dorset is an ex-service-man. Nothing, perhaps, so very remarkable about that, except that when he left the forces in his late forties, he was a successful high-ranking officer. He chose to leave forces life and reject a variety of opportunities in industry and commerce because he thought the rewards he would get from continued work at a high level did not compensate for the costs which this kind of life would force upon him. Now he finds that his milk round is through by 2 o'clock in the afternoon, leaving him plenty of time and energy for a round of golf. He is able to indulge in village political life, he is on most of the local committees, and is a staunch member of the local parish council. His earnings are much lower than they might have been; his power in the country is much less; but he is a happy and contented man.

'Peter Gay' is 30. He has a degree in economics and is a qualified chartered accountant. He has been married for five years and has two children. For just over a year he has been chief accountant at a large subsidiary of an international company situated on the south coast. His salary is well in excess of £3,000 a year. Peter knows that he is earmarked for higher things – but he doesn't think it is worth leaving his present location for them. He has decided that he wants to remain in the town in which he works at present because then he can continue to be on the beach with his family five minutes after leaving work and they can all go riding and sailing at low cost. In his present job he has time to enjoy the company of his wife and children. He feels this also would disappear if he returned to London and to head office and to the promotion that awaits him. He is now actively searching for another job in the same locality even though this may mean a substantial cut in salary.

One of the largest airlines operating out of Great Britain had a vacancy in Germany for one of its trainees. The company had been recruiting from the universities for many years and had six trainees who would have fitted the bill ideally. The job was a good one: there was a substantial increase in salary and it gave the young graduate a chance to be his own boss after a few months' training. Not one of the six would accept the job, despite the promised rise in status and pay and the opportunities for further promotion. The reasons for their refusals were all personal: one was thinking of getting married, another's wife did not fancy living in Germany even for the short period of time involved, and a third did not want to leave his parents.

These are just three examples of a group of people who do not appear to regard work as a 'central life interest'. Other things take priority over achieving success in the work sphere. We would estimate that the actual number of such individuals is still small; their importance lies in the fact that certainly among the middle classes, they seem to have been practically unknown over ten years ago.

Another group of middle-class individuals who are of interest in this context are those who, while they may still be deeply involved in their work, are becoming more and more concerned with the relatively low level of their financial rewards. This group is typified, perhaps, by the young doctors who threatened to go on strike.

They were fed up with having to work ludicrous hours for a pittance largely because they were supposed to be dedicated and involved. They willingly accepted the involvement required by their work but do not see why they should sacrifice the rest of their lives to it. Their desire for more time to themselves and more particularly their desire for more money became a major preoccupation at the expense of their work. With a few adjustments, this story could fit a number of other similar groups such as teachers, insurance and bank employees and even airline pilots. All have turned to militant trade unionism to improve their financial status.

These two groups we have outlined are important because they may reflect a change in the meaning attached to work by different social classes. In the past, the stereotype was that the 'working class' was concerned primarily with financial rewards and with work as a means of passing the time. In contrast, the 'middle-class' concern was with the nature of the work and the scope it offered for responsibility, achievement and purpose in life. Basically, the working-class attitude was supposed to be one of self-interest. It was typified by the expectation that every moment spent at work should be paid for, and once one left the work environment, work ceased. In contrast, the picture of the middle class was more one of dedication in which financial reward had a less central role and in which the individual was expected to act well beyond the minimum call of duty. A useful dividing line in the past was between those who did and those who did not get paid extra for overtime. The middle-class concern with the intrinsic aspects of work was said to extend into a commitment to the organization and an identification with its values and goals, and this implied that any kind of militant trade unionism or attempts at collective bargaining were unnecessary.

The two groups we have described may, in their different ways, be pointers to a swing away from this traditional middle-class involvement in work. The status, purpose, challenge and achievement in the job may no longer be sufficient compensation for a financial return which is diminishing in relation to rising costs measured in terms of mental stress and social upheaval.

The kinds of pressure to which we are referring are many and varied.

One of the most obvious is the ever-increasing pace of technological change. Redundancies are sometimes one of the more publicized results but there is the increased dissatisfaction felt by many at the introduction into the organization of a few persons, such as systems analysts, at salary levels which make nonsense of the previous payment structure. Those in middle management and supervisory positions sometimes feel that they have suffered a marked loss of status. There is an increased attention to detail required on many jobs, with consequent mental stress. And the harm that technological change can do to personal relationships is in some cases irreparable.

On top of that, technological changes often bring about a tightening of control. There is an increased attention demanded to detail. However, the impact of the computer must not be over-emphasized. For the great majority of middle-class jobs, it has had no impact on one of the fastest-growing problems, that of 'information overload'. The amount of new and ever more detailed information relating to most types of job is growing at such a rate that it can be almost a full-time job just trying to keep up-to-date. The costs in time and possible stress, which are incurred in trying to stay informed, mean that many, who may formerly have taken a deep interest in new ideas relating to their work, may now no longer be prepared to do so. In many jobs there is increasing pressure put on by the related problem of making decisions about what information is important and what can be ignored. It becomes increasingly difficult to maintain full commitment to a profession or skill about which one knows less and less.

Apart from the anxiety often engendered by change, there can be additional fears resulting from the insecurity, the changed hierarchies of status and the possible wiping out of promotion channels. These can often be very important for managers, as was demonstrated in Cyril Sofer's study of managers and technical specialists in mid-career. His sample had a high degree of involvement in work which was particularly strong in relation to promotion. Promotion itself seemed, for many, to be the goal rather than the rewards that accrued from it. This seems to have reflected a commitment to a relatively stable social system in which promotion paths could be clearly visualized several years ahead. If the speed of change in the social structure of organizations is likely to increase with the impact of mergers and changes in technology, then perhaps we can expect some weakening in this commitment.

Technological advances have resulted in some jobs being changed radically, although the public image of the job has remained the same. This is especially true in some traditionally middle-class occupations where young people are entering the job with expectations which cannot possibly be met. For example, work of our own has shown that most girls still go into nursing because they want to help other people. The major satisfactions they are expecting are: firstly, the perception of being able to help patients, which really means being able to see them get better; and secondly, the ability to get on friendly terms with patients. Both of these goals are becoming harder and harder for nurses to achieve. Advances in technology, and in treatment generally, have meant that only the really sick ever spend long periods of time in hospital. This means that nurses' chances of having patients whom they can perceive to be recovering under their care are much lower now than they used to be, and patients often do not feel well enough to really appreciate their nurses. This is especially true in children's wards, where nursing used to be a major source of gratification to student nurses. Also, the introduction of much more automatic monitoring equipment into hospitals is taking aspects of patient contact, such as pulse and temperature taking, away from the nurses. In this profession, as in many others, the public image is way behind the technological reality – and the result is that many of those entering the profession are likely to become quickly disillusioned.

These trends lead us to the conclusion that the scope for involvement, previously found in many of those jobs in industry, commerce and the professions, which have traditionally provided employment for the middle classes, is diminishing. To find the fulfilment which they previously obtained through work, they may have to look elsewhere. It is unfortunate that this seems to be happening at a time when the concept of industrial democracy is receiving ever-increasing support. There is a widespread belief that workers at all levels should participate more fully in management policies and decisions. Related concepts, such as 'job enrichment' – which tries to make each individual worker's job as meaningful and personally fulfilling as possible – are gaining more and more acceptance. Some time soon, the competing demands of technical control for efficiency and human control for fulfilment in work seem likely to come into conflict. At some point, the human costs of technical 'progress' may have to be more widely debated.

The Experience and Meaning of Work Today
Stanley Parker

Reprinted with permission from *The Future of Work and Leisure*, MacGibbon & Kee, 1971.

We shall look at the different ways in which men and women earn their living in our society and the different meanings that work has for them. The various sources of satisfaction and dissatisfaction that people have in their work tell us something about how well or how badly the content and organization of the work is suited to their needs. The different meanings that people tend to attach to work according to the type of job they do, and the widespread feeling of alienation from work, are other aspects that merit attention. Finally we may consider the probable changes in the occupational structure that are likely to affect satisfaction, meaning and alienation from work.

The statements that follow are based on data from two sources: 1. surveys carried out by various social researchers, including myself, and 2. case studies from *New Left Review*'s two volumes of *Work: Twenty Personal Accounts*. It is hoped that this mixture of the statistically respectable with the humanly interesting will be more acceptable than either source alone.

Work Satisfaction

Many occupations have been the subject of work satisfaction studies, though factory and office work have predominated. Among skilled factory workers and craftsmen intrinsic satisfaction with the work itself is frequently found, especially when the job involves the completion of a whole product. Assembly-line workers attach more importance to being able to control to some extent the pace and methods of their work. Variety of operations is a source of satisfaction to both factory and office workers, and among the latter the friendliness of the working group is often mentioned (particularly by women). In comparing proportions of satisfied workers in different occupations, there seem to be separate scales for manual and non-manual jobs, with more satisfaction found at the higher levels of skill in each group. Professional workers are most satisfied, and semi-skilled and unskilled manual workers least so.

Of 'special situation' factors which influence satisfaction, social interaction seems to be most important. Insecurity in a job, even when accompanied by good objective conditions, adversely affects satisfaction. Autonomy in the work situation – freedom to make decisions and take responsibilities – is positively related to satisfaction. If three individuals are engaged on the same work with mates doing respectively a better, worse, or the same job, the first is likely to show least job enjoyment. Permissive supervision and leadership, and being consulted in advance about changes in work processes, are conducive to satisfaction. In general, jobs which involve dealing with people provide more satisfaction than those which do not.

The above is a brief summary of some of the main findings from surveys of work satisfaction. These findings give us some idea of the sources of satisfaction and the features of jobs which produce satisfaction, but we need the benefit of more personal accounts to understand the full richness – and also the relative poverty – of people's working lives. If we put these personal accounts within a framework then we can preserve both a personal approach and a systematic one: we understand *people* more fully and we understand *society* more fully.

Let us consider some of the main themes which emerge from people's statements about what makes work satisfying to them:

1. *Creating something.* This is compounded of a feeling that one has put something of oneself into a product and a deep sense of pleasure in the act of creation itself. It is perhaps the most common of all the expressed feelings of satisfaction and felt by the widest range of workers, both manual and non-manual. Referring to steelmaking in the early years of the present century, a steelman writes that 'every pot of steel was an act of creation. It was something derived from the absorbed attention of dedicated men.' An account describes his work partly as 'an act of creation, i.e. if the thing is right there is a form about it, a kind of beauty which comes from its structure; it exists that way because it has been made from the right bits and pieces.' Sometimes the feeling of creating something is linked to how the thing created fits into the scheme of things. Thus tool-making 'was obviously a source of much ego-contentment and status. Each man made a complete tool, jig or punch and die by himself.' Even a product which is in fact created by a number of people can give satisfaction to the one who can feel that it is really 'his'. A journalist, otherwise indifferent to his work, writes that 'for the time it took me to re-read one of "my" stories in the papers next day, I too felt the satisfaction of having created'.

2. *Using skill.* This is often associated with creating something, but it lays more emphasis on what the work does for the person rather than the product. Again, the use of skill cuts across the manual-non-manual division of work. 'The skilled worker has to work out, from drawings, the best method of doing the particular job; he has to set his own machine, he has to get the necessary tools out of the stores, he has to grind his own tools and so on. Using his ingenuity and his skill, the worker is constantly made aware of his active and valuable role in the productive process.' The bricklayer finding 'a certain joy in being able to do something competently with one's hands and in using muscular force with common sense to overcome obstacles', and the computer programmer delighting in the scope his job has for technical ingenuity are other examples of the different ways in which satisfaction can be gained from the use of skills.

3. *Working wholeheartedly.* Various restrictions on full productive effort by workers (attempting to beat the rate-fixer or

time-study man, working to rule, 'go-slows' etc.), are common in industry today. But there is no evidence that these are *preferred* patterns of working and they mostly exist as weapons in the battle to get more money. More enlightened management policies than most existing ones could surely turn to better account the knowledge that most people enjoy working wholeheartedly provided that they do not feel that they lose financially by doing so. A salesman expresses this idea clearly and simply: 'Like most people, I enjoy working wholeheartedly when I work.' A brick-layer says that 'the jobs I have enjoyed most are those where I have worked the hardest'. A slight variation of this theme is the fact that few people like to turn out sub-standard work.

4. *Using initiative and having responsibility*. This theme includes a feeling of freedom to take decisions and a certain independence of authority in the sense of people telling you what to do. To some extent the satisfaction derived from a job having these characteristics is a matter of personality and upbringing. Some-one who has been raised and educated in the tradition of con-formity and subservience to authority may not wish to use his initiative or have responsibility in his job. But it seems that most people value the opportunity to think and act in their work as responsible and relatively autonomous individuals. Even those workers who are 'not paid to think' often find it helps the job to go well if they do. A machine minder will replace the broken part of a machine without calling the supervisor because 'it's quicker and more interesting to do it yourself'. Another aspect of responsibility is well expressed by the doctor's secretary who found that 'one of the chief attractions of the job for me is the feeling of being in charge, feeling that I matter . . . I would cer-tainly be missed if I left'.

5. *Mixing with people*. This is an outstanding source of satis-faction to people whose work involves dealing with customers or clients. The attraction may lie in the variety of people one meets, the feeling of being able to help or teach others, the use of in-dependent judgement as in casework, or simply the pleasure derived from social contact. A teacher writes that his job is 'concerned with growing and developing individuals who are never predictable, and so provide a variety of experience which is always stimulating'. Those whose work brings them into regular contact with other people may not always feel (as does

one minister) 'increasingly refreshed and healed by personal encounter', but at least they will mostly agree with the doctor's secretary that 'it is much more interesting to follow cases than costs'.

6. *Working with people who know their job.* The 'human relations' school of industrial sociology stresses how important it is to have good communication between managers and workers and that it helps if managers show a friendly and interested approach towards their workers. However, if this is merely used as a technique, people tend to 'see through it'. A deeper respect seems to be accorded bosses who really know their job. Among the things that one town planner looks for in a job is the opportunity 'to work for people who know how to get a job done and who are not afraid or ashamed to be seen to be responsible'. Mutual respect is looked for; in the words of a steelman, 'to know that a manager knew his job and that he respected one reciprocally was a good thing all round, good for the metal, good for the melter, and good for the manager'.

So far we have described some of the positive satisfactions that people gain from their work. What can be said of the things that cause dissatisfaction? Obviously some of these are simply the opposite of the things discussed above – not being able to create anything, using no skill, and so on. But the emphases are rather different. Again, drawing on a number of *New Left Review*'s accounts, we can see several themes of dissatisfaction:

1. *Doing repetitive work.* This produces a feeling of never really achieving anything and of failing to use one's human faculties. It has long been recognized as a problem in industry and attempts to ameliorate it include shifting workers from one job to another as frequently as possible (job rotation). The full effect of repetitive work on human beings is incalculable, but we have the evidence of a few articulate victims. 'Nothing is gained from the work itself – it has nothing to offer . . . Either one job is followed by another which is equally boring, or the same job goes on for ever: particles of production that stretch into an age of inconsequence. There is never a sense of fulfilment.' Sometimes fully mechanical work may be preferred to work which requires a little attention because it enables the person to absent himself mentally from the job. Thus a housewife complains of 'the sameness of jobs that require perhaps less than a quarter of one's

mental awareness, while leaving the rest incapable of being occupied elsewhere'.

2. *Making only a small part of something.* Long ago Karl Marx drew attention to what he called the excessive division of labour under capitalism: the forcing of men into a specialization of function that becomes more and more narrow and less and less inclusive of their various potentials of ability. Despite some attempts to give people more of a whole job to do (job enlargement) there is still plenty of work that in effect makes the worker, in Marx's phrase, an appendage to a machine. One operative expresses the view that 'the worker's role is becoming more and more that of an onlooker and less that of a participant . . . The loss of dignity and restriction of talent compatible with modern factory life cause a lack of quality in the factory worker.' To a toolmaker, 'the normal lot of the industrial worker is a very unsatisfactory work experience of performing a fragmented task under conditions he can only marginally control.' These observations suggest that fragmented tasks not only mean less participation by the worker in the total work process but also affect his whole way of life and restrict his personal development.

3. *Doing useless tasks.* It can be argued that any work for which someone is prepared to pay or to authorize payment presumably has a use. But this ignores the extent to which the whole system of production and distribution has become remote from direct personal needs as it has become 'mass'. Much of the growth in the service occupations has to do with protecting property. A nightwatchman describes his work group as 'a hive of men guarding the sleep of capital. Producing nothing, this labour exists to make nothing happen, its aim is emptiness.' Another type of task commonly felt to be useless is form-filling. In offices, factories, schools and hospitals the amount of paperwork is steadily increasing. The occupations it provides are seldom satisfying to the people concerned. Writing about himself and his fellows, a clerk remarks that 'unlike even the humblest worker on a production line, he doesn't produce *anything*. He battles with phantoms, abstracts: runs in a paper chase that goes on year after year, and seems utterly pointless.'

4. *Feeling a sense of insecurity.* The recurrent economic difficulties of the country, combined with technological and organizational changes, have resulted in an increase in the number of

workers being made redundant. This, in turn, has led to mounting fears about the security of jobs. A feeling of insecurity seems to spill over into dissatisfaction with many other aspects of a job. Few people seem able to analyse their feelings of insecurity but many of them mention it in talking about their work. 'There is a general feeling of frustration, a feeling that life has little purpose in such insecure conditions where everyone is threatened with the loss of his job.' (Warehouseman). Sometimes the loss of a job is at least partly looked forward to. 'You feel dispensable, interim: automation will take [the job] over one day, the sooner the better.' (Clerk).

5. *Being too closely supervised.* Much has been learned by industrial researchers about the most appropriate and acceptable forms of supervision, but few of the lessons seem to have been learned by management. Office workers are more often the victims of inhuman supervisory systems than are factory workers. The clerk quoted above describes the worst kind, 'those that have you lined up in rows facing the front, with the eagle eye on you and no excuse for moving at all'. In social work and teaching the grievances concerning supervision take a rather different form. A child care officer explains how the 'hierarchy' is a drag on growth and change: 'What each of us needed in the job was the awareness to know what people were really saying, or trying to say, and to then decide how we could help them. To be assigned a role in a hierarchy contributed nothing to that.' Similarly a teacher complains that the bureaucratic structure of the school means that the school governors and senior staff 'wish to supervise the minutest details of the projects they organize'.

The themes of satisfaction and dissatisfaction discussed above cover many aspects of the jobs that most people do today. Perhaps the most remarkable thing about the findings in general is the large gap they show between the most rewarding and the least rewarding kinds and conditions of work – a gap that cannot be entirely justified by the differences in the actual and potential abilities of the people concerned.

Meanings of Work

The concept of 'meaning' overlaps that of satisfaction (or dissatisfaction). When someone says that he finds his work satisfying because it is, for example, creative, this is a way of saying that the work has meaning for him, that he can see the purpose for which it is done and that he agrees with this purpose. On the other hand, a worker may be dissatisfied with his job because he feels it to be 'meaningless' in the sense of not understanding where his contribution fits into the whole, or even (in the case of highly fragmented work) not knowing what that contribution is. Strictly speaking, of course, any kind of work must mean *something*, even if it is nothing more than a way of earning a living.

Undoubtedly there *are* broad differences in the meanings attached to work, but we must beware of too-sweeping generalizations. Not all middle-class and professional occupations are 'fulfilling' to their holders although a desire to achieve status or success may lead to exaggerated claims about the most trivial and socially useless occupations. On the other hand, the poor economic and social rewards of many so-called working-class occupations should not obscure their real value both to society and (less often) to the workers themselves.

The meaning of work varies with three factors: type of occupation (skills used), industry (use to which the skills are put), and status (position in the employing organization or in society). In many cases the content of the work will vary with employment status, but even where the content of the work is the same or very similar work attitudes may vary according to status. Thus laboratory workers were found to differ in their work values according to whether they were 'professionals' or 'technicians' even though both groups had roughly the same kind of tasks. The professionals were far more likely to say that the kind of work they did was the most important thing about a life's work, while the technicians more often said that security or pay was the most important thing.

A notable difference in status, or *social* position in society, is perhaps better understood as a difference in class, or *economic* position in society: that between workers and capitalists.

Those highly paid employees at managerial level who approach the economic position of capitalists are able, because of their stronger bargaining position, to obtain favourable terms of employment, often including the ability to determine their own working hours. Their work, though more demanding, is usually intrinsically more interesting, partly because they make decisions instead of having to conform to other people's decisions. In short, we may divide people into three broad groups with regard to work experience: the capitalists, who have no need of employment but may work if they wish (minimum constraint); the managers, who are employed on favourable terms (medium constraint); and the mass of employees, who are compelled to work for a living (maximum constraint). Inevitably, work must mean different things to these three groups.

Alienation from Work

The theme of alienation from work is widely used to describe the disengagement of self from the occupational role. As some of the personal accounts showed, workers tend to become frustrated by the lack of meaning in the tasks allotted to them and by the impersonality of their role in the work organization. Such workers are virtually forced to turn to non-work life for a sense of values and identity: 'I only work here, but if you want to know me as I really am, come to my home and meet my family.' Alienation can also take subtler forms among professionals and executives, for whom it may be fashionable to be cynical about one's work but quite 'satisfied' with one's job. Experience of alienation is not confined to a few special occupations, though it tends to be associated with certain characteristic work situations. In bureaucratic organizations it is apparent in the administration of men as if they were things. In an automated factory or office it takes the form of increasing the number of people who deal with the world through abstractions.

Further Reading: The Experience of Work

H. BEYNON AND R. M. BLACKBURN, *Perceptions of Work: Variations within a Factory*, Cambridge, Cambridge University Press, 1972.

T. BURNS, *Industrial Man*, Harmondsworth, Penguin, 1969.

P. CURRELL-BROWN, *Smallcreep's Day*, London, Pan Books, 1973.

R. FRASER (Ed.) *Work: Twenty Personal Accounts*, Harmondsworth, Penguin Books, 1968.

C. L. HULIN AND M. R. BLOOD, 'Job Enlargement, Individual Differences and Worker Responses', *Psychological Bulletin*, Vol. 69, 1968, pp. 41–55.

A. TURNER AND P. R. LAWRENCE, *Industrial Jobs and the Worker*, Boston, Harvard University Press, 1965.

C. R. WALKER AND R. H. GUEST, *The Man on the Assembly Line*, New Haven, Yale University Press, 1957.

D. WEDDERBURN AND R. CROMPTON, *Workers' Attitudes and Technology*, Cambridge, Cambridge University Press, 1972.

5 Current Thought on Job Satisfaction

As we saw in Chapter Three, many of the ideas which form the basis for the current interest in job satisfaction are derived from American theories. However, a great deal of work in this area has been and is being done in Britain. The purpose of this chapter is to give an indication of some of the theoretical work which is being undertaken in this country, in developing these theories further.

The first article by **Robert Cooper** discusses the motivational knowledge on which job design theory is based. The practice of job design is concerned with enhancing the intrinsic rewards of work on the premise that effective performance and job satisfaction derive from the intrinsic content of jobs. Cooper outlines a model for considering work as a means by which an individual's needs and wants can be converted into desired outcomes, particularly need satisfaction and effective performance. One of the problems with current job design Cooper suggests, is that commonly used terms such as 'challenge' and 'responsibility' are inadequately defined. He goes on to propose a framework of intrinsic job characteristics in an attempt to improve the understanding of the motivating qualities of tasks.

Our second piece, by **Emery and Thorsrud**, was originally published some years ago but it seems valuable to reprint it it here, since it echoes Cooper's concern with understanding how organizations 'can contribute to the quality of our work experience and personal development'. The extract outlines hypotheses derived from work of the Tavistock Institute about the ways in which tasks may be grouped into jobs based on a number of general psychological requirements. They emphasize that these requirements are not specific to factory work, nor can they always be met in the same way, since work settings and people obviously differ. Rather they provide general guidelines which may be useful in the practical situation of trying to assemble tasks into jobs to take account of the psychological needs of people.

The following three readings provide examples of the ways in which the differences between work settings and people are being taken into account. **Birchall and Wild** discuss changes which are being made in the method of working from traditional forms of organization to 'group working', in an attempt to offset the ill-effects of repetitive jobs with little scope for responsibility or a sense of achievement. They present a useful categorization of the types of groups found in work situations. They also outline the nature and purpose of work groups which have been created in industrial situations where methods of group working have been adopted to restructure the work organization. They conclude that efforts to improve jobs may be more successful if introduced for groups rather than individuals, so that each group member has some choice about whether or not they wish to take on added responsibilities. The semi-autonomous work group seems to offer the greatest opportunity for the achievement of both organizational and individual benefits.

Another use of the concept of grouping has been developed as a means of reorganizing batch manufacture, known as cellular manufacture or group technology which is described by **D. T. N. Williamson**. He defines the fundamental principle of cellular manufacture as 'pockets of self-contained responsibility in which man's skill, intelligence and enthusiasm are harnessed in somewhat specialized working groups which can extract the best possible result from the level of manufacturing technology in the context of the particular circumstances which apply at the time'. The basic idea is that similar components are manufactured in a 'cell' comprising a family of machines capable of producing those components from start to finish. The cell is operated by a group of men who need to be versatile to cope with the variety of components, and also the different machines within the cell. It is easier for the men to control their work and correct errors because they are operating within a small group and this allows more time for creative ideas and the growth of a team spirit. Williamson suggests that group technology is exactly what is needed by the engineering industry in Britain at the present time, to 'rectify a century of decaying work methods'.

Enid Mumford, the author of our fifth reading, would agree with Williamson that the mechanistic concepts of scientists and engineers have encouraged a belief in the superiority of the machine, creating 'a ludicrous vision of industry where computers will do the decision-making, while men provide low-grade motive or brain-power to carry out increasingly simple and repetitive tasks'. She quotes from the instruction manual of a leading computer manufacturer to highlight the mechanistic design philosophy of most systems analysts and systems designers. That this philosophy should be so prevalent is a tragedy, since the introduction of a new computer system may afford a rare opportunity to actually design the technology to provide for human needs, rather than is usually the case, having to accept a fixed technology and then alter the human situation to try and introduce some improvement. She outlines a method which is being developed to enable computer based systems to be designed using a socio-technical approach, so that both technical efficiency and job satisfaction are increased.

The final article in this chapter is by **Peter Warr and Alan Little** from the Medical Research Council's Social and Applied Psychology Unit at Sheffield. They suggest that job enrich-ment, or any other attempt to improve the quality of jobs, will only be successful if certain background factors are work-ing in its favour. They discuss the factors which they consider important in three categories, job factors, people factors, and organizational factors. If these are taken into account, then they feel there is a better chance of a job improvement programme being effective.

This chapter has been concerned with some of the theoretical ideas developed in Britain during the past few years. The next chapter will show how these ideas have been put into practice in attempts to improve jobs in several different situations.

How Jobs Motivate

Robert Cooper

Reprinted with permission from *Personnel Review*, Vol. 2, No. 2, Spring 1973, pp. 4–12.

The theory of job design, as we know it today, rests largely on the premise that effective performance and authentic satisfaction in work follow mainly from the intrinsic content of the job. The practice of job design is concerned with designing the content of jobs in order to enhance intrinsic rewards such as feelings of achievement and worthwhile accomplishment.

There is of course a tendency to single out mass production jobs as the paradigm of rationalized work having little or no intrinsic attraction. But we should not overlook the fact that many other areas and levels of work are also deficient to varying degrees in intrinsic rewards. Even managerial jobs can be low on intrinsic content.

Currently, most job design applications embody changes in job content rather than job relationships, and are usually described as job enlargement or job enrichment. Both these terms really refer to a particular form of job design – building up jobs that are deficient in content. Jobs may be augmented by means of *horizontal enlargement*, that is, increasing the number and variety of existing task operations, or by means of *vertical enlargement* which refers specifically to the addition of skill, autonomy and responsibility to the job. Job enrichment is another term for vertical enlargement. In theory, job design knowledge can be just as readily applied to overloaded and overly stressful jobs or to situations which offer possibilities of creating new job designs such as are sometimes found in the development of new work systems.

Motivation in Jobs

Job design theory is only as valid as the motivational knowledge on which it is based. Essentially, motivation is concerned with three features of behaviour:

1. personal needs or wants,
2. rewards or outcomes of behaviour, and
3. the means by which needs or wants are translated into outcomes, i.e., how needs become satisfied.

The motivational significance of work lies in its provision of the means by which needs and wants can be converted into desired outcomes. Job performance requires that the employee manipulate the means offered by the job so as to realize outcomes which both satisfy his own important needs *and* meet certain organizational requirements for effective performance. This definition focuses attention on the key role of means both for performance and for need satisfaction. It is clear that performance and satisfaction depend on the appropriate means being available to the employee in the job. Figure 1 illustrates the process. It begins with the employee's needs, grouped here according to their extrinsic and intrinsic natures. The employee *uses* the job as a means for realizing a variety of outcomes which serve to satisfy his needs. Two aspects of the job affect his ability to realize desired outcomes: 1. the means available in the job, and 2. the role requirements. *Means* refer to those features of the job which support or make possible behaviours required to attain outcomes successfully. (The absence of means or the presence of constraints will of course preclude or limit required behaviours.) *Role requirements* represent the organization's and the employee's own expectations of the behaviour required in the job. Foremost are expectations of good performance and low absenteeism and turnover. The role requirements are, in effect, the standards by which effective job behaviour is judged. The job outcomes or rewards are contingent upon satisfying the role requirements. Figure 1 indicates that means are causal to the attainment of role requirements.

Note that outcomes are of two types: first-level and second-level outcomes. First-level outcomes are those which are *directly* contingent upon job performance – pay, promotion, job accomplishment, etc. In themselves, first-level outcomes have no value but acquire value through their ability to secure second-level outcomes such as food, clothing and shelter. Outcomes feed

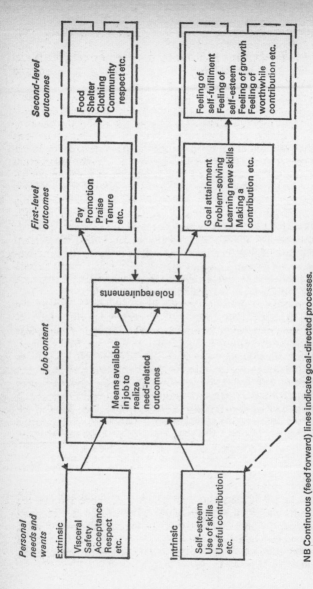

| Personal needs and wants | Job content | First-level outcomes | Second-level outcomes |

Extrinsic
Visceral
Safety
Acceptance
Respect
etc.

Intrinsic
Self-esteem
Use of skills
Useful contribution
etc.

Means available in job to realize need-related outcomes

Role requirements

Pay
Promotion
Praise
Tenure
etc.

Goal attainment
Problem-solving
Learning new skills
Making a contribution etc.

Food
Shelter
Clothing
Community respect etc.

Feeling of self-fulfilment
Feeling of self-esteem
Feeling of growth
Feeling of worthwhile contribution etc.

NB Continuous (feed forward) lines indicate goal-directed processes.
Broken (feed back) lines indicate need-satisfaction and role-maintenance processes.

Figure 1. How the job satisfies employee needs and role requirements.

back (see broken lines in figure 1) to satisfy personal needs and maintain the probability of occurrence of role-required behaviours.

Extrinsic and intrinsic rewards affect motivation in quite different ways. Extrinsic rewards like money and praise are given to the employee by an external agent (e.g., an employing organization or an individual manager) in exchange for attaining standards of behaviour laid down by the latter. Intrinsic rewards are under the direct control of the employee himself. A major assumption of current motivation theory is that intrinsic motivation contributes more to job behaviour and satisfaction than does extrinsic motivation. The reason for this lies in the employee perceiving that, under intrinsic conditions, he is the prime cause of both his performance and his rewards whereas, under extrinsic conditions, performance and rewards depend more on external factors. In practice, this means that rewards in intrinsic motivation are more directly tied to performance and are less subject to temporal lags and organizational mediations than is the case with the performance-extrinsic reward relationship.

The relevance of job design lies in its ability to identify the specific characteristics of jobs that will optimize intrinsic motivation. Terms such as challenge and responsibility are commonly used to describe the motivating qualities of tasks. The problem with such terms is that they do not readily lend themselves to scientific study; they are poorly defined and they lack an underlying theory by which they can be causally related to such dependent variables as performance and satisfaction. Elsewhere, I have proposed a framework of intrinsic job characteristics which attempts to deal with these deficiencies. The framework outlines four conceptually distinct intrinsic job dimensions: Variety, Discretion, Contribution, and Goal Characteristics.

Variety

Variety describes the amount of physical differentiation in the job and its immediate surroundings: differentiation in prescribed work place, in physical location of work, in prescribed work operations, and in the number of people available for interaction in the working area. The variety here is essentially among the prescribed and known features of the job.

There is ample evidence from industrial studies to testify to the influence of Variety on employee behaviour and satisfaction. The consensus of these studies is that little Variety in the job has a definite detrimental effect on performance, satisfaction and absenteeism.

Job Variety assumes two different forms which appear to have different motivational implications. In one form, Variety describes the complexity of the *spatial* environment; in its other form, it refers to the complexity of the *temporal* environment. Spatial variety is the amount of variety within the immediate spatial setting of the job and is exemplified particularly by the variety of operations performed, their cycle times, as well as by features outside the task itself such as the number of people available for social interaction in the immediate work area. Temporal variety in work is usually characterized by a change in the type of work as in job rotation or by scheduled stoppages such as those designed for rests or meals. In the case of spatial variety, it seems likely that performance and satisfaction will be affected largely by 'stimulus satiation' (a form of boredom produced by continued exposure to the same stimulus pattern) which can be dissipated by perceptual alternation among the various elements in the situation. In the case of temporal variety, which involves change in job or environmental content over time, it seems that 'hope' of an expected, desired change after a period of monotonous activity becomes the major determinant of performance and satisfaction. The work curves of routine tasks, for example, are invariably characterized by an upward swing towards the end of the work period.

It is doubtful if Variety is a true motivator. Its value is probably limited to routine, repetitive-type jobs which characteristically induce feelings of boredom; an increase in Variety simply means a decrease in boredom. There is reason to suppose that the general relationship between Variety and the dependent variables of job behaviour will be of an accelerating form with lower levels of Variety exerting a particularly degrading effect on behaviour, the severity of this influence falling off gradually with increasing amounts of Variety. In other words, higher levels of Variety simply serve to make the job tolerable rather than positively attractive.

Discretion

Discretion means being free to exercise choice. Discretion in work takes two forms: 1. choice in organizing the means and tools of one's work, and 2. choice of appropriate knowledge in the solution of problems. For convenience, we shall call the former *Means Discretion* and the latter, *Skill Discretion.*

In skilled work, the two forms of Discretion are functionally related in that the successful application of Skill Discretion depends upon the freedom to manipulate the backup operations (i.e., Means Discretion) as required. Blauner puts it thus:

> The freedom to determine techniques of work, to choose one's tools, and to vary the sequence of operations, is part of the nature and traditions of craftsmanship. Because each job is somewhat different from previous jobs, problems continually arise which require a craftsman to make decisions. Traditional skill thus involves the frequent use of judgement and initiative, aspects of a job which give the worker a feeling of control over his environment.

But in semi-skilled work the two forms of Discretion tend to be dissociated. Because of the largely routine, non-problematic nature of semi-skilled work, Skill Discretion exists only at a vestigial level. However, semi-skilled work does offer some scope for the exercise of choice in the way that methods, tools and pace of work are used. In fact, this is often the basis for the enlargement of semi-skilled jobs.

Specifically, Means Discretion includes deciding the pace one wishes to work at, the methods to be used, and may extend to choice in accepting or rejecting the quality of incoming raw materials and in securing outside services. This form of Discretion is often referred to as Autonomy or Responsibility. Its motivational value derives particularly from the perception that one is responsible for one's own job behaviour and the experience of being free from externally-mediated pressures; these enhance job commitment and satisfaction.

Skill Discretion is, of course, a key characteristic of skilled work. When faced with a job problem, the employee refers to his store of appropriate knowledge and from it selects a set of responses which he believes will lead to a solution; this is the essence of Skill Discretion. The choice of an appropriate response is usually effected through the exercise of logic or trial-and-error. A high level of Skill Discretion in a job produces a keen sense of challenge which leads after successful performance, to a feeling of achievement. It is this which makes Skill Discretion probably the most satisfying aspect of job content.

Goal Characteristics

It is assumed that people pursue goals because they value the *content* of the goal. That is people act in order to gain food, money, promotion, love, favours, or whatever: in so doing they consummate some (usually explicitly recognized) need or desire. Goal-content motivation is often referred to as extrinsic motivation: that is, one performs the task for some reason external to the task itself. But the content of a goal may also cover intrinsic motivation if one likes working on the task for its own sake. Instrumentality Theory represents a sophisticated formalization of the goal-content approach to motivation. In addition to their content, goals possess a certain structure or form which is constituted by 1. *the clarity of the goal*, and 2. *the level of difficulty of the goal*. It is these structural features which directly affect task behaviour.

Goal Clarity: Performance goals may differ according to the degree of clarity or specificity with which the performance criteria are described. If I instruct a student to 'write a paper for me', I present him with a goal of low clarity; he is unclear as to how long the paper should be and when he should complete it by. The clarity of his goal is increased to the extent that I provide this additional information.

Goal Difficulty: Goals which are either too easy or too difficult are less motivating than those of medium difficulty – the latter provide a manageable degree of challenge to the employee and thus draws on his motivation.

Contribution

Most work results in constructive changes which contribute to some end product or service. If the job is to create a sense of involvement and satisfaction, it must represent a fair-sized contribution to the total task. Consider the task of completing a jigsaw puzzle. Our imaginary performer begins by selecting all those pieces having at least one straight side – his strategy is to complete first the outside frame of the puzzle and then fill in the middle 'picture' pieces. In these early stages the fitting together of each jigsaw piece does not add spectacularly to the total puzzle, but, as the salient characteristics of the picture emerge, each added piece contributes more significantly to the task, its significance being proportional to the extent of the information it adds. Many organizational jobs are like this. Compare the job of press operator in a car factory, whose machine presses out car doors from sheet steel, with the job of the assembler, who fixes the same doors to the visible car body. The latter job contributes *centrally* to the total configuration of the product whereas the former contributes only *peripherally*. Adding a door or a steering column or a wheel represent important contributions to the making of the vehicle. Early production contributions have little psychological value because they do not contribute visibly to the vehicle's essential character and contributions which come late in the production process add relatively little because at this stage the vehicle's essential character has been established for some time.

Implications for Job Design

Each of the individual characteristics of our framework implies a unique consequence for job behaviour, as we noted above. Variety benefits performance and satisfaction by reducing the inhibiting effects of boredom; at best, it makes the job tolerable rather than positively motivating. Skill Discretion is the characteristic most likely to produce achievement feelings, while the influence of Means Discretion is especially marked in job commitment. Goal clarity and difficulty are the characteristics most directly related to performance. Contribution adds meaning to one's job activities and thereby enhances feelings of worthwhile accomplishment.

Maximum motivation seems likely only when all four characteristics are amply represented in the job (with Variety being the least important). This follows from 1. the largely additive effects of the individual characteristics, and 2. the apparent fact that they influence job behaviour in different ways.

In practice, most job enlargement programmes fall far short of the maximum motivation ideal, being limited largely to Variety, Means Discretion and Contribution. This is especially evident in the enlargement of low-skilled industrial jobs.

Many job enlargements are also somewhat limited in the extent of their augmented features. Whatever motivational gains they make arise largely by comparison with frustratingly meagre pre-enlarged job content.

It is clear that organizational characteristics, such as technology and the nature of the organization's task, are important limiting (and, in the extreme, probably immutable) factors in most enlargements but the degree to which they actually circumscribe the extension of job content is a question which has not been seriously discussed by theorists and practitioners of job design. The potential for organizational choice may be greater than we think. For example, evidence suggests that several important job content variables are only partly determined by technology.

In contrast to blue-collar job changes, white-collar enlargements, though again stressing Means Discretion and Contribution, tend to be represented by more generous increments in job content. This may be one reason why their motivational effects appear to be so much more remarkable when compared with the results of blue-collar enlargements. Another likely reason is their typically greater emphasis on performance requirements, particularly through the systematic use of performance feedback and/or performance expectations. Perhaps these serve indirectly to shape up goal clarity and difficulty levels for it is significant that reports of white-collar enlargements often note quantity *and* quality increases.

Beyond Job Content

Job motivation does not stop at job content. The individual is embedded in a matrix of organizational forces which can have considerable reinforcing value for job-derived motivation. This view recognizes the systematic properties of the organization as interlocked sources of motivation and meaning in work. Cultivating these sources involves the creation of a *vital system* which optimizes the system's salience for individual, group and organization simultaneously. Job content is a key system variable at the individual level. At the wider level, work systems derive vitality 1. from having autonomy, 2. by engaging pro-actively with their environments, and 3. by contributing to leading societal values.

Vital systems thinking requires a conceptualization of individual work roles as dual-facet structures – one facet being autonomous and intrinsic to itself, the other being dependent on and integrated with its immediate system. The facets correspond to two basic motivational tendencies – the *self-assertive* and the *integrative*. Man's '*self-assertive*' tendency is the dynamic manifestation of his unique wholeness as an individual; his *integrative* tendency expresses his dependence on the larger whole to which he belongs, his partness'. Job design has articulated the conditions required to realize self-assertion; it now must do the same for integration.

Some Hypotheses about the Ways in which Tasks may be more Effectively put together to make Jobs

F. E. Emery and Einar Thorsrud

Reprinted with permission from *Form and Content in Industrial Democracy*, Tavistock, 1969, pp. 103–5.

1. *Optimum variety of tasks within the job*. Too much variety can b: inefficient for training and production as well as frustrating for the worker. However, too little can be conducive to boredom or fatigue. The optimum amount would be that which allows the operator to take a rest from the high level of attention or effort in a demanding activity while working at another and, conversely, allows him to stretch himself and his capacities after a period of routine activity.

2. *A meaningful pattern of tasks that gives to each job the*

semblance of a single overall task. The tasks should be such that, although involving different levels of attention, degrees of effort, or kinds of skill, they are interdependent. That is, carrying out one task makes it easier to get on with the next or gives a better end-result to the overall task. Given such a pattern, the worker can help to find a method of working suitable to his requirements and can more easily relate his job to those of others.

3. *Optimum length of work cycle.* Too short a cycle means too much finishing and starting; too long a cycle makes it difficult to build up a rhythm of work.

4. *Some scope for setting standards of quantity and quality of production and a suitable feedback of knowledge of results.* Minimum standards generally have to be set by management to determine whether a worker is sufficiently trained, skilled, or careful to hold the job. Workers are more likely to accept responsibility for higher standards if they have some freedom in setting them and are more likely to learn from the job if there is feedback. They can neither effectively set standards nor learn if there is not a quick enough feedback of knowledge of results.

5. *The inclusion in the job of some of the auxiliary and preparatory tasks.* The worker cannot and will not accept responsibility for matters outside his control. In so far as the preceding criteria are met, then the inclusion of such 'boundary tasks' will extend the scope of the worker's responsibility for and involvement in the job.

6. *The tasks included in the job should entail some degree of care, skill, knowledge, or effort that is worthy of respect in the community.*

7. *The job should make some perceivable contribution to the utility of the product for the consumer.*

8. *Provision for 'interlocking' tasks, job rotation, or physical proximity where there is a necessary interdependence of jobs.* At a minimum this helps to sustain communication and to create mutual understanding between workers whose tasks are interdependent, and thus lessens friction, recriminations, and 'scapegoating'. At best this procedure will help to create work groups that enforce standards of cooperation and mutual help.

9. *Provision for interlocking tasks, job rotation, or physical proximity where the individual jobs entail a relatively high degree of stress.*

10. *Provision for interlocking tasks, job rotation, or physical*

proximity where the individual jobs do not make an obvious perceivable contribution to the utility of the end-product.

11. *Where a number of jobs are linked together by interlocking tasks or job rotation they should as a group:*

  (i) have some semblance of an overall task which makes a contribution to the utility of the product;

 (ii) have some scope for setting standards and receiving knowledge of results;

(iii) have some control over the 'boundary tasks'.

12. *Provision of channels of communication so that the minimum requirements of the workers can be fed into the design of new jobs at an early stage.*

13. *Provision of channels of promotion to foreman rank, which are sanctioned by the workers.*

The above hypotheses are merely intended as an illustration of the sorts of matters we would wish to keep in mind.

It will be noted that these hypotheses are concerned with a limited number of general psychological requirements:

(a) the need for the content of a job be reasonably demanding of the worker in terms other than sheer endurance, and yet to provide a minimum of variety (not necessarily novelty);

(b) the need for being able to learn on the job and to go on learning; again it is a question of neither too much nor too little;

(c) the need for some minimal area of decision-making that the individual can call his own;

(d) the need for some minimal degree of social support and recognition in the workplace;

(e) the need for the individual to be able to relate what he does and what he produces to his social life;

(f) the need to feel that the job leads to some sort of desirable future.

These requirements are not confined to operators on the factory floor, nor is it possible to meet them in the same way in all work settings or for all kinds of people.

Group Working

Dave Birchall and Ray Wild

Reprinted with permission from *Work Study and Management Services*, October 1973.

Introduction

Considerable interest has recently been focused upon the replacement of more traditional forms of work organization in manufacturing by methods of 'group working'. Critics have suggested that many jobs such as machine operating, machine minding and assembly-line work, are highly repetitive, lacking in responsibility, and offering little scope for the worker to gain a sense of achievement. 'Group Working' has been advocated as the basis of a possible solution. Companies such as Volvo and Saab have been reported as introducing group methods of assembly, whilst accounts are to be found in the literature of group working in situations as diverse as logging and heavy engineering. These reports have perhaps helped demonstrate the importance of group working amongst blue-collar workers as well as the extent of potential applications, but as yet the precise nature of group working remains unclear and there appears to be no detailed assessment of actual or potential application in any one industry.

The types, characteristics and function of work groups

Three basic types of worker activity might be observed in most production situations. The principal activity derives directly from the nature of the work content of the task, which places certain demands on the skills of the worker. Exercise of such skills constitutes a form of *technical activity*. The demands of the workplace, and the nature of the work to be done, also necessitates some interaction amongst workers, thus a second type of behaviour – here referred to as *socio-technical* – is required, and includes any form of social interaction necessary for the performance of the task. The third level of behaviour is purely *social*.

These three basic types of activity are inter-related, hence technical organization and socio-technical activity must be examined in order to understand worker behaviour. For example, the formation of many types of work groups is considerably affected by the technical and formal organization of the work place.

TYPES OF WORK GROUPS

Any number of workers sharing certain characteristics and relating one to another in such a way as to differentiate them from others might be considered to constitute a work group. The form and purpose of the groups may vary enormously, but they have in common the fact that some form of interaction takes place between their members.

Groups within organizations may be categorized in several ways, the principal distinction being as follows:

1. *Formal groups*, created to achieve specific goals and to carry out specified tasks which are clearly related to the total organizational mission. They may be either permanent or temporary groups depending upon the purpose of their formation.

2. *Informal groups:* relationships will develop between members of the organization which extend beyond functional objectives. If the arrangement of the work area, the work schedule and the nature of the work permit, these informal relationships may lead to the development of 'informal groups'. Such groups arise out of a particular combination of 'formal' factors and human needs and are affected by, among other factors, the degree of interaction between individuals, personal characteristics, and external influences. Such groups may be the result of a shared interest such as a common economic objective or they may be purely friendship cliques, members gaining certain satisfactions from their interactions.

Formal groups can be classified by the type of dependence between members, i.e.:

1. Operational interdependence, in which members are dependent for completion of their task upon other members. Groups working in progressive manufacturing systems such as assembly lines are operationally interdependent. Earnings often depend upon the collective performance of the group in which case pressures are often exerted by the group upon those deviating

from group norms. When these groups are found at the shop-floor level there is usually status homogeneity among members.

2. Functional interdependence, in which members are dependent upon others with complementary skills in order to achieve completion of the group's objectives. This category includes such groups as those manning process equipment and maintenance teams. Individual earnings may be related to the group productivity, and the different skills possessed by group members may lead to status differentials.

3. Structural interdependence resulting from organizational design, giving members common supervision and normally common territory. Payment may relate to group or individual effort, and members may be heterogeneous in respect of skills and responsibilities.

Organized or formal groups are divided by Dubin into:

1. *Team Group* in which members designate the positions to be filled and the people to fill them, changing allocation of members to positions as required. Such groups are fairly autonomous, receiving very little supervision, and often working within broad terms of reference established by supervision.

2. *Task Group*. The jobs are clearly defined and each individual is assigned to one and only one job. The group will have some flexibility over method of work adopted and also the rate of work, but little other discretion.

3. *Technological Group*, in which work content and method are specified and individuals are assigned to the jobs. Speed of working is also controlled. The individual has little scope for the use of discretion. He has, however, in most cases the opportunity for some degree of social interaction. The overriding importance of the technology allows the group members little autonomy in determining or varying the operating activities.

The types of work group itemized above are included in the approximate relationship, given in Figure 1 which although containing only a small proportion of the types of group identified in the literature, illustrates the essentially two part and overlapping structure of group working in industry.

CHARACTERISTICS AND FUNCTIONS OF WORK GROUPS

Dubin suggests that in general formal groups are more likely to support individual innovation in connection with the job since they will have generally been established specifically to carry out work. Group innovation, however, is not necessarily beneficial to the organization since the goals of the group may differ from those of the organization. Conduct standards developed by, and learned in, organized work groups are oriented specifically with respect to work, some appertaining to working activities, others to ideas about the work performed. Voluntary

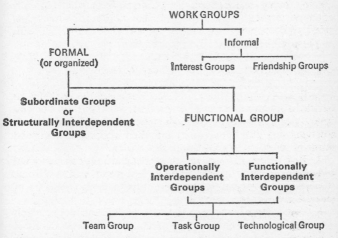

Figure 1. Summary of Types of Work Group (emphasis being placed on Formal Groups).

groups, on the other hand, develop their own conduct standards, largely concerned with interpersonal relations among members. The individual may gain increased confidence through the acknowledgement of his work skills by other respected members of the organized work group.

Work groups, particularly formal groups, facilitate the subdivision of tasks in order to fulfil formal organizational functions. In addition to satisfaction of economic objectives, groups offer members opportunity for social and psychological satisfaction.

Affiliation needs may be satisfied through acceptance by a group, which may further offer individuals the opportunity for the development or enhancement of a sense of identity and self-esteem. Members may acquire the opportunity to exercise influence. The effectiveness of social skills can be tested and improved, whilst the group may also provide the individual with reinforcement and security.

Tannenbaum has suggested that the support offered to the individual by the group is an especially important basis for the member's attraction to the group in the context of the frustration individuals face in their jobs. Such support may be of several types:

1. comfort or consolation to members
2. help or protection to members by acting against the source of threat or frustration
3. strengthening the individual member in his opposition to the source of adversity.

Group norms are developed in most types of functional work group, especially norms relating to the objectives and important aspects of behaviour of the group, e.g. output, work methods, attitudes to management and unions and attitudes on other work subjects, and social activities. Argyle summarizes – 'Norms are created as a solution to the external problems of the group (the work and environment to be dealt with) and as a solution to the internal problems (how to survive as a harmonious social group).' Such formulation of rules and standards often results in groups becoming conservative and resistant to change. Highly cohesive cliquish groups may exhibit hostility to other groups and to external authority and this together with norms relating to group performance perhaps represents the principal forms of group counter productive behaviour.

Survey of exercises in group working

Clearly, irrespective of the type of production system adopted in industry, work groups of various types will exist and possibly exert significant pressure which could be counter- or pro-productive. Equally it is clear that the types and characteristics of the groups existing in any situation are greatly affected by the technology and organization of the work, and that those responsible for production systems design are in a powerful position to influence the nature of work groups relations at shop-floor level.

In this section we shall attempt to identify the nature and purpose of the work groups that have in general been created in industry. We are especially concerned with exercises or experiments in which a method of group working was adopted to replace or supplement an existing work system, and therefore primarily with deliberate attempts to re-structure work organization through the creation of formal or organized work groups.

NATURE AND PURPOSE OF GROUPS

Group size ranges from three to twenty with an approximate mean of nine. Where reasons are given, the majority of exercises appear to have been undertaken in an attempt to overcome manifest problems, typically relating to productivity and quality. In certain cases changes external to the work place promoted or provided the opportunity for the experiments, e.g. changes in output requirements, the introduction of mechanized equipment, the need for expansion etc., whilst apparently in a minority of cases the exercise derived from some concern for the nature of the worker's role or tasks (e.g. to increase work variety, complaints about work conditions etc.) Problems relating to worker absence and turnover are given as the reason for change in very few cases.

WORK GROUP RESPONSIBILITIES

The allocation of greater responsibility for the production process was a significant feature in many of the exercises. Two basic categories of group responsibility could be identified, firstly those responsibilities which call for *regular* decision-making or activity from the group or its members and secondly, responsibilities which might not necessitate recurrent action. In a majority of cases groups have been established for the principal purpose of assuming greater responsibility for the day-to-day operation of their part of the production process. In such cases the groups have normally been given responsibility for tasks such as inspection, allocation of work, supply of materials etc., i.e. regular 'day-to-day' production responsibilities. Such *functional groups* correspond to the autonomous work groups widely recognized in recent literature.

The second category includes the creation of groups whose responsibilities are primarily of the intermittent, even perhaps, 'once only' type.

Detailed descriptions of these latter exercises reveal their essentially *consultative* purpose. Such groups were not, it seems, established in order to permit the re-organization of planning and control activities previously undertaken by inspectors, supervisors etc., but rather to facilitate communication, permit joint management/worker decision-making, etc. The formation of such groups does not diminish the responsibilities of first level supervision or of technical or service staff although it may considerably affect the relationships between worker and supervisor. In contrast, the formation of groups with 'regular' production responsibilities often appears to obviate the need for chargehands, separate quality inspectors, progress chasers etc.

The distinction between these two categories of formal work groups are summarized in Figure 2. The groups as described above are of course stereotypes, and in practice it is likely that some overlap will exist, more so in the inclusion of the responsibilities of consultative groups in functional work groups than vice versa.

Most of the exercises (70 per cent) involved the establishment of functional work groups. In most cases the groups were fairly autonomous, working within fairly broad terms of reference (team groups) or had some degree of control over the rate of work and the method adopted (task groups). The majority of task groups replaced groups where there was little opportunity for the use of discretion and whose work content and method were clearly specified (i.e. technological groups). Team groups, on the other hand, were created in similar proportion from both task and technological groups. Consultative groups were essentially created where the technology of the process controlled the worker's activities.

In general the pattern of development evident from these exercises involves the following movements:

1. In cases where the main objectives of exercises were quality or quantity improvement and for cost reduction the

groups created were given greater flexibility over work method and over the rate of work (i.e. task groups). In 62 per cent of the cases where assembly-line working was changed, task groups were established, whereas only 33 per cent of changes introduced into other situations, e.g. job shops, resulted in the formation of this type of group.

2. When companies were experiencing personnel problems and expressed concern about the motivational content of the work, they tended to introduce much greater degrees of group autonomy (team groups).

3. Task groups were typically achieved in assembly-line situations by a reduction in group size and the addition of responsibility for inspection; work allocation usually remained the duty of the supervisor.

4. In process operations changes often led to the formation of fairly autonomous or team groups. The changes were usually introduced as part of a productivity agreement.

It is of interest to note that whilst the exercises reported here were all selected because of their emphasis on formal group working, they demonstrate a surprisingly diverse pattern of changes. Whilst over one third of the exercises involved the creation of virtually fully autonomous functional work groups ('team' groups), very many exercises involved the allocation of significantly less freedom to the work groups.

RESULTS OF GROUP WORKING

Improvement in quality is cited in a majority of those exercises in which results are discussed, whilst a large proportion of exercises also benefited from improvements in output. Mainly the benefits obtained correspond to the reasons for the introduction of group working, emphasis generally being on the practical benefits of group working. The other benefits associated with the introduction of consultative groups relate to improved worker attitudes, motivation and relationships.

Discussion

Groups of workers are essential to organizations. Manufacturing organizations have acknowledged the importance of social

Type of Formal Group	Primary Role	Principal Responsibilities might include	Relationships with	
			Supervision	Specialist Staff
Functional Work	Day to day operation of part of the production process	Quality inspection Supply and requisition of materials Planning/Scheduling of work Maintenance and housekeeping tasks Requisitions of maintenance repair Production control and progressing Work allocation Work rotation Rectification work	Assume some of routine responsibility of supervision Supervision takes on more of a technical role	Assume some of routine responsibility Group may be given direct access to specialist staff
Consultative Work Group	Communication representation and joint decision-making with management and ancillary workers	Appointment of representatives Problem solving Setting goals for output and quality Determining work hours, breaks, shift, etc.	Joint discussions, problem solving, decision-making	Joint discussion, problem solving, decision-making usually with group representation and supervision

Figure 2. Types of Formal Work Group.

groups and provided, in many cases, excellent facilities for off the job social contact between employees. They have also made use of work groups as a convenient arrangement for supervision, payment etc., and also to enable the efficient achievement of ends beyond the individual's capability. However, the opportunities for the satisfaction of the individual's social needs through formal work group membership have often been ignored by the job designer. These needs that may be satisfied by group membership may be more intensive when the job itself is of little interest to the individual. Workers whose jobs provide little inherent achievement together with little opportunity for satisfaction of social needs are unlikely to be oriented to the achievement of company objectives with consequent adverse effects on quality, absenteeism, timekeeping, non cooperation and even possibly grievance action.

The type of work organization considerably affects the interpersonal contact required by the job, the organization of the work place considerably affects the possible pattern of social interaction. It may be argued that social relationships interfere with the quantity and quality of the work produced. For most individuals, however, work which does not permit interpersonal contact fails to fulfil a basic human need. Moreover, this often essential interpersonal contact may be provided when, for satisfactory completion of the task, a group of workers are required to coordinate their individual activities. Many organizations are attempting to improve the quality of working life by improving the work content of jobs, adopting such techniques as work rotation, job enlargement, and job enrichment. Such changes suit many workers but ought not to be forced upon those who do not wish them. Thus it may prove more successful if changes are introduced for work groups rather than individuals. When additional responsibilities are given to a work group the individual member has the freedom to choose between active participation and passive disinterest. Those who seek peer group approval and recognition will be given the opportunity to achieve this, whereas those who wish only to perform a simple task can also remain a group member.

An examination of reported experiments and exercises in group working has revealed that organizations which have attempted to make better utilization of formal work groups have established groups of two basic types. Those which have been established solely for the purpose of management/worker consultation have often been employed to aid the implementation of change. In many cases, functional work groups have been created with additional responsibilities for the day-to-day operation of part of the production process. These added responsibilities are, in some cases, restricted to functions such as quality inspection and rectification. In others, however, the group has been made fairly autonomous being assigned many tasks formerly undertaken by the supervisor. This use of the work group as a semi-autonomous unit appears to offer the greatest opportunity for the achievement of the formal organizational functions whilst offering the individual the opportunity for satisfaction of his social and psychological needs through group membership, the possibility of exercising influence over decisions directly relating to his immediate job and a job which is inherently more interesting.

The Anachronistic Factory

D. T. N. Williamson

Reprinted with permission from the Proceedings of the Royal Society, A331, 1972, pp. 139–60.

Manufacture is central to our way of life and is our primary source of wealth as a nation. Along with agriculture, mining, construction and power generation, it supports our other activities like education, commerce and trade, transport and distribution, public services, entertainment and recreation. Our current and future welfare depend on its success, and it has for some time been obvious that we are not succeeding as well as other industrial countries. There are many reasons for this decline, but low effectiveness of the manufacturing process is certainly a major and very direct one, and improving that would be one of the surest ways to reverse the trend.

Technological change in manufacture is inseparable from the people who are a necessary, even if decreasing, part of the manufacturing process, and many of our present difficulties have been caused by considering changes to the mechanics of the process in isolation from the people who have to make them work.

The development of factory and business organization at all levels has continued logically from precepts which were, to say the least, doubtful, and in order to cope with increasing size and complexity, has become increasingly authoritarian and inflexible. Decision-making is becoming more and more centralized in an analogous manner to military organization, but the development of western society has taken an opposite direction: authority is everywhere in decline, individuality is more prized, and there is a yearning to participate in decision-making; to shape events rather than be shaped by them.

The blame for this national lack of recognition of the overall goals of society falls not only on the shoulders of management and management education. It must fall also on the scientist and the engineer, who, by their mechanistic concepts, initially in the relationship between man, machines and processes, and continued more recently in the field of computers and information handling, have encouraged a belief in the superiority of the machine. We seem to be encouraging a ludicrous vision of industry where computers will do the decision-making, while men provide low-grade motive- or brain-power to carry out increasingly simple and repetitive tasks. A little reflection reveals the ultimate lunacy of such a proposition, and it can be recognized for what it is, a misuse of technology, and a misunderstanding of the proper functions of man and machine.

Unless considered against this general industrial and social background, technical developments which would point the way to the future have little relevance. We need to place the processes and apply the technologies in their proper perspectives in relation to human beings, so that each can contribute effectively and continue to develop fully its different potential. Machines are only a means to an end, and the happiness, motivation and continued development of people is clearly the most important aspect from every standpoint, including that of efficiency.

One of the three major lines of development in industrial manufacture, and the earliest of these, and still by far the largest in terms of employment, is batch manufacture.

By a happy coincidence of needs and means, a method of

reorganizing batch manufacture, using essentially the same tools as at present, has been developing over the past decade, which is capable of overcoming most of its shortcomings. This has come to be known as cellular manufacture, or group technology, the latter term being the less specific because of the frequent change of meaning which it has undergone, although it is now more commonly used.

Cellular Manufacture

HISTORY

The first publication on the subject was in 1959, when S. P. Mitrofanov published a book in the USSR called *The Scientific Principles of Group Technology*, which was subsequently translated into German and English. It marked the beginning of the first phase of group technology development, but was much more concerned with improving machine tool utilization by reducing the proportion of setting time by classifying and grouping 'technologically similar' parts together to be manufactured conventionally, rather than forming groups of machines or cells, within which groups of people could work more effectively. Almost in parallel with this, development work was being conducted in Europe and America on classification and coding systems with a view to variety reduction, that is, eliminating the duplication of components at the point of design, and it is not surprising that the existence of these systems led to attempts to use them for grouping similar components together for manufacture.

In Britain around this time Audley Engineering (now Serck-Audco Valves) were wrestling with their factory problems, and a total rethink of their business led them to create separate manufacturing cells as a logical solution to their problems. They coined the term 'cellular group production', and this was its first true implementation, and it remains the only known example of total implementation in every facet of the business. In the 1960s there was considerable confusion over terminology, caused by the quite different objectives of the various participants, and at one time classification and group technology were almost synonymous terms, but the confusion is beginning to resolve itself and the term group technology is becoming synonymous with true cellular manufacture, and classification and coding systems are coming into their proper perspective as merely one facet of a wider reorganization of batch manufacture, and of limited use for component family formation.

The fundamental principle behind cellular manufacture which it is much more important to grasp than the mechanistic nuts and bolts of the process itself, is that it consists of pockets of self-contained responsibility in which man's skill, intelligence and enthusiasm are harnessed in somewhat specialized working groups, which can extract the best possible result from the level of manufacturing technology in the context of the particular circumstances which apply at the time. It is to be thought of, not as a static, but as a dynamic structure capable of adapting to change, where productivity gains are not once-for-all-time, but can continue up to a physical limit set by the character of the manufacturing processes. Experience so far goes to show that this can always be better, more efficient and more personally rewarding than the amorphous system, which is in widespread use today.

OPERATING PRINCIPLES AND ADVANTAGES

The operating principle behind cellular manufacture is that components of a like class are grouped together into families and made, from start to finish, in a 'manufacturing cell' consisting of a group of people operating a number of machine tools which, taken together, are capable of all the manufacturing operations necessary. There is not necessarily any set pattern of organization within a cell, and the object is, as far as possible, for them to be self-adapting so that, when changes to the work pattern occur, they are capable of matching them.

The men in a cell are trained to be versatile, and are often capable of operating more than one type of machine or process. Correspondingly, there are usually more machine tools than men in a cell. It is this surplus of machine tools over men which leads the uninitiated to assume automatically that there must be a poorer machine utilization with cellular manufacture than with a conventional arrangement. But this is not so. There is evidence that, because of greater familiarity with the work, the more limited range of machining and correspondingly reduced set-ups within a given cell, the utilization of individual machines rises very significantly, so that the overall utilization is as good as, or even better than, that achieved by the conventional arrangement. It is quite usual to require fewer machine tools after changeover, and this without all the detailed machine-loading scheduling previously necessary.

Because all the machining capacity is available in a compact arrangement, and the machining operations are carried out in rapid time sequence, the time to complete a given part need be little more than the aggregate time for the individual operations. Since the set-ups may be common to the range of components, and therefore used repeatedly, set-up time is reduced, and may even be eliminated.

Comparison of figure 2 which is a flow pattern for cellular manufacture, with figure 1 illustrates the magnitude of the improvement.

The overall time to make a component can be reduced below a tenth of conventional time, and great benefits can be derived from this. It is important to realize that this concept, like the computer-controlled manufacturing systems, departs from the idea of batches and replaces it with a nearly continuous flow of a family of parts through a given cell, and makes it practicable to manufacture parts as they are required.

Breaking these traditional constraints provides great opportunities to reorganize the other facets of the business, with far-reaching implications. Shrinking the manufacturing cycle reduces the inventory dramatically, freeing the money so tied up for more useful purposes, and, in conjunction with the ability to make parts as required, could slash delivery times.

ADVANTAGES IN TERMS OF HUMAN VALUES
So far we have considered the gain in purely mechanistic terms, but the improvement in communication and human values is equally dramatic, and probably more far-reaching. It is common experience and can be demonstrated mathematically that the maximum number of people who can work and communicate together effectively rarely exceeds ten, except for the simplest routine jobs. Under cell conditions the optimum number is nearer six. A group of this size can always follow what is going on in detail, and can correct errors and omissions immediately

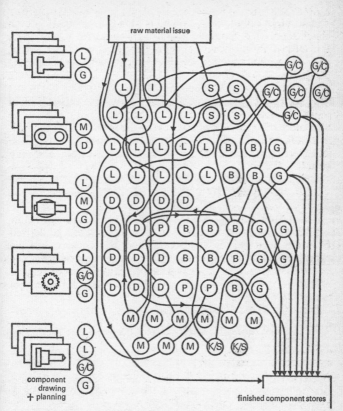

Figure 1. Some routing patterns under functional layout. (Courtesy The Machinery Publishing Co.).

they arise. This is a continuously self-optimizing and self-healing process not readily matched by any inanimate control system, and its value can hardly be overrated. Once an activity is expanded beyond its effective span of control it starts to go wrong, because minor errors and omissions are not detected and corrected immediately and become cumulative. These

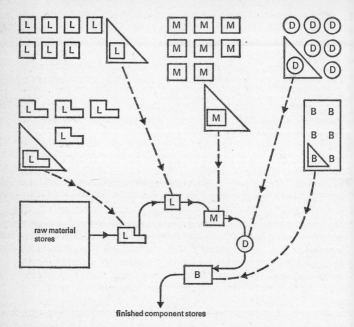

Figure 2. Improvements in factory layout. (Courtesy The Machinery Publishing Co.).

undetected errors have bedevilled attempts to use electronic data collection and processing systems to control large-scale batch manufacture. Only by redesigning the process to shrink the span of control, so that all the people concerned work in a closely knit environment conducive to detecting and eliminating errors as they occur, does data collection become reliable and control easy. A cell becomes the unit of control, and central control gets its progress information from the cell leader. This consists simply of progress towards completion of the allocated task, uncluttered by the usual interchange of detailed information about the latest tragedy, which forms the essential gossip between foremen in conventional manufacture.

Freed from this previously almost full-time occupation, the cell leader can now devote himself to maintaining the morale of his men and encouraging them continually to improve their working efficiency by collective ideas and action. This atmosphere can be achieved in a small group even in the environment of a large workshop, providing that the group is given sufficient autonomy to take their own day-to-day decisions at the cell leader's discretion. Such helpful attitudes can be greatly encouraged by methods of payment, like a group bonus system, which reward collective initiative.

A man working in this environment really feels that he is contributing to his own well-being and that of the company. He can see what he is producing, and how it fits into the overall activity of the company. He can see that day-to-day working improvements which he makes react immediately and are not lost in some endless pipeline. All this fosters rapid growth of skill, team spirit and pride in achievement, which are now almost totally missing in our over-organized industrial society. In my view these are quite priceless assets which cannot be replaced by any kind of job manipulation. Human beings are not by nature automatons, and, if forced into such a mould, quickly lose any interest or enthusiasm. They may continue to do the job as a means of support, but they will seek other outlets for their creative energies, and we need look no further than this for the inexorable rise of industrial unrest. This is rarely to be found in companies which have given people a proper job to do and a creative environment in which to do it. Where relations have deteriorated, frequently owing to changed managements, formerly contented people become restive and attempts to cope by authoritarian methods only aggravate the situation. Once such a pattern has started to unfold, it is difficult to change. One small thing leads to another, and before long we are on the downhill path, with steadily decreasing room for manoeuvre.

The only way to break this is by an imaginative fresh start, and cellular manufacture provides just such an opportunity. Although I do not wish to over-emphasize its role in the long-term scheme of things, I think it is unique in its potential to rectify a century of decaying work methods quickly and at relatively trivial cost. If this opportunity is not grasped or is misused, nothing which so exactly fits the present needs of the engineering industry in the UK is likely to recur. The attractiveness of cellular organization, which gives rise to hope that it may catch on rapidly, is that there is something in it for everyone. The engineer gets a better product more quickly; the salesman can offer better delivery, lower prices or higher margins, and increased flexibility in meeting his customers' needs; the accountant is pleased by the reduction of stocks and work in progress; the manager welcomes the ease with which the system can now be controlled; the shareholder can see a better business with a higher turnround on investment, leading to higher profits; and the artisan works in a different world, where his intelligence is once again put to proper use and where he can take home a higher pay for doing a more satisfying and productive job.

QUANTIFIED BENEFITS
It is difficult in this stage of an emerging technology to present a coherent picture of the benefits achieved so far by the companies which have implemented cellular manufacture. This is partly because only one company has so far 'gone the whole hog', partly because companies have had different criteria and goals in mind, and partly because frequently there was little accurate information about the relevant parameters in the pre-cellular era.

WIDER IMPLICATIONS
There is a mismatch between the trends of professional management in industry and commerce, and the values, aspirations and expectations of the people who have to make the industrial system work and I have tried to show how important it is that the correcting of this divergence must go hand in hand with improvements in technology if we are to achieve any lasting benefit. Unfortunately, while we may dream of a better tomorrow, we always seem to be shackled to an industrial and financial structure which perpetuates yesterday. Few of the decision-makers concern themselves with shop-floor problems, and further down the line the production managers are too harassed by the day-to-day hurly-burly to have the time or inclination to make sweeping changes. So we continue to stumble along the same well-worn path, patching the potholes, but rarely making a new road. Only when conditions verge on the impossible do we think of change, and by that time we are in no shape to change

successfully. For the majority the view seems to be that it is better to travel hopefully than to arrive.

The mass-production industries are large and powerful, and well able to cope with their future. Competition is an effective spur to concerted action. Capital goods industries vary greatly in size and capability, and here concerted action is much less likely. One can only hope that, in a flash of enlightened self-interest, they will appreciate and grasp the advantages of 'going cellular' as a stage on the way to manufacturing systems. The benefit to the national economy of industry-wide improvements on the scale which the pioneering firms have achieved would be dramatic, and is within our grasp. Halving stocks and work in progress alone in the batch engineering industry would release over £1,000 m for much-needed investment.

Although we are not exactly renowned for making swift changes, there is a likelihood that future improvements in productivity could outstrip the rate of growth of the economy, with consequent unemployment. This is especially true where improvements are made by changes in organization, and there-fore not restricted by the maximum rate of capital investment. We are experiencing a foretaste of what will become a worldwide industrial problem as the use of labour shrinks in the manufac-turing industries, and we have currently the spectacle of Govern-ment spending large sums of public money in panic measures to alleviate and reduce unemployment, while executives in indus-try are simultaneously spending money on processes and methods of working which will increase it. Quite apart from the human misery, society has to pay the real cost in the end, but it is to be hoped that the present widespread and uniformly adverse reac-tion to this state of affairs will serve to emphasize that industrial policy and social policy can no longer be kept in separate water-tight compartments.

Designing Systems for Job Satisfaction
Enid Mumford

Reprinted with permission from *Omega*, Vol. 1, No. 4, 1973, pp. 493–8.

Introduction

Work systems are usually designed in technical terms to meet technical and business objectives, with little thought given to the needs of people operating the system. That is, the concept of an optimal socio-technical system which is recognized to contain both man and machines and is designed to enhance the capabilities of both, is not used by systems designers. Instead the task structure that emerges during implementation is merely a by-product of the technical part of the system, and its rigidity is attributed to constraints assumed to exist in the technical system. Recently computer systems in particular have tended to produce jobs which lack interest and challenge and this seems to be a product of the current design philosophy.

Computer Design

This design philosophy can be ascertained by examining the computer literature. For example, the instruction manual of a leading computer manufacturer defines systems analysis as embodying the following:

1. Defining the requirements of a new system.
2. Designing the new system, including the functions to be performed by the computer.
3. Specifying the following in exhaustive detail:
(a) The initial inputs and final outputs of the system.
(b) The content and logical structure of the files.
(c) The logical processes whereby input to files interacts to produce output.
(d) The ordering in which processing takes place.
(e) The allocation of items to files or streams of data and the prescription of sorts or other handling methods at appropriate points.
(f) The methods to be employed by users to operate the system.

The criteria set out for evaluating proposed systems designs are:

(a) *Cost considerations:* Site; Equipment; Staff salaries; Maintenance costs; Taxation relief.
(b) *Reliability:* Of computer hardware.
(c) *Accuracy and security:* Here systems designers are asked to consider the extent to which manual systems can be standardized.
(d) *Control and Flexibility:* Is the system easy to manage?
(e) *Integration:* Can the system be integrated with larger systems?
(f) *Expansibility:* Can it be expanded?
(g) *Availability:* Are hardware and staff available?
(h) *Acceptance:* Will the system be accepted by auditors, line management, unions and staff?

This last criterion is the only gesture towards the human aspects of the system. There is no recognition that acceptability and job satisfaction may be important design factors. This approach appears standard to the technical literature on computer systems design.

Human needs are sometimes catered for in a negative sense, as when systems design takes account of man's limitations. Meister and Rabideau describe the simplification of equipment in the American space programme so that man can cope with it. This, too, has been the approach of the ergonomists. But up to now little attention has been paid by either engineers, computer systems designers or sociologists to identifying the extent to which particular technologies embody human design flexibility. By human design flexibility is meant an absence of those technical constraints which cause human activity within a system to be restricted and specific. New production systems have emerged based on a logic of production needs which pays little attention to human needs. These systems are introduced with the implicit assumption that the human being will and must adapt to the demands of technology. Managers and academics have tended to accept this approach uncritically and, while a great deal of research has been directed at identifying the impact of different kinds of technology on work organization, until recently little attention has been paid to establishing how a technology can be manipulated so as to better provide for human needs.

Job Satisfaction

Sociologists who have perceived problems of human adaptation and have tried to do something about these have generally left the technology alone and manipulated the human situation so as to introduce some ameliorating features. The early experiments in coal mining were of this kind as are present day attempts at job enrichment. It may be that these previous technologies were unavoidably deterministic, although we have little evidence here as their flexibility has never been investigated. But there is reason to believe that this is not true of computer technology which at present appears quite flexible and has the potential to become increasingly flexible in the future.

If this is the case then the current approach of defining systems in purely technical terms with little thought for the human consequences and no attempt to design for human variables is assuming unnecessary limitations in a technology which has the potential to meet technical *and* human needs at one and the same time. Sackman points out that relatively few people working with computer systems have received formal training, or have experience, of techniques for dealing with both men and machines in computerized settings. He suggests 'humanistic automation means that computers serve human ends and that automation is not an end in itself. Computers are there to elevate man's intellect and increase his control over his environment.'

In order that the flexibility of computer technology can be exploited to serve human ends, particularly those of the individual in work, a great deal needs to be known about the design opportunities and limitations of this technology.

The research programme which the Computer Research Unit at Manchester Business School is at present undertaking will, we hope, provide this information. Our work is directed at the development of a socio-technical approach for the design of computer based systems. This means the formulation of a set of principles which assist the systematic and integrated design of both the technical *and* human parts of any system so that both technical efficiency *and* job satisfaction are increased.

Satisfactory socio-technical systems cannot be designed unless human needs in work can be clearly identified. This information is required on what individuals and groups are seeking from their work environment and on the kinds of work situations which will assist an individual to develop his innate capabilities.

Unfortunately no coherent theory on job satisfaction exists in the literature. There are a number of schools of thought, each of which has concentrated on a different component of job satisfaction. For example one school, represented by Maslow, Herzberg, Paul and Robertson, has directed its attention to psychological needs in work; in particular to those factors which lead to positive work attitudes and work motivation. A second school, represented by Lupton, Gowler and Legge, has concentrated on work controls and the effort reward bargain. A third school, Gouldner, Crozier and others, has looked at social values and the creation of industrial structures which provide opportunities for joint management worker participation in decision taking. A fourth school, Davis, Hall, Lawler, Herbst, Gulowsen, Cooper and others, has seen task structure as the most important element in job satisfaction and has concentrated its researches on job design. Work by the Computer Research Unit has led to the formulation of an integrated theory of job satisfaction which embraces all these different approaches, and to the creation of a diagnostic tool for identifying needs in work and for measuring job satisfaction on a number of variables.

This diagnostic tool incorporates a job satisfaction model, developed by the Computer Research Unit, which examines the 'fit' between what the employee is seeking from his job and what he is receiving on five variables which are seen as directly related to feelings of job satisfaction:

	The employee wants
The knowledge fit	His level of skill and knowledge to be used and developed.
The psychological fit	Status, recognition, responsibility, advancement, self development.
The efficiency–rewards fit	An acceptable effort reward bargain. Acceptable work controls.
The social value fit	An employer who does not violate his personal value system.
The task structure fit	A set of tasks which meet his needs for variety, interest, challenge and autonomy in work.

If there is a bad fit on any of these variables then the fit can be improved by the opportunities for change presented by the new computer system. The psychological, efficiency–reward and social value fits will be improved through alterations in personnel policies. The knowledge and task structure fits can be improved through a socio-technical approach to systems design which creates forms of work organization and individual job structures related to people's needs.

During the design process, work organization and the content of individual jobs are discussed with employees to obtain their views on how their jobs may be more effectively structured to improve job satisfaction.

We hope that this research will contribute to the theory of job design. The work done so far on this subject has been mainly in the traditional areas of industry including coal mining, pulp and paper manufacture and, lately, the car industry. Our research extends these applications into the tertiary sectors and into one of its newest areas, that of computer technology. It is believed that the research findings will prove to be of practical value to systems designers and managers faced with the problems of designing, implementing and operating computer systems.

The Computer Research Unit is already assisting a number of firms to cater systematically for the human factor when introducing computer systems. In these firms we are doing the following:

(a) Identifying human needs by means of our diagnostic tool;

(b) Helping managers to set human objectives;

(c) Assisting systems designers to design systems in socio-technical terms to meet technical and human objectives;

(d) Monitoring the human aspects of systems implementation;

(e) Evaluating the success of systems in terms of increased job satisfaction.

Conclusion

Our ability to contribute as expertly as we would like to the socio-technical design of computer systems could be improved with additional knowledge of the human impact of different computer applications, of their technological constraints and of their human design flexibility. We are now commencing research to fill this knowledge gap and hope soon to be able to answer the following questions:

(a) Are some types of computer applications less flexible in human terms than others? Preliminary investigations suggest that this is true of production control systems where a great deal of discretion is removed from the worker.

(b) Do particular man-machine interfaces in the computerized system present flexibility problems? Data input seems to suffer from major constraints in this respect. At present input is via punch tape, visual display units or document readers, the first two resulting in tedious and repetitive work activities.

We are also developing a number of training modules to provide systems analysts and managers with experience in socio-technical systems design. We would hope that eventually our approach would become a part of all systems analysts' training courses. But perhaps we are too optimistic.

Who's Afraid of Job Enrichment?

Alan Little and Peter Warr

Reprinted with permission from *Personnel Management*, Vol. 3, No. 2, February 1971, pp. 34–7.

It is likely that job enrichment, in common with any other personnel procedure, will succeed only if important background factors are working in its favour. In some settings job enrichment is the natural next-step, whereas in others it is doomed from the outset. The problem is therefore to identify the conditions which must be satisfied if job enrichment is to live up to its promise.

There is a real need for more research to investigate and specify these conditions but the results to date already suggest a number of influential factors. These may be grouped under the headings of job factors, people factors and organizational factors.

Job factors

Although it has sometimes been implied that jobs at all levels are amenable to job enrichment, the evidence so far suggests that the approach is more readily applicable to administrative, clerical, supervisory and technical positions where there is inherently more scope for initiative. Some jobs obviously present real difficulties for the enrichment approach, being so routine and repetitive that the introduction of planning or controlling elements is well-nigh impossible. This may have nothing to do with the people holding these jobs, but be a feature of the processes involved.

For example a highly automated food factory may have vestiges of human intervention at points where automation has not yet proved possible (gently turning over confectionery for instance). With automated activities on either side, the obvious development here is not enlargement but further automation so that the job is eventually eliminated.

A shorter-term solution (but one which is not welcomed by all workers) is the introduction of some sort of rotation system between different tasks in order to introduce a little more variety into the job. However, such rotational schemes often suffer from the same faults as naïve job extension, since all tasks may be equally tedious.

Difficulties are also likely to arise if the job which is to be altered is a piece-work one. Planning and controlling functions are notoriously difficult to measure and to incorporate as elements on a rate sheet. This means that employees who are paid by results may well see proposals to enrich their jobs as round-about attempts at rate-cutting. In situations where manual employees get high earnings by continuous productive effort, they naturally will be suspicious of invitations to 'more challenging work' when these invitations appear to take away their current piece-work advantages.

It seems on the whole then that jobs at rather higher skill levels offer the greatest opportunities for job enrichment. We have seen that this typically involves the introduction of planning and controlling activities and that the potential for such extensions without disrupting pay levels must exist before job enrichment is worth considering.

People factors

Just as there are differences between jobs in their potential for enrichment, so are there major variations between people. There is little doubt that many workers take a largely instrumental view of their work – they want to maximize their financial gain and are little concerned with the higher level needs of Maslow's scheme or with Herzberg's motivators. These people may see little value in job enrichment. Other workers may be worried about having to take additional responsibility when they feel themselves sufficiently stretched already while still others may feel that their work is not as boring and restricting as outside observers suspect.

Certainly, the assumption that specialized jobs *inevitably* produce monotony and boredom does not hold water. Workers whose jobs are repetitive and simple are not in every case bored by them: some may indeed prefer the short cycle-time operation where they can develop a steady rhythm which in effect 'pulls them along'. Many others appreciate the safety of not being allowed to take decisions and prefer repetition and specified work to change and variety.

This does not necessarily mean that some of these groups might not benefit were job enrichment introduced, but it does mean that real difficulties might be encountered in getting operatives to accept the changes required by a job enrichment programme. There are also cases where employees lack the intellectual capabilities to organize and further plan their own work. In such cases, the universal application of the job enrichment philosophy is obviously inappropriate.

The practical question is, of course: how can we determine whether employees carrying out a particular job can benefit to a worthwhile extent from enrichment? Once again, this takes us back to the need for research to better spell out the relevant personal characteristics, but it seems apparent that some kind of market research will always be required. What do employees in fact feel? What are their abilities and aspirations?

One important issue is the breadth of variation within the group which is performing a job. If the people involved range in age from their teens to their sixties, are male and female and are of widely differing intelligence then it is unlikely that they will be uniformly able to accept a job enrichment programme. On the other hand an all-inclusive recommendation is much more plausible for a single-sex group of similar age and intelligence. Generally, though by no means always, job enrichment has proved more successful with younger, more adaptable staff. For older staff, the change from traditional supervised methods to the new approach with no one looking over their shoulder may be more difficult to adjust to.

Other people factors which have been found to affect attitudes to work are those to do with geographical location. There are some consistent differences between urban employees and those from more rural areas so that the same job situation, in companies with employees in different parts of the country, may need to be handled differently.

Organizational factors

In addition to these job factors and people factors, there are several important organizational factors which affect the outcome of a job enrichment programme. The attitude of trade unions to such a scheme is one obvious consideration; there is no doubt that moves towards job enrichment can present difficulties for a union.

In some respects workers may be being asked to take over managerial functions and, in so far as this threatens the traditional union role, it could reasonably be resisted. This will naturally be partly dependent on the job and people factors already noted, but it will be apparent that union attitudes cannot be neglected when the possible success of job enrichment is being evaluated. Further, introduction of enrichment could lead to demands for higher pay or better conditions to match the greater responsibilities involved in the new job designs. It is likely that this is largely a question of the working relationship which exists between unions and management.

Another important organizational factor is the position and status of those supervising the employees whose jobs are to be enriched. Since enrichment involves channelling responsibility further down the organizational hierarchy, it could result in job impoverishment for the supervisors.

It follows that job enrichment is unlikely to succeed unless the supervisory role is adjusted to fit the new scheme of things. Supervisors will need to change their behaviour in the direction of greater consultation, and such a change is not always an easy one. They may also have to assume quite new fields of responsibility – for example, involvement in the more active training programmes which the new methods are likely to call for. Their own training has of course to be expanded to meet their changed responsibilities.

Perhaps the greatest hindrance to the success of any scheme is managerial and supervisory resistance. This might arise out of perceived threats to one's own position or from a more general incompatibility between the job enrichment philosophy and the traditions and climate of the company.

In general, many of the results from job enrichment programmes have been extremely encouraging. If care is taken in changing the job design to ensure real enrichment and to avoid mere meaningless extension, and if the programme is introduced sensitively with due regard for the psychological climate of the organizations, and most of all if the programme is consistently supported by management throughout the organization, then there is much evidence to suggest that enrichment can be effective in a variety of different situations. If we check up on the mediating job, people and organizational factors before venturing into a scheme then we can be much less fearful about its outcomes.

Further Reading: Current Thought on Job Satisfaction

R. COOPER, *Job Design and Job Motivation*, London, Institute of Personnel Management, 1974.

W. W. DANIEL AND N. MCINTOSH, *The Right to Manage?*, London, McDonald, 1972.

J. W. DICKSON, 'What's in a Job', *Personnel Management*, June 1971, Vol. 3, No. 6, pp. 38–40.

S. MILLS, 'Job Design: a review article', *Personnel Review*, Vol. 2, No. 2, 1973.

E. MUMFORD, *Job Satisfaction: a study of computer specialists*, London, Longmans, 1972.

D. WEDDERBURN AND R. CROMPTON, *Workers' Attitudes and Technology*, Cambridge, Cambridge University Press, 1972.

R. WILD AND D. BIRCHALL, 'Means and Ends in Job Restructuring', *Personnel Review*, Vol. 2, No. 4, Autumn 1973, pp. 18–24.

The readings in this chapter provide illustrations of the practical applications of the theoretical ideas we have been considering in preceding chapters. The general term 'job improvement' has been used, because the readings cover a wide range of projects with very different objectives and actions, but all with the direct aim or side benefit of achieving an improvement in the quality of jobs.

It may be helpful to provide a framework for these various case studies by suggesting a classification scheme to highlight the differences between them. The cases seem to fall into three main groups, depending on which factors in the situation were changed:

(a) The first two readings describe cases where the main changes were made in the administration and control of work, but not in the actual work content. Forms of autonomous working groups were established which had responsibility for some aspects of administration including allocating work among the group members, and controlling quality, but the tasks of each individual did not alter significantly.

(b) The second group of four readings are concerned with cases when changes were made in the content of work, that is the actual tasks which people perform, but no significant change was made in the 'technology' or the plant and equipment used.

(c) The final reading deals with a case where the introduction of new 'technology' was used to try and create a socio-technical system from the start, by including social variables into the design of the new plant, rather than designing the equipment only on technical criteria, and then expecting the people to adapt to it.

The other aspect of the cases which is worth considering is the reason why the firms in question undertook the various job improvement schemes described. In most cases, the schemes

The classification is summarized in the following table:-

SUMMARY OF CASE STUDIES

Main change in:	Case Study	Group involved
Administration and control of work	Blake & Ross	Women – Valve assembly
	Hallam	Men – Warehousemen
Content of work	Paul & Robertson	Men – Sales representatives
	McDavid	Women – Order clerks
	Cotgrove et al	Men – Nylon spinners
	Edwards	Men – Engineering workers
Technology	Hill	Men – Refinery workers

were started in response to a particular problem which was being encountered, whether on the personnel side, such as absenteeism, or on the production side e.g. the need to reduce errors or increase output. As a result, the job improvement achieved may only be an indirect consequence, whether or not it was hoped for as an additional benefit, and the evaluation of success may be in terms more understandable to the accountant than the social scientist, as suggested by Cherns in Chapter Two. Many companies would echo the words of a personnel director who wrote 'Philosophy in our Company is that we should involve people as much as possible in planning their work and make work as satisfying as possible, but, only where this is consistent with increased efficiency.'

Having considered some general points about the readings in this chapter, it may be valuable to look at them individually.

Blake and Ross describe a project which they undertook in setting up a series of autonomous work groups among women in a valve assembly factory. This exercise was part of the extensive 'work structuring' programme undertaken by the

Philips electrical organization in this country and Holland.
Although in this case no changes were made in the actual
tasks of the women, other exercises conducted by Philips in
this country have involved such changes, for example in the
complete assembly of fan heaters undertaken in the plant at
Hamilton in Scotland.

The second piece, by **P. A. Hallam**, also deals with a group
working situation, set up among warehousemen working for
John Player and Sons, the cigarette manufacturers. The
objective was to increase the flexibility of the men and to
delegate some of management's responsibility. The job
previously done by the foreman was delegated to the work
group itself, leaving the foreman free to deal with paperwork
and occasional unusual problems. The removal of the hierarchical system and demarcation between jobs resulted in a
much higher level of mutual assistance and increased job
satisfaction for the men, as well as a higher wage based on
increased knowledge.

One of a series of widely known experiments carried out
in ICI is described in the third extract. This is the only example
included here where a controlled experiment was carried out,
and therefore it is particularly interesting, since this is rarely
possible in an industrial situation. **Paul and Robertson**
describe the changes made in the jobs of a group of sales
representatives, who were in fact reasonably well satisfied with
their jobs and already had considerably more freedom and
flexibility in their jobs than some of the other groups described
in this chapter. The comparison highlights the fact that many
of the ideas applied here are relevant to most working
situations, though the people and jobs may differ widely, as
pointed out by Emery and Thorsrud in Chapter Five.

A clerical situation is described by **Ian McDavid**. Sales
order clerks working for BOC were given the responsibility
for dealing with the total order processing procedure for a
group of customers. As a result they came to regard them as
their customers and gained considerable satisfaction from providing a better service than had previously been possible.
The company also felt the changes were beneficial from their
point of view.

The two readings just described provide examples of what

is generally known as job enrichment, that is where a job is loaded vertically to give a greater say in the planning and decision-making associated with a particular job, so that it provides a more challenging job and greater opportunities for individual fulfilment in work. The next case study is an example of job enlargement in which the job is loaded horizontally by adding to it more tasks of a similar nature, to provide greater variety of work. **Cotgrove, Dunham and Vamplew** describe the changes in the jobs of a group of men in an ICI nylon process plant which were associated with a productivity agreement. As the authors make clear, the job was monotonous before the agreement and indeed still rather boring afterwards, largely because the constraints of the technology left little room for manoeuvre. However, the organizational changes which were made led to improved motivation and performance, as well as reductions in fatigue, boredom and labour turnover. The most interesting point is that although most of the men went into the agreement for the money, they welcomed the reduction in boredom and the added responsibility which they gained through the agreement.

The sixth piece concludes the group of case studies in which job improvement was achieved through organizational changes rather than through changes in the technology. **Graham Edwards** describes three cases where group technology has been implemented on lines similar to those outlined by D. T. N. Williamson in Chapter Five. In each case, a 'family' of machines was created to manufacture components which required the same sort of machining, so that large numbers of components could be made without having to re-set the machines. Most of the benefits achieved are in terms of reductions in setting-up times and stock levels, but there were also improvements for the men since typically a group of five men operated a cell of twelve machines, so that they have greater variety and more control over their work as well as a sense of cooperation with the rest of the team.

The final case study in this chapter by **Paul Hill** is an example of a new refinery being built from the beginning on the basis of socio-technical ideas, rather than from a largely technical standpoint. The building of the refinery by Shell offered a great opportunity to put into practice a philosophy which had been developed by the company during the previous years. The company issued a 'philosophy statement' part of which read:

> People cannot be expected to develop within themselves and to exercise the level of responsibility and initiative that is required unless they can be involved in their task and unless, in the long run, it is possible to develop commitment to the objectives served by their task. The Company recognizes that it cannot expect its employees at all levels to develop adequate involvement and commitment spontaneously or in response to exhortation. It must set out to create the conditions under which commitment may develop.

A good example of the way the technology may be designed to help job satisfaction, as suggested by Enid Mumford in Chapter Five, is given in the description of the way the interface between the computer and the operator was designed to achieve joint optimization, that is the best match between the capabilities of the man and the machine.

The seven case studies presented in this chapter illustrate the variety of situations and ways in which attempts have been made to improve jobs. All the studies here were successful to some extent and most achieved benefits for both the individuals and the companies concerned. Obviously this is an unrealistically rosy picture because there have been some projects which have not achieved the improvements which were sought, and had to be abandoned. Unfortunately, descriptions in the literature of projects which failed are virtually non-existent. No one, it seems, likes to discuss their failures in public, so that knowledge of them is confined to the folk-lore, though it would be valuable if they were discussed more openly. The next and final chapter will deal with some of the doubts and queries which have been raised about job improvement projects.

Some Experiences with Autonomous Work Groups

Jenny Blake and Shirley Ross

This extract was specially written for this volume and has not previously been published in this form.

In the late sixties and the early seventies, Philips UK began investigating the cost of labour turnover and absenteeism. In the parent factory of our component complex in the north west, a small team of people of differing disciplines and backgrounds set out to examine the problem in our own part of the company. A great deal of data was collected and analysed and although external factors began to influence labour turnover, absence figures remained high.

The idea behind the exercise was to present data in a meaningful form to managers and for members of the team to be available as resources should any manager wish to call upon them.

One valve factory manager found that his absence figure was 17 per cent and still rising. His budgeted level of absence was 8 per cent and he asked for two team members to help him investigate problems of absenteeism – the two consultants were one person from the Personnel Department of the parent plant and a colleague from the Central Personnel Department of the organization.

This particular valve assembly factory is located some 25 miles from the parent plant, employs approximately 300 operators, all female, has ancillary departments such as stores and administration with a mixed labour force, 4 mechanics, 12 first line female supervisors, and reporting directly to the factory manager, an industrial engineer, a personnel officer and 3 foremen.

Both consultants believed very strongly that in any problem-solving exercise there is a need for all levels of the organization to be involved and moreover, there is a need for total commitment and understanding on the part of management to the problems and their solution.

To be meaningful, it was felt that consultants should begin to work with the management team, but that this work had to be task rather than policy orientated. If absence was to show a long-term improvement, operators must be involved and not because of techniques forced on operators by management; we, the consultants, approached the problem from two directions. It was felt that management should study closely the composition of the factory population and find within it a small 'unit' of people making the same type of valve numbering about 20 to 30 people and whose age, marital status and work background reflected the spread of these variables within the total population of the factory.

Quite by chance we discovered that the factory was due to be redecorated. This seemed a good opportunity to let ourselves be known to both operators and first line supervisors. We invited the cooperation of all employees in deciding the colour scheme for the factory. As the exercise was fun but also effective, we very quickly became known to most of the factory.

We felt that one way of beginning to tackle the problem of what we called 'temporary withdrawal from work' would be to invite the selected groups of operators to answer a questionnaire on absence. Our next step was to involve first line female supervisors in the questionnaire design and also through them to keep operators informed of developments.

First line supervisors in this factory are called coordinators – their role being that of coordinating the various aspects of production such as training, quality and balance of production. We felt that any 'task' group should be clear about its objectives. The aim of this group of coordinators became:

To design a questionnaire which operators could answer individually, and in complete confidence, containing questions broadly connected with temporary withdrawal from work – that is, to ask questions about what people found stressful and boring in their jobs and asking for their comments and advice about how to decrease absence.

Both tasks were completed. The twenty-five people from the representative unit were asked by the consultants if they would participate in completing the questionnaire. Whilst this was being done, the rest of the factory was being kept in touch by the coordinators. It seemed important then and we still feel it is, that things out of the ordinary are explained clearly to as many people as possible over as short a time as possible.

Analysing the completed questionnaire, we found that both stress and boredom appeared to be factors in the decision to withdraw temporarily from work. The answers to the open-ended questions were also very interesting – many of the twenty-five mentioned 'if only' type of things. For example: 'if only I could be trained to do some other jobs, I could then move around', 'if only I could plan my week as I want it, instead of coping with the daily fluctuations imposed on me by my fore-man' and 'if only I had more say in the acceptance or non-acceptance of the components for my valves'.

The management team, plus the twenty-five operators, met with us to discuss the answers. We told the operators that we felt convinced that it should be possible to re-organize work to take care of some of their particular points, but we stressed that we would all (and that included them) need to give the matter a great deal of thought. They expressed a willingness to continue and so, for the next few months, we spent one or two days of every third week in this factory. One day was spent with the management team, the other with 'our' unit of operators.

The work with the management team was on two sorts of levels. One was a fairly clear educational level – where we talked about behavioural science theory, about the socio-technical systems approach – talking often about the hypotheses that the Tavistock Institute of Human Relations have formulated concerning requirements the work organization must satisfy in order to be effective. We also talked with them about Maslow and his hierarchy of needs, about Herzberg and his theories of hygiene and motivation, about Rensis Likert and his management styles. These were the things then discussed at the educational level. The other role we played was that of enabling the management to diagnose their own activities and decision-making processes.

Work then, at managerial level, was going well. Work at operator level though was not promising. We were very conscious of a need not to impose, not to push ideas at the unit of twenty-five operators, thus they tended to use us as a complaints bureau. Eventually, in an effort to make a change from the routine of our visits, we showed them a film of one of our Dutch factories where television sets, formerly made by rows of thirty people were now being assembled from start to finish by groups of seven people. They liked this idea and felt it answered quite a lot of the points they had made in response to the questionnaire.

Some people were clearly for the idea, some clearly against. The decision was to take an anonymous vote and twelve of the original twenty-five operators felt that they would like to attempt to become a 'team'.

Again we stressed the importance of feeling the motivation to attempt a new approach to the organization of work and also the importance of feeling capable of accepting new responsibilities. However, they still felt very keen to go ahead.

Again it became important to state our common objectives which at this time were:

1. to cause a decrease in absenteeism.
2. to cause a decrease in the stresses which appear to cause or affect absenteeism, by offering operators, more interest in their work, more opportunities for involvement and commitment and for developing flexibility and adaptability.

So, during December 1971 and January 1972, we, the team of operators and the management team embarked on first the design and then the carrying out of a training programme to equip the operators to become an independent unit, at the end of January. There was a strong feeling with all of us that we needed to propose a firm date for the setting up of the new unit and we felt two months was about right for our purposes.

The management team defined their task as being to communicate with various linked groups back at the parent factory. Valves are assembled in this feeder factory. Components for them are made in the parent factory as is the enscupulation of the product before it is despatched to the customer. Computer department now had to be asked to cooperate in the production of separate data on quality and quantity for this new group. The 'contacts' in the component areas had to be altered and then be given an outline of the project to give them an understanding of the kinds of problems the operators might have. Also in the past, the majority of such contacts had been approved with coordinators only – never with operators – we had to explain the basic philosophy behind such a change. We were helped in both cases by the fact that back in 1970, both computer depart-ment and one of the production foremen from the component area had been involved in the original data collection exer-cise. Although it had not been planned, these people were, in effect, seeing a result from some work in which they had been involved two years previously – a useful motivating factor perhaps.

To start their training programme, the operators visited the parent factory. The objectives were to see components of their valve being made, which hopefully gave them a greater under-standing of the specifications of such components and to bring them face to face with people who would now be their contacts. They also visited the valve finishing area and concluded with a lecture session in the laboratory on the working properties of a valve.

Before the re-organization, the operators generally made only one stage of their particular valve. The team decided that each member should be at least capable of making two stages in the valve before the end of January – the second stage to be performed at a comfortable degree of competence. The teams began to define further what it saw as being its new responsibilities. These were to include the quality of their output and some aspects of administration and being able to 'balance' a unit – that is, to be able to finish up the end of each day with the appropriate number of finished valves for the number of components drawn from stores.

These operators were now ready to move geographically to another part of the factory. Hierarchically the team now reported directly to a foreman. It seemed fairly obvious that for some time yet, many meetings would be held on a fairly regular basis. Should all these people be tied up at these meetings? Had they all a valid role – or were we just desperately trying to be partici-pative by involving everybody all of the time? One foreman of the three was responsible for this particular valve type. It seemed better for him to attend meetings with his twelve operators.

The operators had already mentioned to the two consultants that they felt 'overfaced' when eight other people were present. For a week or two we tried meetings with the team and their foreman. The team again asked to see the consultants. They complained that their foreman had too many good ideas which they adopted quickly during problem-solving exercises. They said they were used to him being right so they tended to adopt his suggestions immediately. This they felt meant they were not maturing in terms of decision-making.

We went back to the management team to discuss this problem. A solution was found which has now become standard practice – the foreman would still have his meetings, but a second member of the management team, namely the Personnel Officer for the factory, would act as an observer at the meetings. Her task was to make sure that the team was allowed its say in decision-making and to make certain that the team had enough relevant information to complete its decision-making. Because the foreman was technically extremely competent it was difficult for him to explain things in easy stages. He was fond of using abbreviations for example. The Personnel Officer's role was to make sure by testing out if necessary that each team member understood what was being said. Because of her role too, this person had a good idea of the mix of personalities in the team and could, we hoped, ensure that those who were basically shy had a chance to speak.

The two consultants also felt at this time that we should now begin to take a back seat – we had to ensure that the management team continued to develop, but we had also to ensure that this participative form of group working belonged to the factory not to the consultants. We found this to be a rather delicate balancing act. To know when we were being too possessive about the factory on the one hand and on the other not moving too far away too soon.

The team continued to have fairly regular meetings with the foreman and Personnel Officer, but these were becoming less and less cries for help and more and more fact-finding missions, on some operational problem or other. The team had also now decided it would call in specialist help only if it as a group decided it was necessary.

We have already noted that this first work group had decided that as well as undertaking many tasks formerly tackled by the first level supervisor, they would also embark on learning one job other than that which they could do already. Formerly this would have involved an instructress but they decided to instruct each other. They found that this did not operate well, but they still seemed to be reluctant to face the idea of outside help. We suggested that perhaps it might be a good idea for the group to have what we called 'stand-by' instructresses. It was suggested that two of their number could be given a crash course on instruction and that they could eventually become responsible for all training in the team. This particular compromise worked well.

Since the early days of the project, we had not included first-line supervision in our thinking. The management team and ourselves had realized that labour turnover in this group was problematical. It was both fairly common and predictable due to the sex, age and marital status of this level of the hierarchy. It had originally been openly discussed that natural wastage in this group of supervisors should enable us to test out autonomous group working without coordinators feeling that their jobs were in jeopardy – an essential basis of our approach.

From the beginning we had set up a series of monitoring devices to check progress. From them we noted that cost of meetings and training time was decreasing. The management team were also working well and had coped successfully with a top managerial change in their area. After six months we assessed the qualitative results of Team I. Since the factory management had already had an approach from some members of another unit and Team I expressed a desire to continue group working it was felt appropriate for Team II to begin working.

An educational process was begun by the two service department people in the factory who had discussions with any unit who might be off production for one reason or another, outlining the philosophy of teamwork and answering any queries on the concept and practice of teamwork.

The development of teamwork in the factory is as follows:

Team I	February 1972	7 stages	13 people
Team II	October 1972	2 stages	9 people
Team III	February 1973	7 stages	12 people
Team IV	July 1973	5 stages	9 people
Team V	January 1974	4 stages	8 people
Team VI	March 1974	5 stages	10 people
Team VII	April 1974	7 stages	11 people

| Team VIII | May 1974 | 5 stages | 12 people |
| Team IX | August 1974 | 4 stages | 7 people |

Two points need to be made concerning firstly trade unions and secondly payment. Local representatives of the trade unions were involved at all stages in the change process. On the second point, when considering the format of payment schemes for teamwork, it was thought that two main factors should be built into the scheme, 1. retention of the individual element and 2. the need to make team payments based on team results. Thus a scheme was devised which offers an incentive for both individual and team improvement.

Some learning which has developed from this approach is as follows:
1. Firstly, there is a need for total commitment and understanding on the part of a. management, b. the trade union(s) and c. the service functions concerned, in order to provide a supportive atmosphere in which new ideas can be tried out and 'grown'.
2. There is a need to use every opportunity to develop and perpetuate a participative climate.
3. There is the need for an enormous amount of education and communication *at all levels* of the organization (even amongst people who are in no way directly involved in the situation).
4. Some understanding of the processes involved in change were demonstrated by the consultants and were found to be useful.
5. The initial cost of time and effort invested by all concerned was greater than anticipated.
6. The problem of supervisor(s) feeling threatened by the additional responsibility offered to their subordinates needs to be understood.
7. The inevitability of disappointments – both of operators and of management during the change process – must be considered.
8. There is a need to be flexible and pragmatic in approach. This method requires great tolerance of ambiguity, particularly on the part of management, who must ultimately be

responsible and accountable in this 'open-ended' situation.
9. It is useful to apply some 'technique' in order to 'loosen' the initial situation e.g. a questionnaire.
10. There is a need to inform, yet 'keep at a distance' other interested parties.

Furthermore, the implications of such an approach are various, including for example, having begun to involve individuals and groups, it is not possible to deny or retract this offer of involvement in the future, without incurring high psychological costs. In terms of the disciplinary and supervisory systems practised by management, there also needs to be an awareness that such an approach involves commitment of employees through participation. Finally, the implications of teamworking to the structure of the organization need to be understood, since these are changes in the physical structure and in the power structure of such a situation.

Managers and others who may be contemplating such an approach need to be aware of the risks involved, as well as the likely 'pay-off'. However, given the changing needs of individuals, and organizations, such an approach may prove to be a constructive method of coping with change and offering long-term viability both to the organization and to the continuity of work for its employees.

An Experiment in Group Working

P. A. Hallam

Reprinted with permission from *Work Study and Management Services*, April 1973, pp. 240–44.

Introduction

Group working, where factory employees can get on with their routine work without close supervision, is taking place in a number of areas at Player's for the first time. Trials were held in each location first to see if the system would work and when it was found to be successful it was introduced permanently.

Teams of men who have a leader are left to carry out all the daily routine work without being told what to do all the time. They decide amongst themselves who will do what and when. They receive higher wages and get job satisfaction from the extra responsibility. The foremen are happy because it leaves them free to do all their paperwork and supervise anything out of the ordinary.

Summary of events leading to group working

The warehousing facilities are situated in two buildings, a main store and a subsidiary store.

The warehouses jointly contain an average of 11,750 pallet loads of packaging materials required for the making and packing of cigarettes. Material is delivered by road transport and almost without exception is unloaded by fork lift truck, to designated areas within the store.

On demand, these materials are sent to the factories for use in the cigarette-making and packing departments. The composition of the lorry loads varies from adhesives, cigarette paper and filter tip plug rods used in making cigarettes; to foil, cellophane, wrapping paper and associated printed cardboard for the packing department. Also held in stock are the packing materials required for pipe tobaccos.

In 1969, as a result of joint consultation between Management and the Work Study Department, improved methods were introduced which included:

1. Re-organization of the yard layout to improve traffic flow.
2. Removal of obsolete stock.
3. Re-organization of the stock storage area and the introduction of a reference grid for stock locations.
4. A pre-loading area for outgoing materials.
5. Staggered lunch breaks for fork lift truck drivers.
6. Improved housekeeping in the dock area.

Following the completion of these changes, it was decided to adopt a system of group working which offered considerable advantages in flexibility of labour, as well as providing the opportunity to appoint leaders and delegate some of management's responsibility; which was a highly significant objective in the exercise. On paper it appeared like this:

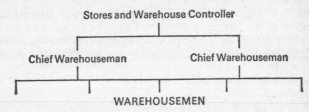

Stores and Warehouse Controller

Chief Warehouseman   Chief Warehouseman

WAREHOUSEMEN

After consultations with union representatives, and subsequent preliminary training, the scheme was fully implemented in the main warehouse only, for a trial period of one month.

At the end of the trial period, it was decided that group working should continue, and that the completion of training within the group be continued as a routine exercise. It was recognized that to ensure a satisfactory level of competence a period review system would be carried out to monitor the effectiveness of the personnel, as it would not be possible to forecast how long it would take to achieve it. At the end of eleven months' operation, no changes had been found necessary in methods, or personnel, to overcome lack of efficiency. It should be noted that the major skills required by this group were fork lift operation and clerical recording work.

The group system called for everyone to learn the skills of storage and warehousing in order to site incoming goods in correct location and in a sequence which would enable withdrawals to be made correctly.

Job definitions and personnel

The men available were very suitable to meet the initial requirements of group working which, with its increased job knowledge, enabled management to offer an improved salary scale. Clearly, also, company policy would not have encouraged a major change in the personnel unless there was incontrovertible evidence demanding this. The group selection was not based on any technical or social compatibility.

In discussions with the men and union representatives, how-ever, it was unanimously agreed that if after a reasonable period of training any employee did not reach the required standard, a replacement would be found.

Some of the men in lower grades were eager to participate because of the overnight promotion and the financial reward. Conversely, there was a nucleus of more highly qualified per-sonnel who felt that they saw the erosion of their hard-earned promotion at the same time. The acceptance of the scheme was in no small way due to the majority benefiting from the former.

The average age of the twelve men at the introduction of the scheme was 43 years (only three men being under 40); 33 per cent of the men had been with the Purchasing and Stores Depart-ment for less than two years; 33 per cent (not the same personnel as previously mentioned) had never been promoted before. In fact, no one had been promoted for almost a year.

With the abolition of established supervision, it was necessary to find leaders with the ability to coordinate the activities of the group, and to accept wider responsibilities, without reverting to the role of foreman.

Job descriptions were compiled for the two jobs within the group, i.e. Chief Warehouseman and Warehouseman. These were subjected to job evaluation and remuneration fixed accord-ingly, which provided a small pay differential but did not impair the ideals of group working; nor did this in any way preclude the Chief Warehouseman from carrying out the duties of Ware-houseman. However, it was recognized by all concerned that, to some extent, two specialist members existed.

It was logical to promote the existing Head Storekeeper and one of the Storekeepers to be the new Chief Warehousemen, because both of them were competent, and had great experience. They were fully conversant with all aspects of the job, and were held in respect by management and men alike. They had been involved in the planning which led to the introduction of group working, and were fully committed to it.

A year later

To set the results of the first year's working in true perspective it is necessary to remind ourselves of the dissatisfactions which obtained before the project was undertaken.

There were many anomalies in the work load assigned to each person under the previous system. The warehousing of pipe tobacco materials was not equitable with that of cigarette making plug rods. By making half of the group responsible for all outgoing materials, and half for incoming, and having total flexibility within each sub-group, there was no chance of anyone doing a major portion himself.

The previous divisions of work and the grading system meant that information was localized with individuals. There was a certain aura surrounding the clerical duties and the office.

To some extent there existed an imbalance in the work loads due to the somewhat semi-rigid lines of demarcation which existed. Management were concerned with the amount of time spent by the Head Storekeeper on clerical duties, which to some extent prevented him from dispensing his practical knowledge to good effect in the warehouse.

The first year's working was felt by management to have demonstrated the success of the scheme, although clearly some local difficulties had been highlighted. Initially the flexibility which was a primary objective was to some extent lacking, partly due to insufficient formal training being undertaken. There was, therefore, some retention of specialization, some members endeavouring to insulate themselves in familiar tasks, and showing reluctance to undertake unfamiliar ones. The Chief Warehouseman endeavoured to live with this situation by allocating particular people to specific jobs, which was rather contrary to the underlining philosophy. In the main, however, the extra responsibility and job rotation brought its own extra job satisfaction. There were fewer worries because everyone, being on the same grade, could assist each other with problems and make concerted efforts to overcome a backlog of work, or an urgent task, whereas before, individual effort was the measure of performance.

Furthermore, information and knowledge was now being dispersed, and all members could psychologically feel that they were equal, and had the right to be aware of the on-going situation.

In other words, the previous hierarchy had been removed.

More than one person was now aware of the procedures, and anyone who had previously felt that information was hard to discover – because of cliques withholding knowledge – now had a better chance to progress.

There was an obvious financial inducement which was primordially important in the acceptance of group working. If the duties of the Chief Warehouseman grade were an overlap of the Foreman and Head Storekeeper, then the duties of the Warehouseman were on a par with the Storekeeper. The financial increment due to promotion from fork lift truck driver or labourer grades was also attractive.

The fact that all were responsible for the movement of materials lessened total individual responsibility, but gave each a bigger share of it. Few admitted to being overawed by the acceptance of extra responsibility but there were members of the group who felt that they would not desire any more.

Training

There was a strong feeling of dissatisfaction amongst some of the experienced members because of the extra work load of having to train the less experienced members in the duties involved. It was felt that this may have been due to the loss of the mystique that some people had built into their job over the years. One member stated that initially information was not forthcoming so easily because of this. Generally, it was felt that the scheme was introduced more smoothly than anticipated.

Job rotation

There was much more job rotation now that the system was much more well known. The majority of the inexperienced members stated that they were given the opportunity to attempt the irregular tasks – e.g. despatches to other companies within the Imperial Tobacco Group – but lack of job knowledge did not account for the fact that certain jobs were done with reluctance, even by experienced members.

There was evidence of a lack of rotation in certain jobs, particularly the manual tasks of housekeeping and pallet sort-out for return to the manufacturers. Dissension was caused, and had had the effect of forcing others to take their turn.

Job rotation had meant a greater awareness of the system. Mistakes, which might have been concealed previously, were rectified more easily, because of exposure to all other members. The Chief Warehousemen should have noticed those who required assistance to help them to bring their work up to standard.

The role of the Chief Warehouseman

The reduction of the number of grades had meant an overlap of job responsibilities. It was obvious that the removal of the supervisory grade of foreman had called for a broader range of duties to be carried out by the Chief Warehousemen, who felt at times they had to absorb duties previously carried out by the foreman.

Whilst keeping in mind the concept of a group working and its inherent flexibility, the Chief Warehousemen's responsibilities gave justification for a higher rate of pay. The problem was whether to give them a small differential which would retain the feeling of group working, or a greater one which could be seen as a continuation of the 'foreman-men' relationship. This was not universally popular because it was felt that this sort of job differential was not suited to the mutual assistance situation of group working.

Job evaluation, therefore, assessed the grade and a small pay differential was awarded to the Chief Warehousemen, who felt that this was not sufficient reward for the extra administrative duties that they had to undertake, particularly in the absence of the Warehouse Controller.

A situation now developed in that the Chief Warehousemen had become office-bound, attending to clerical and administrative duties. They preferred to be on hand to ensure that no mistakes were made and to be aware of all happenings. This might have been due to an 'indispensable' attitude or to the fact that they felt that they had previously carried out all warehousing duties in their career and were now unwilling to make what they considered to be a retrograde step. The recent appointment of a younger Chief Warehouseman was significant, because since then he had continued to do routine warehousing duties as well as his wider responsibilities.

Active participation in routine duties by them, even on an infrequent basis, appeared to play an important psychological part in dispelling fears that they were assuming a supervisory role.

Promotion

A small percentage, the more ambitious members, recognized before the system was introduced, that there would be fewer opportunities for promotion after the system was in operation, because of the reduction in the number of grades; but this did not deter them from accepting the system. They also felt that they would require to gain experience and promotion by means of a transfer to the stores' functions within the factory.

However, the make-up of this particular group, accepting its average age and the length of service of its members, and through personal discussion, pointed to a particularly settled group in respect of long-term ambition and 67 per cent were satisfied to stay in the present environment without directly pushing for promotion.

Discipline within the group

The removal of the foreman had had no marked effect on the attitude of the men in terms of discipline. Most felt that they preferred to work without close supervision. The previous foreman was inclined to help men to carry out their duties.

The fact that many members of the group were still learning the routine meant that a certain tolerance existed. The definition of discipline centred on lack of effort or failure to rotate jobs, etc. Even inexperienced members became disgruntled with the work output of the experienced members, such was the democracy of the situation.

One member of the group suggested to the Chief Warehouseman that the latter was not a strong enough disciplinarian. His reply was that this was a group scheme with no established supervision, and he had no authority to act as a foreman.

In the present system, a direct confrontation between individuals was probably the most satisfactory, and there was evidence of this situation having occurred, although the majority preferred not to risk trouble by confronting a slacker. They hoped that the Chief Warehousemen or the Warehouse Controller were sufficiently aware of those who failed to engender group spirit and would take the necessary action.

Conclusions

Management on the whole were well satisfied with the way the group had reacted to the challenges and with the way in which they had adapted themselves to the new and, to them, unique working arrangement.

As far as the men were concerned, there was unanimous approval for the new system attributable, in the main, to the following factors:

1. The financial increase awarded because of the extra knowledge required for the job.
2. The job satisfaction due to the variability of work content.
3. The delegation of responsibility leading to increased job status.
4. The imbalances of work loads of the previous set-up were redressed, by redistribution.
5. Lack of demarcation, which allowed mutual assistance with work.

The size of the work force and the somewhat local area in which they operated clearly favoured this type of experiment. Nevertheless, the main conclusions to be drawn are that, given careful planning and good communications, job participation can be made successful.

Job Enrichment and Employee Motivation
W. J. Paul and Keith Robertson

Reprinted with permission from *Job Enrichment and Employee Motivation*, Gower Press, 1970, pp. 23–38.

Structure of the Studies

The ICI studies were concerned with ascertaining the importance of job content for a single factor in the total work situation. For this purpose, job enrichment had to be isolated, change restricted to that one area, and the results measured.

EXPERIMENTAL CONSTRAINTS

The need to measure results introduces certain constraints which do not exist in the normal managerial situation. As a consequence, three main features were common to all the studies.

1. Hygiene factors were held constant. That is to say, no changes were made, as part of the study, in matters such as pay, security, status or working conditions.

2. Experimental and control groups were established. The criterion for an adequate control group was that it should be a similar group of people, doing similar jobs, for whom changes could have been made analogous to those actually made for the experimental group. Extraneous influences could then be assumed to affect both groups more or less equally, and any diverging trends in the performance or satisfaction of the two groups could be more surely attributed to the changes connected with job enrichment.

3. The studies were kept confidential. This was a regrettable but essential precaution to avoid, as far as possible, the confounding influence of the 'Hawthorne effect' – people's well-known tendency to behave in an artificial way when they know they are the subject of an experiment.

PROCEDURE FOLLOWED

The procedure of setting up the various studies followed a consistent pattern.

First, discussions were held with division directors and senior managers to ascertain their willingness to take part in the studies and to identify those areas where motivational change seemed particularly necessary or desirable.

Next, in discussion with departmental heads and their senior staff, the exact composition of experimental and control groups was decided. A meeting was held at which all the managers concerned were brought together to suggest and agree on changes which might be made for the experimental group. This meeting usually involved line managers down to but not including the immediate supervisors of either group; also present would be other interested parties such as the manager of a closely related department or a representative from the personnel function. All participated in a brainstorming session during which any idea for changing the job in question was entertained. These ideas were then 'screened': all suggestions dealing with hygiene were ruled out, as were any felt by the managers themselves to be in any way impractical or undesirable. Only those changes which met with the full approval of local management and which had an impact on job content were used as the basis of the study.

Once the changes were agreed, ways had to be found to measure any change in the performance or satisfaction of the experimental and control groups during a trial period. Whenever possible, measures of the quantity, quality and cost of work done were devised; such performance measures were always specific to the group concerned and were determined by local management. On the question of job satisfaction, use was made of a job reaction survey, devised by Herzberg, which measures how satisfied people are with the motivators in their jobs as they themselves perceive them. This survey was given both before and after the trial period in order to detect any improvement or deterioration which might have taken place. In order not to draw attention to the experimental and control groups, and because the information obtained would be useful in any case, the survey was normally extended to cover the whole works or department concerned. In one or two cases, the selection of experimental and control groups was postponed until the results of the first survey were known.

When all preliminary work was completed, the agreed changes were introduced as gradually and naturally as possible, for the experimental groups only. The trial period during which performance and satisfaction of both experimental and control groups were monitored, ran from the time when all the changes had been implemented for as long as possible, before results had to be collated and the programme of studies wound up. The trial period normally lasted a year, and was never less than six months.

Sales Representatives

OPENING SITUATION

An opportunity arose in one part of the company to investigate the effects of motivation in the sales field. A decline in market share in one product range had been halted before the study began; nevertheless sales in 1967 showed no improvement over 1966. As far as could be judged, the company's products were fully competitive in both price and quality: the critical factor in the situation appeared to be the sales representative's effort.

Sales representatives' salaries and conditions of employment, however, were known to compare well with the average for the industry. Furthermore, when the job reaction survey was given, the representatives' mean score turned out to be higher than that of most employees of equivalent seniority, suggesting that they also enjoyed considerable job satisfaction.

The specific problem in this case, therefore, was that to achieve the vital business objective of recapturing the initiative in an important market, sustained extra effort was needed from a group of people who were already comparatively well treated and reasonably satisfied with their jobs.

THE CHANGES

1. Sales representatives were no longer obliged to write reports on every customer call. They were asked simply to pass on information as they thought appropriate or request action when they thought it was required.

2. Responsibility for determining calling frequencies was

placed wholly with the representatives themselves, who kept the only records for purposes such as staffing reviews.

3. The technical service department agreed to provide service 'on demand' from the representatives; nominated technicians regarded such calls as their first priority. Communication was by direct contact, paper-work being cleared after the event.

4. In cases of customer complaint about product performance, representatives were authorized to make an immediate settlement of up to £100, but only if they were satisfied that this could be done without prejudice to the further liability of the company.

5. If faulty material had been delivered, or if the customer was holding material for which he had no further use, the representative now had complete authority, with no upper limit in sales value, to decide how best to deal with the matter. He could buy back unwanted stock even if it was no longer on the company's selling range.

6. Representatives were given a discretionary range of about 10 per cent on the prices of most of the products they sold, especially those thought to be critical from the point of view of market potential. The power limit given was often below any price previously quoted by the sales office. All quotations other than at list price had to be reported by the representatives.

The theme of all the changes was to build up the sales representative's job so that it became more complete in its own right. Instead of always having to refer back to headquarters, the representative now had authority to take decisions on his own. He became someone with whom the customer could really do business. Each change implied a greater responsibility; together they gave the freedom and challenge necessary for self-development.

EXPERIMENTAL DESIGN

The company sold an extremely wide range of products to many different customer industries, or 'trades'. In view of the initial effort required to determine the discretionary range on prices and to make the technical service arrangements, it was decided to limit the study to three trades, chosen to be typical of the business as a whole. Each was an important trade with an annual turnover of between £¼m and £½m. Together, they gave a good geographical spread and covered many different types of customer.

The experimental group (N = 15) was selected to be representative of the sales force as a whole in terms of age, experience and ability. An important part of each member's selling responsibility lay within the nominated trades. The rest of the sales force (N = 23) acted as the control group. The changes were introduced for the experimental group during December 1967, and the trial period ran from 1 January to 30 September 1968.

The background of static sales and the objective of recapturing the market initiative dictated that sales turnover in the nominated trades would be the critical measure, checked by gross margin. The difficulties of comparing unequal sales values, allowing for monthly fluctuations and seasonal trends were overcome by making the comparison on a cumulative basis in terms of the percentage gain or loss for each group against the equivalent period of the previous year.

Since they were selling in the same trades in the same parts of the country, the performance of both groups can be presumed to have been influenced by the same broad economic and commercial factors. In one trade the two groups were evenly matched. In the other two, the experimental group had the bigger share of the business and tended to sell to the larger customers; in these cases it may be surmised that prevailing market conditions would affect the experimental group's performance, either favourably or unfavourably, more than the control group's. As it happened, in one of the two, commercial trends were favourable, while in the other they were distinctly unfavourable. Taken as a whole, therefore, it would seem that the comparison is as fair as any that could be obtained between the performance of sales representatives under the two sets of conditions.

RESULTS

During the trial period the experimental group increased its sales by 18.6 per cent over the same period of the previous year, a gain of £130,000 in sales value. During the same period the control group's sales declined by 5.0 per cent. The equivalent change for both groups the previous year – that is January to September 1967 against January to September 1966 – had been a decline of 2.9 per cent. The difference in performance between the two groups in 1968 is statistically significant at the 0.01

level of confidence: it would occur by chance much less often than one time in a hundred.

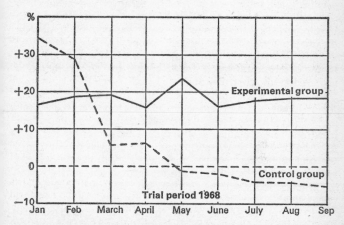

Figure 1. Sales Turnover within nominated Trades during trial period in 1968 (Percentage change against corresponding period of 1967 plotted cumulatively).

Figure 1 shows the month-to-month performance of the two groups, plotted cumulatively. It can be seen that the control group in fact started the year extremely well, with January/February sales in the region of 30 per cent above the equivalent 1967 figures. This improvement was not sustained, however, and by May cumulative sales had dropped below their 1967 level. By the last five months of the trial period, performance was running true to the previous year's form, showing a decline of about 3 per cent. The experimental group, on the other hand, started more modestly, not exceeding a 20 per cent gain during the first quarter. During the second quarter, high sales in May compensated for poorer figures in April and June; the third quarter showed a steady if slight, rise in the rate of improvement over 1967. This sustained increase of just under 20 per cent is in marked contrast to the previously declining performance of the trades as a whole.

In view of the greater negotiating authority granted to the experimental group representatives, it is important to check whether their substantial increase in turnover was achieved at the expense of profit. As all quotations other than at list price were reported by the representatives, it was possible to analyse the gross margin achieved by both groups. This analysis showed without doubt that the gross margin per £ of sales value achieved by the experimental group was as high, if not higher, than that achieved by the control group.

Comparisons with other trades suffer from the disadvantage that different economic and commercial factors affect the various parts of the business. Nevertheless, when the experimental group's performance was compared with that of the rest of the business, it could be seen that a performance differential of between 6 per cent and 7 per cent was maintained, both across different groups of trades and throughout the trial period. At 1967 rates of turnover, this would be worth at least £600,000 per annum in sales value.

It is always possible, of course, to find other feasible explanations for the sales results achieved. Some specific cases where an experimental group representative had achieved a breakthrough with a given customer were investigated in depth. In the majority of such instances the representative stated that the ground work for the breakthrough had started before the job enrichment study was put into operation and that the actual sales achieved could not be related to his greater responsibility alone. For this reason it is important to record the views of the sales managers concerned. They were unanimous in the belief that job enrichment had been successful in motivating the experimental group representatives. No figures, over such a relatively short period of time, they felt, could ever properly substantiate the 'enormous improvement' they had observed in these men, who were 'mentally much keener' and had developed 'a much sounder approach to the job'.

One or two of the managers felt somewhat deprived by receiving fewer reports than previously, but no one wanted to go back to the old system; it was agreed that management should sort out what kind of information it needed and why, and communicate this to the representatives. Managers were unanimous that the concept of a direct relationship between the sales representative and his opposite number in the technical service department was sound, even though there had been some practical difficulties. All agreed that the representatives had in no way abused their negotiating authority. Turn around time on complaints had been speeded up, and the customer now felt that he was talking to a responsible person. There was a distinct impression that representatives had actually used their price discretion less often than they had previously asked the sales office to quote special prices. In the opinion of the Home Sales Manager, once the representatives were given negotiating authority, they learned for the first time what the real obstacles to sales were in each individual case. The job itself had become a learning situation in which each man had the opportunity to develop his own professional expertise.

In order to measure the sales representatives' job satisfaction, a job reaction survey was given twice, once before the trial period started, then again at the end. On both occasions the response rate for both groups was over 90 per cent. Results are given in Figure 2.

Scores are out of 80. Despite the fairly high starting point, above the company average for staff of equivalent seniority, the experimental group's mean score showed a clear 10 per cent gain over the trial period, while the control group's mean score remained static.

GROUP	Mean score Dec 1967	Mean score Sept 1968	Percentage change
Experimental	50.1	55.4	+10.6
Control	51.8	52.0	+ 0.4

Figure 2.   Job satisfaction – Sales representatives

Improving Job Satisfaction in an Office
Ian McDavid

This extract has not previously been published in this form.

Introduction

For a number of years, BOC has been interested in the question of employee motivation and in 1971 a two-day seminar devoted to this subject was introduced into the programme at the BOC Training Centre at Chartridge. The Manager of Operation, Technical and Supply Centre (OTSC) Rotherham (Gases Division), attended one of these seminars in February 1971 and felt that the techniques discussed on the seminar were particularly relevant to a problem that existed in the OTSC Stock Control section.

Background and Problem

One of the functions of OTSC is to produce or obtain spares for customers installations within Gases Division and Cryoplants Ltd (this includes an active overseas requirement). In the past these parts were ordered on a multi-part order form processed in the stock control office at OTSC by seven clerks on a sequential basis i.e. acknowledge, record, define (2), type, process (2). These clerks were supported by four more people in an information room who dealt with queries on outstanding orders. The stock control office and the information room were each controlled by a supervisor.

The perennial problems of the stock control office were a high percentage of errors in processing the orders and unsatisfactory delays in meeting them. The internal consequences of these problems were low morale and high labour costs through frequent use of overtime and hiring of temporary clerks. Management action, including two changes of junior and middle management responsible for the order office, had failed to deal adequately with these situations.

Discussions at Chartridge

The Manager of OTSC and five other BOC managers in the same syndicate on the seminar discussed the work of the OTSC clerks and 'brainstormed' the following list of changes which they felt would deal with the problems:

1. Provide better desks
2. Take clerks on a coach trip round the company
3. Give the clerks new titles
4. Replace with better calibre staff
5. Give the clerks responsibility for specific product groups
6. Re-plan the office
7. Increase salaries
8. Merge the operation with the nearby Gases Division offices, at Brinsworth
9. Re-decorate the offices
10. Give the clerks product training courses
11. Provide the clerks with regular trips around the works and stores at OTSC
12. Give the clerks responsibility for stock control.

However, most of these ideas, on closer study, did not appear to tackle the core of the problem which seemed to be one of improving the clerks' attitude to their work. They were either too general, peripheral to the work itself, or did not increase the opportunities for the clerks to get a feeling of achievement and recognition from their efforts. Only item (5) – the reorientation of the work to give the clerks responsibility for specific products and the order processing associated with them seemed to offer a significant improvement in these areas.

Therefore the syndicate recommended that:

1. Each clerk should be made responsible for the total order processing procedure
2. The work should be divided between them on the basis of each clerk dealing with specific products or groups of products
3. This responsibility should be made known to all other sections of OTSC and to the various customers.

Discussions at Rotherham

On his return, the OTSC manager discussed the problem with

the manager directly responsible for the stock control office, and, as a result, it was decided to invite the tutor who had run the seminar at Chartridge, to assist in devising a solution. A meeting took place at Rotherham where it was re-affirmed that the major problems of the sales order office from the management's point of view were:

1. no specific person was responsible for the complete order procedure
2. promised delivery dates were frequently unfulfilled and changes in them rarely notified to customers unless they complained
3. the level of errors and performance standards of the clerks were unsatisfactory
4. the clerks were only aware of their mistakes, not of their successful processing of 90 per cent of the orders.

On re-examining these problems it was confirmed that giving each clerk the total order processing procedure was a sound move. But it seemed that rather than divide their work between specific products it might, for the following reasons, be an even better solution to give each one responsibility for particular customers:–

1. it would develop a feeling of responsibility – the customers would be *their* customers
2. it would be in line with the organization of the despatch, scheduling and transport departments
3. it would be more likely to help with the communication problem between OTSC and its customers
4. it would establish natural promotional paths in the department i.e. upwards through the various sizes of customers.

The decision was therefore taken to re-align the work of the sales order office clerks on this basis.

The Changes

The changes came into effect on 5 April and the new structure was one supervisor supported by four regional sales office clerks. Each clerk was given an assistant and clerks were given total responsibility for processing and progressing the orders in their region. The stock control office was renamed the sales order office and the information room was integrated into it by placing its main feature, the out-of-stock board, near the clerks. The changes took place with the minimum of physical disturbance, although after a few weeks' experience the office layout was reorganized and each clerk given a telephone. Some extra training was given to the clerks as they were not at all conversant with the complete order processing cycle.

Result of the Changes

By June, local management's comments on the changes were as follows:

1. Cost saving. Staff had been reduced by two, saving approximately £2,000 per annum. The use of temporaries had ceased and overtime had been cut, saving approximately £1,000 per annum. Thus the total savings were approximately £3,000, representing nearly 20 per cent of the department's total wages bill.
2. Management control. This had improved in three ways. The manager, supervisor and accounts department all knew who was responsible for any query; the problem of outstanding orders was more under control with responsibility clearly assigned and nobody between the customer and the clerk processing the order; the performance of individual clerks could be closely monitored.
3. Customer confidence. The changes had made possible reciprocal visits between the regional materials managers and customers installation engineers and the clerk who dealt with them. This had helped to improve relationships and had given each side a better understanding of the other's problems. Since the changes OTSC has actually received compliments from its customers and these have been recorded at their management meetings. As confidence grows the investment that customers are making in stocks is falling thus providing another saving to the Company.
4. Flexibility and cover. Because each clerk was doing a total job and also had an assistant it had become far easier to cover

holidays and absences and also to plan for training and promotions.

5. Highlighting of priorities. Under the new system despatches to each customer took place on a specific day of the week. This enabled the whole work of the department to become more focused on the immediate priority of the orders due out on that particular day. In several cases, by working together, it had been possible for the clerks to process emergency orders which would have previously been left until the next despatch date.

6. Work Satisfaction. This had shown a positive improvement. It was reflected in the more keen and enthusiastic approach that the order clerks were showing to meet the increased responsibility they now had.

Conclusion

All the problems of the OTSC sales order office have not yet been fully controlled and resolved, although if the present improvements continue, by the end of 1971 the situation will be *substantially* better than before the changes.

The changes made may in retrospect appear small and obvious and the achievements attainable through a variety of other problem-solving approaches. Yet the sales clerks thought they were radical and clearly no lasting solution had previously been found despite continuous management concern. The approach used by the OTSC management, often called job enrichment, did ensure that the human side of the situation was taken into account rather than taken for granted as is so often the case when day to day operating pressures are severe.

It is difficult to calculate the total benefit to the company of the changes. Some, like the reduction of the wages bill are quantifiable but others, like improved morale and better management control, depend largely on subjective evaluation. The key criteria must be for management to be confident that following the changes a real financial gain has accrued to the Company. On this occasion there was no doubt on this score.

The Nylon Spinners

S. Cotgrove, J. Dunham and C. Vamplew

Reprinted with permission from *The Nylon Spinners*, George Allen & Unwin, 1971, pp. 40–103.

The tasks which men perform are to a considerable extent shaped and determined by the technology. There are obviously significant differences in the tasks performed by a craftsman, compared with those of the man on the assembly line, in levels of skill, and in the length of the job cycle. The relations between men and machines then, may usefully be thought of as a socio-technical system. And the socio-technical system of a craft technology, an assembly-line technology, or a process technology, will clearly each differ in significant ways; ways which have important implications for the motivations and satisfactions of the men on the machines.

The Socio-Technical System and Motivation

We are here exploring a particular socio-technical system. The fact that the technology involves the extrusion of molten polymer through fine holes to produce thread largely determines the tasks which men do. One of the characteristics of much modern machine technology, is the way in which the production process is broken up into distinct elements, so that the worker performs only a narrow range of tasks on a small part of the total product. Consequently his daily work is largely meaningless; he is unable to see the contribution which his activity makes to the total product. Moreover, the pace of work, the methods to be used, and the organization of the plan of work, are all decisions taken out of his hands, mainly by those who have designed the machine. In short, the worker is virtually powerless to exercise any control over the tasks he performs. Under such conditions, work ceases to be a form of self-expression and becomes primarily instrumental – a means to other ends; the worker becomes a *thing* – an appendage to the machine – in short alienated. One of the most potent indices of such estrangement from the self is a heightened awareness of time. There is no involvement in the present; only an anticipation of the end of work, of release from the monotony and boredom, the heat, the noise and fumes.

Such studies of the relation between technology and the meaning and satisfaction of work focus attention on the characteristics of the production process and their significance. And although the vocabularies used by psychologists and sociologists differ, there is a substantial convergence of ideas. Blauner talks of alienation; but he does so in a way which is almost indistinguishable from Herzberg. 'When work provides opportunities for control, creativity, and challenge – when, in a word, it is *self-expressive* and enhances an individual's unique potentialities – then it contributes to the worker's sense of self-respect and dignity . . .'

But the technology is not the only determinant of the tasks men perform and of the daily conduct of their working lives. The precise allocation of tasks and the mode of their performance has still to be determined. And this is the function of the organization of work. Indeed, a major preoccupation of the literature on the management of industrial organizations is concerned with devising the most effective means of organization. What is particularly interesting is the growing awareness in such literature that the needs of individuals must be taken into account. Previously, emphasis was on devising strategies for decision-making and coordination. The general outcome of such strategies was dependence and submissiveness which increased as one went down the chain of command. The result was not only the lack of opportunities for self-actualization, but the generation of a variety of *strategies of independence* as a protection against organizational demands.

Side by side then with the increasing awareness of the importance of motivation there has been a growing literature emphasizing the need to increase involvement in the decision-making process at all levels, of which the most influential in industry has probably been R. Likert's *New Patterns in Management*. Participative group organization, to use Likert's term, 'tends to develop greater organizational flexibility, commitment, responsibility, effectiveness in problem solving . . .' In short, these are the organizational conditions necessary 'self-actualization'.

The technology leaves some room for manoeuvre. The way in which tasks are organized may be a key factor influencing the meaning and satisfaction of work.

What is particularly interesting about this experiment is the fact that the technology remained unchanged. The innovations were organizational ones. Such changes were of necessity limited, and could only take place within the parameters fixed by the production technology. Nevertheless this study will indicate the very considerable impact of such organizational changes, and can be interpreted as a challenge to any narrow view of technological determinism.

We need not spend long on describing the process itself, but a brief outline is necessary. The process starts from the charging floor where the polymer chips from which the yarn is made are loaded into hoppers. It is released from these to the unit floor where it is melted and whence it is pumped to the extrusion floor. Here is it extruded through dyes as molten filaments and air-cooled. On the spin-doff floor the yarn is wound on to cylinders. The process thus far described takes place mainly in the spinning section through which it passes in a continuous vertical stream. When it reaches the last floor it is doffed, or taken off the machine on cylinders. It is transported from here to the last major section, the drawtwist area, where it is wound on to bobbins. In the course of this operation it is stretched and twisted to make what is called true yarn. The auxiliary areas deal with inspection, low-grade yarn, residual yarn on cylinders, empty bobbins and cartons returned by customers, packing, warehousing, and so on.

For nearly all of the low-skilled operatives the work was characterized by a division of labour that allowed only for the repetitive performance of a limited set of standardized tasks. Moreover, particularly for spinning and drawtwist operatives, their work was organized for them to the extent of informing them on which machines to perform their tasks, the precise time to do this, and the time limits for carrying out the tasks. In the auxiliary areas operatives had to fulfil work quotas either in teams or individually. Thus, virtually no scope was given for initiative or autonomy. The operatives were in a strait-jacket of standard practice and generally fairly tight supervision.

The Agreement

It is against this background that we must discuss the agreement which came into effect at the beginning of 1968. For the management at ICI, this was intended as more than a straight effort bargain. It was hoped that the changes in manning which were to be introduced would lead to job enlargement, and job enrichment and would thus result in more satisfying work, offering more scope for individual responsibility and initiative, and thus, for self-actualization.

Organizational Changes

A major objective of the agreement was to achieve a reorganization of work so that the operative was subject to less detailed control by the rule book and by supervisors. Accordingly, supervision was reduced and much responsibility which was formerly borne by supervisors was transferred to operatives. The most important change here is that operatives now plan and organize their own work. For example, in the drawtwist area the system of working to a planned schedule has been replaced by a free-queuing system whereby operatives determine which machines to doff, string-up, or whatever the task may be. They also plan their own meal breaks and rest periods themselves. One result of this is an increasing independence of supervision so that, even though operatives generally consider that some foremen will be necessary in future in case of emergency and to give technical advice, they foresee drastic reductions.

In addition, there has been some job enlargement. Although proposals to add minor maintenance tasks to the operatives' jobs had not been agreed with the craft unions at the time of the inquiry most have since come into operation. The extent of these changes varies considerably from area to area, and it is evident on a broad view of the data that most change has occurred in the spinning area. Whereas formerly most operatives mainly worked in teams confined to either the extrusion or spin-doff floors, the teams are now organized vertically over three floors. Spinning operatives are now trained to work on any of these three levels with the object of creating greater flexibility of labour and consequently more efficient utilization of manpower. There is no job rotation scheme as such, but rather a movement of labour to where it is most needed, when it is needed. In fact, generally speaking, operatives still work mainly on one floor – on the tasks that they tend to be best at – switching from floor to floor or team to team if the necessity arises.

In the drawtwist area, operatives have been cross-trained to work on other drawtwist machines, although the differences in technique are not great. They have taken over responsibility for machine scheduling previously determined by a computer. They also perform additional jobs such as packing bobbins directly into polythene bags (formely done by auxiliary operatives). This involves inspecting the bobbin and taking complete responsibility for its condition when it reaches the customer. They now segregate cylinders according to the amount of residual yarn left on them preparatory to their being transported to auxiliary areas. In common with spinning operatives, they are now responsible for checking machinery – gears, draw ratios, etc. – but this is a relatively infrequent task for most workers.

In common with the above two areas, greater flexibility has been introduced into the auxiliary areas, resulting from the cross-training of operatives. Moreover, a good deal of rationalization has taken place making the coordination of work more efficient. Some jobs have been enlarged, combining hitherto separate tasks into one job.

Changes in Payment

One other major change introduced was more directly related to the role of direct monetary incentives. Before the agreement, an incentive scheme was in operation which functioned essentially in a negative way, in that a bonus was awarded and deductions made from it for mistakes leading to a lowering of the quality of the yarn. In order to enforce this scheme quality patrollers were employed to examine the work. For workers in the auxiliary area the system worked differently. Either in groups or individually, production quotas had to be met in order to earn the bonus. Production over this quota earned no extra bonus.

Under the new agreement this scheme was discarded in

favour of a fixed annual salary paid weekly. This was done partly because it was assumed that since the worker's main concern was his weekly pick-up, and changing sections might mean losing money, there would be resistance to such changes. But more important, a system which involved close checking would be inappropriate in the new situation where the worker was to be given more responsibility.

Under the new payment system, each operative was allocated to one of eight payment grades. The grades had been reached after considerable consultation during which specifications for the new jobs had been drawn up and interviews had been held with representatives of each grade in order to estimate the skill and responsibility involved. As a result of the new grading, the average increase in pay was around £3 per week. Only a very small number had increases of less than £2.

What then were the effects of the agreement – of the involvement discussions, the abolition of the bonus scheme, and the substantial decrease in supervision and increased flexibility of work tasks?

Conclusions and discussions

Our evidence does not really lend support for the view that changes in the context of work (as distinct from the job itself) are of relatively little importance. Indeed, noise, heat and shift work were major sources of complaint tolerated by many only because pay was high. Moreover, dissatisfaction with conditions spilled over into more generalized attitudes towards company management.

Little could be done about such factors, at least in the short run, but where changes were possible, in methods of payment and supervision, there are strong grounds for believing that the effects went beyond reducing dissatisfactions and resulted in increased productivity by creating a situation in which there were no dis-incentives to attaining high levels of output and quality. Here, of course, we must stress the part played by the constant efforts to 'educate' operatives to the importance of quality so that quality-consciousness became part of the ethos of the job.

Most important, perhaps, were the changes in supervision

with the introduction of shop-floor participation. The improvements in teamwork, cooperation and communications have been documented. Equally important, and more difficult to document, are the more subtle changes in attitude, involvement and motivation. The involvement discussions in some cases stimulated such enthusiastic proposals for job enlargement that supervisors felt it necessary to try to soft-pedal and to focus on more realistic goals. There is little doubt, too, that knowledge and experience were tapped that had previously lain dormant. As one supervisor said: 'It was fantastic the constructive suggestions, the constructive criticism about the way the place was running at the moment.' Not only were group decisions more fully accepted ('Once they'd agreed to something it was in, no question about it'), but there was a stronger motivation to see that they succeeded.

In short, participation does more than provide a therapeutic outlet for grievances, important as this may be. There was certainly a reduction in the number of grievances reaching higher managerial levels, 70 per cent being settled on the shop floor. It is also a source of positive satisfaction: '. . . being forced to do something is degrading, and hence one is both motivated to do something through fear, and motivated not to do it through pride'. There is more likelihood that people will assume responsibility for their own rather than others' decisions: '. . . so long as supervisors set goals and make decisions they behave as responsible individuals and often cannot understand why their employees fail to accept a similar responsibility'. Groups are united with a common aim if they make the decision themselves, and as a result team spirit is high. There is more mutual help as a group responsibility is assumed.

Such gains in cooperation and teamwork should not, however, be interpreted as indicating a radical change in industrial relations. In particular, labelling operatives as 'salaried' does not automatically carry with it any fundamental change in attitudes towards the firm in the direction of any increase in identification with the interests of the firm, more commonly found among salaried workers. Most went into the agreement for the money. And a large proportion, indeed the majority in drawtwist, thought that the company had benefited most from the agreement. In short, it is perfectly possible for an increase in teamwork and cooperation on the job to exist side by side with a tough attitude towards the effort-bargain, and even considerable dissatisfaction with the equity of pay.

Of course, participation is not an easily applied formula with guaranteed results. It depends for its success on a number of conditions, not least the appropriate managerial ideology (e.g. a confidence in their workers' ability) and an employee-centred supervision. But it has been shown, and our evidence tends to support it, that given the right conditions workers will respond eagerly to the chance to exercise control over their working environment in organizationally useful ways as opposed to the usual strategies of independence in the form of restrictive practices and strikes.

Job enlargement plus less supervision had undoubtedly contributed to a marked decrease in boredom. And the work now made greater demands on abilities. But basically the work remained monotonous. Consequently, for most, work had little meaning. It was essentially a means to an end – a source of income. Although reorganization had brought about some improvement, neither the tasks nor the product provided much basis for satisfaction or were seen as in any sense meaningful. This lack of meaning is epitomized in the remark, '. . . what is a bobbin? It looks just like a milk bottle.' In short, however significant the gains from organizational changes, the technology in the last analysis set the limits to job enlargement. Whether these limits have yet been reached is another matter.

What these findings do support is the optimistic view that workers are capable of development, of accepting more responsibility, and of greater initiative. Even the very modest and short period of re-education and the small extensions of responsibility had resulted in marked changes. Again, we can only speculate what are the possible limits, but it is unlikely that they have yet been reached.

Group Technology: Some Practical Applications

Graham Edwards

Reprinted with permission from *Readings in Group Technology*, Machinery Publishing Co. Ltd, 1971, pp. 101–10.

These applications were all carried out in well-known engineering factories, and serve to illustrate the different methods and approaches which have been adopted. They are intended to show that the benefits which have been obtained – and in no case are these to be regarded as not worthwhile – can be related directly to the degree to which management was prepared to implement GT.

Case 1 English Electric, Bradford

English Electric at Bradford manufactured a wide range of 100 – 5,000 hp electric motors, designed almost entirely to customer specification. The average order of about 1.8 machines, and the fact that the majority of component batch sizes was between 1 and 70, made this an ideal environment for the application of GT.

Prior to the introduction of GT, the company was faced with a sales forecast which showed that output had to be doubled within five years. The only answer to this problem was to improve productivity. It was soon realized that the greatest part of the problem lay in the machine shop, which had always been a bad bottle-neck, and to pinpoint the exact area the company took a number of samples to see exactly how productive time was spent. It was found that some $12\frac{1}{2}$ per cent of the eight-hour day was consumed on non-productive work, such as personal time and queuing for tools. As attempts to reduce this did not produce any worthwhile improvements, the management decided to examine areas where large amounts of time were spent, and it was soon discovered that about 50 per cent of the available time was spent on setting up the machines, despite the fact that the company had a good control of machines in the conventional way and efficient production engineers. It was clear therefore that the answer to the problem was to reduce setting-up times.

THE GT EXERCISE
For the purposes of simplicity only lathes were involved, since 70–75 per cent of output started with them. Families of components were collected in which turning was found to be a major operation, the aim being to manufacture large numbers of components without having to reset the machine.

At this stage it was possible to calculate the load. Full machine utilization was the aim, and additional components closely related to the family were brought in. In this way tooling remained unchanged for about 75 per cent of the time, and the set-up was continually refined until one set-up and one family could achieve full machine utilization.

HUMAN PROBLEMS
As with any innovation, GT involves problems of human relations. It was found in this experiment that discipline on the shop floor was essential. The old methods of operating and loading the machines, as dictated by the worker or foreman, had to be discarded, and no changes could be made once the process had been established. Another problem was the skilled men. Many operators enjoy the creative aspect of setting a machine tool, and the results achieved here could not but produce some dissatisfaction, entailing some redeployment.

RESULTS
The results of this work were impressive. Setting-up times were reduced from around 40 minutes to between 5 and $7\frac{1}{2}$ minutes, and output per man increased by about 70 per cent. Planning and rate fixing were left to the men on the machines, whose knowledge of what and where the tools were enabled them to plan the method of manufacture on the machines far more easily and quickly themselves. The planner simply allocated new components to an existing group.

Finally, a word about the limitations. This exercise was conducted from a very narrow viewpoint. The families were chosen without reference to a classification and coding system, on a basis of product knowledge only. They were manufactured on only one machine – the lathe – and the main aim was to reduce setting time. In this the exercise was a success, but it must be emphasized that it was a success in a small area, and that it did little to improve company performance as a whole. This will become clearer when the results are compared to other more ambitious applications of GT which have taken place in other factories.

Case 2 Ferranti, Edinburgh

The main products of Ferranti's Edinburgh factory are complex electronic control systems for aircraft and numerically controlled machine tools. The decision to attempt an application of GT stemmed from a sudden overload which was placed on the turning capacity of the factory, aggravated by the fact that during a previously slack period many skilled workers had left because of the reduction in overtime.

Since 70 per cent of all the firm's turned parts were made from bar of 1 in diameter or less, a family of 304 components was found from the 4,000 parts usually in manufacture. The group or cell of machines to produce this family consisted of three fully utilized first-operation lathes, a second-operation lathe, a vertical mill, a horizontal mill, a drilling and a tapping machine. Some of these machines were considerably under-utilized, so that only four operators were required for the group, three for the three lathes and one man for the other machines.

In order to minimize resetting, the family was split into sub-families, with a simple production code based upon the requirement for a thread, the degree of tolerance permitted, and the material type.

RESULTS

An analysis of fifty-five random jobs from this family produced the following results. Setting time was found to have fallen from 219 hr 52 min to 73 hr 16 min, a reduction of 146 hr 36 min. Throughput time also fell from $26\frac{1}{2}$ days to 3 days, whilst gains were made in standardization and reduced paperwork.

Although satisfied with some of the savings obtained, the company was not too happy about the inflexibility of the system, and it therefore began to reappraise the situation, finally adopting another approach to GT.

The rapidity of change in the electronics industry makes it inevitable that if large batches of components are machined well ahead of schedule some at least will become obsolete owing to modifications. GT, with its shorter throughput times, could help here, as small batches could be produced as cheaply as large ones, and nearer to the required date, so that there would be less chance of subsequent modifications.

THE COMPOSITE COMPONENT CELL

The inflexibility of the first attempt at GT led the firm to alter its approach and turn to the composite component principle. This approach entails the creation of a composite component which embodies the features of the separate family, or subfamily, which can be machined at a single tooling set-up, with little or no setting change. A broader family may contain several composites and here the production control system has to ensure that the components in each composite are, as far as possible, machined consecutively.

The company adopted a method whereby the family was partly manufactured on turret lathes, where the tooling required by each composite was pre-set, away from the machine, on removable turret tops. This procedure reduced the set-up times by about 95 per cent. The company was consequently able to produce parts in fortnightly quantities more cheaply per piece than it had previously been able to produce three-monthly quantities.

Machine loading was simplified because a small group of machines was engaged in making relatively few components. Control over the manufacturing process was improved, since the supervisor of the cell was responsible for the progress and quality of finished components.

THE TOTAL APPROACH AT FERRANTI

All the work conducted at Ferranti had been produced under test-bed conditions, with the writer's research group in close contact at each stage.

The work began at a time when the three main workshops at the factory were being combined. The research took all the components, analysed them by computer, and produced a suggested optimum layout with components and machine groups identified within a total system. Machine utilization was analysed and a production control system developed for subsequent use. The practical men at Ferranti 'kicked the whole thing around' and accepted most of the layout, but made improvements by switching components to increase automation levels.

It can be seen from the variety of cells being used, and the detailed research theses, that Ferranti has investigated GT as fully as any company in the world, and has utilized it in practice very successfully.

Case 3 Serck Audco

THE COMPANY AND ITS PROBLEMS

The Serck Audco factory, situated in Newport, Shropshire, manufactures a wide range of taper plug, butterfly, and ball valves. It was a successful organization operating under much the same difficulties, and with the same sort of deficiencies, as one finds in most job and batch engineering plants. The factory was producing and selling the volume of goods planned, but there was an excessive volume of stocks in hand. More serious was the volume of overdue orders and the twelve-week throughput time. Paper-work was excessive, whilst physical stocks seldom equated with the stock figures. The progress department of the factory was continually attempting to bring order into the production process, but was faced with solving crisis after crisis, caused in the main by failure to meet the unrealistic delivery dates promised to customers.

The crux of the problem appeared to be that no overall plan existed, and the various departments worked in an uncoordinated way. Of the many desirable objectives open to management, the keeping of promised delivery dates, with maximum production efficiency ensuring a minimum of throughput time, was the one chosen.

PLANNING AND IMPLEMENTATION OF GT

The company already had in use a Brisch classification system for the identification of materials at all stages, but to carry out the revision of the production control system an executive team, consisting of six work-study engineers and other leading personnel, was carefully selected. This team soon discovered that by far the greater part of space on the shop floor was taken up by work in progress and space for material transportation. (It should be pointed out that the team was faced with severe resistance from those not wishing to alter the existing system.) Scale models were constructed of standard plant arrangement under what was termed 'cellular group production', and this was found to be admirably suited to the company's requirement.

The new type of plant layout consisted of a number of GT (flow-line) cells of plant arranged alongside conveyors, so that components started at one end and travelled round until they were completed at the other. Each group was designed to produce a specific type of component within the same material and size range.

About twenty-four cells have now been established at the two Serck Audco factories, and they contain between four and fifteen machines. The number of operators is smaller than the number of machines – a typical twelve-machine cell requires about five operators, who travel from machine to machine as necessary. Contrary to present trends in engineering, the machines, together with the jigs and fixtures used on them, are of the simplest type possible. The reason for this is that management did not feel that modern and complex machine tools, such as numerically controlled machines and machining centres, were ideally suited to its production requirements, largely because the components could be manufactured more cheaply on simple machines. Furthermore, the cost of complex machine tools necessitates maximum machine utilization. The continual use of such machines for simple components was thought to be wasteful when the capabilities of these machines were examined.

The decision to opt for simpler types of machine meant that a certain number of machines was always idle in any given cell. This under-utilization usually involved only the simplest tools, such as single-spindle drills. One advantage of this was that when a breakdown occurred work in the cell did not automatically come to a standstill.

Each cell was under the control of a working supervisor, who was allowed, within certain limits, to process the work load as he thought best, provided that certain key operations were adhered to in the sequence. Naturally the system here described demands that the operators must be sufficiently skilled to operate any machine, and that there must be a considerable degree of cooperation between the members of each team of operators. The company attempted to increase the flexibility and versatility of the workforce by permitting operators to move from cell to cell as well as between machines.

RESULTS

Among many of the outstanding benefits which this overall approach to GT brought to Serck Audco was the ability to quote firm and realistic delivery dates much shorter than those previously offered. The following are some of the more concrete statistics which are available, and the scope of these improvements may be compared with the limited benefits which less ambitious implementations have produced:

1. Sales increased by 67 per cent
2. Stocks in hand down by £855,000, or 46 per cent
3. Stocks in hand/sales ratio down by 28 per cent
4. Average throughput time down from 12 to 5 weeks
5. Despatches per employee up from £2,218 to £4,068
6. Average annual earnings up from £714 to £1,163.

Towards a New Philosophy of Management
Paul Hill

Reprinted with permission from *Towards a New Philosophy of Management*, Gower Press, 1971, pp. 135–42.

During the period when the Employment Relations Planning unit was developing its ideas about a long-term plan, the company was designing a major new refinery to be constructed on Teesside. With a planned throughput of six million tons per annum,

Teesport was to be an important addition to the company's refining capacity.

Features of the design were a highly integrated plant layout, with a central control room covering all the units; and a computer installation capable of monitoring and possibly later controlling a large percentage of the actual process operations. Unlike Shell Haven and Stanlow, Teesport was not to be a balancing refinery, so that its operations would be less complex and more stable than theirs. Because of these features, it was envisaged that the whole refinery could be operated with a very small number of operators on each shift.

Since it was planned that the operators would be able to cope with minor running maintenance work on the plants, and since major maintenance during shutdowns would in any event have to be handled by contract labour, it was decided to contract out all maintenance work to an engineering concern in the locality so that there were no engineering craftsmen on the refinery payroll.

Site preparation for the new refinery started in early 1965 and it came on stream, after considerable delays in construction, in April 1968.

Design of Social System

As a new refinery on a green field site, Teesport clearly offered a great opportunity not only to put into practice the ideas of the philosophy statement concerning job design, but also to establish a set of working conditions and practices which could serve as a model for the older refineries to try to follow.

The extent to which this opportunity was seized would depend, of course, on the Teesport management. The key people were all enthusiastic supporters of the philosophy concepts, and were committed to designing, and bringing into being, a social system which would match the technical system – with its novel features – in the best possible way.

After the refinery came on stream in 1968, the Teesport organization proved very successful, with an unusually high level of commitment to refinery objectives at all levels. One reason for this success was undoubtedly the amount of care taken over the design of the organization, and the training of the staff.

Role of Supervisors and Operators

Since Teesport wanted to create roles both for supervisors and operators which would be demanding and challenging, and as they were determined to break away from the established patterns of the older refineries, they decided to eliminate some of the traditional levels from their organization structure. Thus the operators, who would be highly flexible and skilled men, would report direct to a shift supervisor, with no intervening charge-hand or foreman. The supervisors would report direct to the head of operations. The line of command from refinery manager to the shift operators manning the plant would consist of only four communication steps compared with the six or seven steps in the older refineries.

Great care was taken to select people who would be capable of filling these roles and who were sympathetic to the concepts of flexibility and challenge which Teesport planned to build into their organization. The first step was to select the five supervisors who would be responsible for running the shift teams of operators. All five came from other Shell refineries and joined Teesport in March 1966. The refinery superintendent's idea was that after a period devoted to their own training, the supervisors would themselves play an important role in the selection and training of their own teams of operators, and indeed would be fully involved in all matters affecting the building up of the organization.

The time between March 1966 and the start up in early 1968, was longer than originally envisaged, owing to construction delays, but it is interesting that everyone concerned was convinced that this period of training and preparation was invaluable and not a bit too long.

After initial training at Teesport the five supervisors spent six weeks with the refinery superintendent at Shell's Oakville refinery outside Toronto in Canada, where they underwent further training.

On their return to Teesport, the supervisors prepared to assist with the recruitment and training of the operators. This involved coaching – by the training adviser – in methods and techniques for interviewing candidates, and for training the recruits. In the meantime, they also took a hand in such matters as the final formulation of personnel policies, the layout of the control room building, the preparation of an information handbook and the final stages of the drafting of the trade union agreement which would cover the operators.

The refinery was to be manned by twenty-nine operators on each shift, so that there were a total of 116 jobs on the four shifts. In addition, since the intention was to run the refinery without overtime, forty more men were needed to provide cover for all kinds of absence, holidays, and time spent away from the job on training. Thus a total of 156 men had to be recruited.

The supervisors decided on the wording of the advertisements for operating staff which appeared in the local press. For the 156 jobs available over 3,000 men applied. The letter which invited them to complete a formal application form concluded with the following paragraph: 'We are now recruiting operating staff who will be trained on site for approximately six months. No one should under-estimate the difficulties that are bound to arise in starting up a refinery of this complexity. We are seeking men who will accept the challenge of these difficulties and who will prove to be adaptable to changing circumstances. We shall depend a great deal upon the individual effort and sense of responsibility of each member of the staff, who will – after training – be required to work without close supervision.' An intensive interviewing programme was set up and the supervisors were part of the interviewing team. An important element in the process was to obtain from the applicants at their first interview their reactions to the sort of responsible, flexible jobs which were envisaged for operators, so that people to whom this did not appeal could withdraw from the follow-up interview.

Once the teams were recruited, each supervisor assumed responsibility for training his own team, under the general guidance of the training adviser. They did, of course, get assistance from other members of the staff who gave lectures on specialized subjects. Practical training on operations and maintenance was interspersed with theoretical sessions. Aids to training included a complete scale model of the process units and a control panel simulator on which operating techniques could be practised.

During this period of training, the supervisors conducted sessions with their teams on the company philosophy statement. The concepts of joint optimization, and of meeting people's psychological needs, had particular relevance at Teesport, where the whole refinery was to be manned by only twenty-nine operators during any one shift. The need to make the best use of the men's capabilities, and the wish to design challenging jobs, were mutually supporting.

Also vital was the need to develop the operators' capabilities to handle information quickly and effectively. Already identified as the critical human requirement for control of a refinery operating system, information handling was particularly important at Teesport, with its very high level of instrumentation and automation. Any failure or malfunction of the automatic control system would mean that the operator had to take over control himself, knowing that delay was likely to be costly. Some of the implications of this man-machine relationship are examined in the next section.

The payment structure for the operators was fitted to the needs of the system. As it was essential that each operator should be highly flexible, and capable of operating a number of different units, the level of salary was geared not to the specific job he was on but to the extent he had developed and proved his capability to run a number of different jobs. It was envisaged that each operator could learn up to seven different jobs. After training and experience on each job, he would be given a written and verbal test by the shift supervisor. As his range of competence was widened in this way, his salary rate was increased accordingly.

Also essential was the employment of sufficient spare operators, to enable the work to be covered whilst a process of continual training was maintained. In keeping with the general philosophy, it was agreed that each team of operators would handle its own relief arrangements for covering absences of any kind.

The effect of involving the supervisors from the outset in matters which would vitally influence the running of the refinery, and the building of responsible, flexible and challenging jobs for supervisors and operators, was to create in both groups a very high level of commitment to their tasks and to achieving refinery objectives.

Evidence of this commitment is provided by the fact that in the period of over twelve months between the recruitment of the 156 operators, and the start up of the refinery in 1968, only five of these men resigned. This represented an extremely low turnover rate of a little over 3 per cent a year. Wastage would increase later, as the operators found that their training had fitted them for more lucrative jobs overseas.

So far as the supervisors were concerned, one of them has commented on his own reaction to this period of time in the following terms: 'Everyone contributed, it was a wonderful experience and I hope that the marvellous spirit of Teesport today lives on.'

Optimizing the Computer-operator Relationship

Mention has already been made of the computer installed in Teesport's centralized control room, which could carry out much of the data-logging and plant control operations normally done by operators in the older established refineries.

The refinery superintendent, who was concerned with the design of the operator role, and the technologist responsible for the computer programme, both saw the computer–operator interface as a critical factor for the effective operation of the refinery. Both saw it as essential that the way the interface was set up should be governed by the concept of joint optimization, by making the best match between the capabilities of the man and the machine.

One choice available to them was to maximize the use of the computer's capabilities: in other words, to close as many information and control loops as possible, so that the need for intervention by the operator was reduced to a minimum. Whilst such a choice may well have been attractive from a purely technical point of view, the Teesport people were concerned about its implications for the role of the operator. If his role was to be confined largely to monitoring the performance of the computer, this would neither be sufficiently challenging, nor involve him sufficiently in the on-going process of control to enable him at any time quickly and effectively to assume manual control in the event of a breakdown of the computer. Yet it was essential that he should be able to do so, since delay or mistakes could be very costly.

They decided therefore that a balance had to be struck between what was technically feasible, on the one hand, and what was necessary, on the other, to create a role for the operator that would enable him to become internally motivated to perform his task effectively. This meant that certain loops which could technically have been closed, were passed instead, as it were, through the operator, so that he could exert his influence and become part of the control process. The role of the computer was accordingly seen as the logging of data, the automatic control of certain variables, and the rapid provision of information on which the operator or supervisor could take better decisions about the control of other process variables.

The setting up of the computer–operator interface does therefore give an excellent practical illustration of applying the concept of joint optimization. Rather than maximizing the technical use of the computer at the expense of the operator's role, the contribution of both was balanced in a way which would ensure a more effective performance in the long term.

Terms and Conditions of Work

Another significant achievement at Teesport was the establishment of a set of working conditions and terms of employment which were quite different from the traditions of the older refineries in the company. All the features which it was hoped would eventually be introduced at the older refineries through productivity bargaining were incorporated in the Teesport system from the outset.

Whilst clearly it was less difficult in some ways to set up a new system on a green field site than to change long-established systems at older sites, Teesport was also faced with serious problems to overcome. At the time they decided to approach the TGWU about an agreement to cover the operators, there was still in existence a national TGWU agreement with the company, laying down common conditions for all the existing refineries. Furthermore, the overwhelming pattern of custom and practice in the heavily industrialized Teesside area was similar to that of the company's older refineries, and quite different, therefore, from the new pattern Teesport wanted to establish. Some advisers argued moreover that the unions in the area would be very resistant to changes in the normal pattern and that it would be wiser, therefore, to conform.

Teesport, however, saw it as essential that the terms and

conditions of work should be consistent with the philosophy which had guided the way people's roles had been set up. They were determined that all employees at Teesport would be members of the staff: there would be 40 hourly paid employees and no time clocks. Everyone would receive an annual salary, paid monthly into his bank account. There would be no provision for extra payments for overtime. All staff below management level would be compensated for overtime by corresponding time off. Everyone would enjoy the same set of sickness benefits and pension fund arrangements. Everyone would share the same restaurant, although the shift operators would normally eat in the mess-room on the process units.

Rather than await an approach from the union, they decided to take the initiative by contacting the local TGWU officials well before the recruitment of operators was started. After discussions between head office and national officials in London had cleared the way, Teesport talked with the local officials. They were entirely open about their intentions, and their wish to negotiate a separate and completely different agreement from the existing national one. The union officials, far from justifying the warning mentioned above, proved receptive to Teesport's ideas and contributed in joint discussions to their development. The outcome was an agreement covering the operating staff which embraced virtually everything Teesport would have wished. Both sides recognized the experimental nature of the agreement and accepted that changes might be needed in the future.

Undoubtedly, therefore, Teesport had succeeded in setting up a new organization which was a practical demonstration of the value of the two lines of action embodied in the company development programme: the creation of commitment to tasks and objectives through appropriate job design; and the establishment of appropriate terms and conditions of employment.

Further Reading: Case Studies in Job Improvement

J. BLAIR, 'Three Studies in Improving Clerical Work', *Personnel Management*, February 1974, pp. 34–6.

B. DYSON, 'Hoover's Group Therapy', *Management Today*, May 1973.

G. A. B. EDWARDS, 'Group Technology: a technical answer to a social problem?', *Personnel Management*, March 1974, pp. 35–9.

L. KING-TAYLOR, *Not by Bread Alone*, London, Business Books, 1972.

R. PLANT, 'Releasing Supervisory Potential: reflections on an exercise to enrich supervisory jobs in a process industry, 1968–70', *European Training*, Vol. 1, No. 1. Spring 1972, pp. 34–42.

PHILIPS REPORT, *Work Structuring: A survey of experiments at N. V. Philips, Eindhoven (1963–68)*, Eindhoven, N. V. Philips.
(This booklet contains one of the few published descriptions of an experiment which failed.)

D. H. THORNELY AND G. A. VALANTINE, 'Job Enlargement: some implications of longer cycle jobs on Fan Heater production', *Philips Personnel Management Review*, No. 23, January 1968, pp. 12–17.

W. WALSH, 'Enrichment in the Office', *Personnel Management*, October 1969, pp. 42–4.

A. WILKINSON, *A survey of some Western European Experiments in Motivation*, Enfield, Institute of Work Study Practitioners, 1970.

7   Job Satisfaction in Context

In this chapter we will consider some of the doubts which
have been raised about the philosophy or techniques of the
various efforts which have been made to improve jobs, a few
of which were included in Chapter Six. That is not to say
that those efforts were not successful or worthwhile, simply
that they must not be accepted uncritically and without
considering the wider implications, which is what we hope to
do here.

Daniels and McIntosh suggest that some managements
tend to be rather naïve in their expectations of job improvement projects and that this may result in opposition to them
on the part of employees. They emphasize that the needs of
individuals vary over time, according to their particular
circumstances, and that needs are not static as some theories
seem to imply. In their conclusions, they highlight the fact
that in many situations the technology imposes severe constraints
on the possibilities for improving jobs, and that this may
affect manual workers more than white-collar workers. They
also point out that no group can have its jobs improved in
isolation, because others will also be affected, and need to be
considered, for example, the supervisors of groups whose jobs
now include some of their earlier duties.

Hughes and Gregory take a critical look at the current
interest in job improvement, and in particular at the report
'On the Quality of Working Life' which was discussed in Chapter
Two. They quote figures to show that shift working has
doubled in the last twenty years; that the industrial accident
rate has remained constant despite a decreasing proportion of
manual workers; and that low pay is still a problem in Britain.
They suggest that improvements in these basic factors would
be more relevant and far reaching than some of the job improvement schemes which have been taking place.

The development of 'high-trust relationships' is considered
by **Alan Fox**. He feels that many of the efforts aimed at

improving jobs are in fact motivated by economic expediency rather than by altruism or a desire for high-trust relations for their own sake. Fox emphasizes that people are faced with a choice about the patterns of work organization, and this implies that they have a rational understanding of the costs and benefits of the various alternatives. This is no doubt an unrealistic hope, but to think in these terms may raise the choice to a conscious level and make it more likely that choices are made on the basis of critically evaluated knowledge.

The role which the trade unions have to play is considered by **Kenneth Graham**. He discusses how far job improvement projects are likely to contribute to the objectives which the trade union movement has for its members, and where there is likely to be a conflict. The motives of management in introducing these ideas are an important factor, and Graham suggests that where they are more concerned to solve problems rather than genuinely improve job satisfaction, they are likely to meet with resistance. The traditional trade union method of collective bargaining is still relevant to such situations at which the unions intend to 'look hard before they leap'.

The fifth reading is a short extract from a lecture on 'Humanizing Work' given by **John Marsh** to the Royal Society of Arts. This critical extract has been taken out of the context of a lecture which was very positive in tone, but has been included because it explains well the feeling of some managers that they are being overwhelmed by a wave of theory and research of which they have little understanding and which seems remote from the problems facing them in their everyday work.

Our final reading takes us back to the point at which we opened the discussion in Chapter One, in considering how appropriate are the job restructuring exercises undertaken in other European countries to the British situation. **Ray Wild** examines some of the factors which are needed for changes to be effective and points out where there are differences between Britain and Scandinavia in particular. He suggests that concern with restructuring individual jobs is likely to be replaced by efforts to create autonomous working groups within the context of moves towards greater worker participation. However, as has been emphasized throughout this book, people and jobs differ so greatly that no single set of concepts is, nor should be expected to be, adequate to cope with the wide variety of ways in which they relate to their work and hopefully gain satisfaction from it.

Perhaps we cannot do better in conclusion than to quote the final paragraph from the paper by Ray Wild in which he says

the nature of such changes and the manner in which they are pursued must always be determined by local factors and thus simple supposedly 'universal' techniques must always be suspect. This does not mean that certain broad principles or even a general policy might not be identified, but simply suggests that in the final event changes of this type must be approached on a pragmatic basis.

Job Enrichment in Context

W. W. Daniels and Neil McIntosh

Reprinted with permission from *The Right to Manage?* PEP, 1972, pp. 29–52.

Job enrichment is widely feasible and it can bring manifest benefits to workers and to management. We seek to place both concept and practice in context in three senses: by reviewing just how practicable job enrichment is for the mass of blue-collar jobs and workers; by assessing the nature and extent of the benefits that can realistically be expected to follow from applications in those situations where it is appropriate; and by locating the meaning of job content in the social and economic frameworks that are often equally if not more important aspects of workers' jobs. This process of review, and what will essentially be qualification, is necessary as we have detected among some managements a tendency towards quite unrealistic expectations of job enrichment which are unrelated to the reality both of technological constraints and, more importantly, the priorities and interests, of industrial workers, particularly in terms of how they can effectively bring about their own economic advancement.

Fallacies about job enrichment

Though we do not wish to be too unfair, we can illustrate many of the fallacies about job enrichment by reference to a recent pamphlet *The Wages of Fear* dealing with wage-led inflation and incomes policy. (John Nelson-Jones, 1971) Here it is argued that boring jobs and lack of job satisfaction are one of the chief sources of wage inflation. The majority of industrial workers have to endure demoralizing, repetitive jobs, which make them frustrated, aggressive, envious and greedy. Consequently they both join trade unions and put in outrageous wage claims to compensate for their lack of job satisfaction. Thus boring jobs directly contribute to wage-push inflation both by direct stimulation of wage claims and by strengthening, in terms of both membership and support, the position of trade unions. Their collective bargaining position is strengthened and they are consequently better able to achieve inflationary pay settlements.

The author concludes that if only government would initiate a programme of job enrichment throughout industry, making every job interesting, rewarding and responsible, then everyone would be satisfied and content, lose interest in trade-union membership and activity and forget to put in pay demands.

The danger in this type of analysis is not only that it is naïve and impracticable but also that it is likely to be positively harmful, exciting resistance from workers and trade unionists to innovations such as job enrichment because they see them as inspired by a managerial ideology directed towards weakening union strength and depressing industrial earnings. Again these are not views put forward by just one pamphleteer. The ideas and assumptions behind the analysis are shared by many apparently well intentioned managements, who often see job enrichment as a means whereby they might overnight transform militant, organized, industrial workers into contented, compliant staff, no longer attached to ideas of collective protection and advancement through trade unionism. Similarly they have sometimes seen 'job enrichment' as a means of introducing labour flexibility by the back door, under the cover of a more seductive title, and bringing increased job satisfaction for the worker. Breaking down traditional demarcation between different groups of craft workers on the one hand, and between craft and general workers on the other, in order to utilize labour more effectively, has been a widespread objective of many managements in British industry during the last ten to fifteen years. This, however, has normally been pursued quite openly within the framework of productivity agreements which have rewarded workers with a share of the increased productivity ensured by a better labour utilization. For management consciously to try to achieve the same objectives by calling the changes 'job enrichment' and not by increasing workers' remuneration according to their new responsibilities can only result in suspicion of management, charges of 'manipulation', resistance to future changes, and the bringing of the idea of job enrichment into disrepute. This would be a grave loss because job enrichment does have a great deal to offer workers and trade unionists as well as management. Indeed, job enrichment is something which unions should strenuously advocate and strive for. The quality of the work their members do and the level of their job satisfaction should be one of their prime concerns, for trade unions, in seeking to represent the interests of their members and maximize their rewards, should increasingly turn their attention to the aspect of work which is often least rewarding: the work itself. In principle they should be particularly concerned about increasing workers' control which is exactly what job enrichment seeks to do: increase workers' control over their day-to-day work activities, an area in which they can be seen to seek and value autonomy and control spontaneously. But where management and its spokesmen are advocating, and seeking to use, job enrichment as a tool to weaken unions and workers' influence and bargaining strength, it is hardly surprising if they become suspicious of, and hostile to, innovations that could be of benefit to all parties. In fact workers have no real need for fear. Management has no hope of achieving those goals we have attributed to its more ill-advised representatives via job enrichment. Because their members' jobs have been made more interesting trade unions are no less likely to pursue, nor have any less support from their members in pursuing, wage demands related to the cost of living, the earnings of other sections of the community or the profitability of the enterprise. This can be readily illustrated by the way in which at each socio-economic level it is often in practice the groups with the most interesting and rewarding jobs, the greatest responsibility and the highest status, who have the most powerful collective organizations, exercise the most rigid unilateral job regulation and pursue their economic and occupational interests the most single-mindedly and effectively. Examples are skilled craftsmen among industrial workers and lawyers and doctors among white-collar workers.

All too often when people think about work attitudes and motivations they think in terms of a fixed set of priorities, needs or interests. They ask 'What is the worker really interested in?' with the assumption that he is interested in the same thing to the same degree in all contexts.

On the one hand, there is the suggestion that affluence in industrial societies has created a situation where the primary concern of workers is the lack of opportunity for creative activity in work rather than the further increase of their material wealth. On the other hand, there is the conclusion that the advertising, consumer economy, on which the wealth of the advanced industrial societies is based, creates an insatiable demand for consumer goods, which in turn ensures that the economic motive in work remains paramount and will remain paramount for the foreseeable future. But, while offering directly contradictory conclusions, each of the approaches described shares the common assumption that the worker has an ordered and consistent set of needs or priorities in what he seeks from a job; that this set of priorities is reflected and manifested in all aspects of his work behaviour and choices.

But, in terms of understanding workers' behaviour and attitudes, the critical question is often not the one so frequently posed of *what* are people really interested in or most interested in or *whether* they are more interested in job satisfaction and intrinsic rewards than money and extrinsic rewards, but rather, *when* are they interested in intrinsic rewards and *when* are they interested in extrinsic rewards.

The failure to distinguish between what workers are interested in in different contexts has led to some misunderstanding of the significance of Herzberg's findings. Because his form of questioning reveals that, for very many types and levels of employee, the chief sources of positive satisfaction in their work lie in the scope that it provides for achievement, interest, responsibility, recognition and advancement, management has often assumed that workers would welcome changes calculated to increase this type of reward. They have assumed that if they could devise productivity agreements that allowed for an element of job enrichment then workers would be attracted to them for this reason.

Similarly, at the individual level, it is not always true that a job that is richer because it demands more use of abilities will be attractive from the outside. The prospect of such a job may even be threatening and worrying. For instance there was evidence that many of the older men were far from attracted by the prospect of increased demands on their abilities, and the training they would need to fulfil these demands. They were worried that they would not be able to cope with training and that they would not meet the increased demands. All other things being equal, they would have preferred to have continued in their own quiet way, doing tasks that were familiar to them, which if they had become relatively unexciting and uninteresting, were also undemanding. And yet having been required to make the change, they found the fact that they had been able to cope very gratifying, and very often found the new method of working more interesting and satisfying.

Job enrichment and technological constraints

The first conclusion that we can draw is that there are powerful arguments for job enrichment on both economic and social grounds. While it is feasible in a large variety of jobs, there are, however, wide variations in the scope for practical application among different groups of workers in industry. The chief limitation on effective job enrichment for large sectors of industry is the constraints imposed by the primary technology employed in the process of production, which is in turn dictated by the present state of technological innovation. At the moment the general stage that we are going through in industry can be styled as one of sophisticated mechanization which imposes severe limits on the scope of workers' self expression but as automation increases so the scope for both viable organizational choice and the opportunity for designing job structures that permit real job interest, autonomy and responsibility will grow.

While seeking to assess the implications of this type of change for industry realistically, we do not seek to deprecate its very real achievements, but merely to moderate any tendency to see job enrichment as something that could transform the position of manual workers. What does seem true is that while there is likely to be some scope for job enrichment in the large majority of jobs, the scope may be very limited at some stages in the development of technology. It is even more difficult to see any real opportunity in this type of production process for a continuing and progressive process of growth and development for industrial workers.

Job enrichment and collective advancement

The lack of scope for progressive development remains a major distinction between many blue-collar and white-collar jobs and a brief consideration of this distinction will provide a basis for making our second chief qualification about what can realistically be expected of job enrichment when applied to manual workers. First, the nature of many white-collar jobs is such as to provide greater scope for job enrichment even within the jobs that white-collar workers now do. Their jobs tend to provide more scope for organizational choice. They are not subject to the same constraints from the purely mechanical demands of the process of production. But secondly, and perhaps even more importantly, they tend very much more than the blue-collar workers to be able to look forward to the possibility of continuous and progressive growth throughout their working lives, although this is less true for women. The men, however, can expect a succession of different jobs, a succession that is progressively more challenging and demanding, that provides new interest and scope for achievement in mastering the new job and that requires training so that there is a continuous process of personal development and increasingly greater opportunities to use and develop abilities. In short, for the white-collar worker, the concept of a career as opposed to a job still has some meaning, even if at some levels it may be declining. Where it exists, however, it is a powerful force for job involvement and creates a strong link between the fortunes of the individual and those of the enterprise. His individual advancement is dependent upon his performance as rated by his superiors and as the enterprise grows and develops so do the opportunities for the career employee.

The general pattern for the blue-collar worker is very different. For him the probabilities are that he will continue to be a manual wage earner for the whole of his working life. His realistic expectation is that he will continue to do the job he is doing or a very similar level of job until he retires. While it may be possible to enrich the job he is doing, even substantially, it is not realistic to expect that it might be possible to create progressively more interesting, responsible, challenging and demanding jobs for him. Thus, in terms of the components of Herzberg's job enrichment package, the one element that is missing for the manual worker, and which it seems likely that it would be impossible to introduce in anything other than an artificial way, is scope for individual advancement. In terms of involvement in work and attitudes to management and trade unions this is the critical component. Given that the manual worker's realistic expectation is that he will remain in the same type of job that he is in at present and that his scope for individual advancement is limited or non-existent, then any hope that he has of advancement in his status and earnings lies in the advancement of the group of which he is a member. In short his economic and social advancement is linked inextricably to collective advancement, for it is only if the wage or salary grade to which he belongs receives an improvement in earnings, fringe benefits, status or conditions that he will progress.

This does not mean that job content is unimportant or that job enrichment is not practicable or desirable. What it does mean is that as far as these types of manual workers are concerned, job enrichment has to be placed in a collective bargaining context and management has to distinguish between the different attitudes, priorities and strategies that prevail in different contexts. It also means that job enrichment in blue-collar jobs is not going to change the fundamental relationship between management and labour in the way some hopeful managers have assumed, but rather that it will make for improvement within that fundamental relationship.

Indeed, rather than it being possible through job enrichment to transform the industrial worker into the traditional managerial ideal of a committed loyal, staff worker, all the signs are that one trend narrowing the difference that we have distinguished between the job structure of manual and non-manual workers is bringing the relationship of non-manual workers with management closer to that of manual workers. The growth of the white-collar sector and the size of employment units within that sector, with the accompanying formalization of organization and procedures, has tended to bring about a situation in which more and more white-collar workers are finding themselves in the position where their advancement is more closely linked to their grade and group than it is to personal career achievement and progress. Thus they too are increasingly turning towards strategies for collective advancement through unionization.

Job enrichment and management structure

The third main conclusion emerging from our findings and reviews is that the importance of job enrichment for a particular group of workers must not be seen in isolation from the rest of the organization. What comes out clearly is that the type of reorganization we have been discussing has important implications for management style as a whole. This is demonstrated most directly by the effects it has upon supervision or first-line management. The one essential characteristic of any really effective change in the direction of job enrichment is the delegation of greater responsibility to individual workers and work groups, so that some shop-floor decision-making passes from supervisors to the work group. But this immediately changes the position of the supervisor and there will be uncertainty for all at this level. This does not necessarily mean that fewer first-line managers or foremen will be needed or that their span of control will be increased but rather that the numbers at intermediary levels, such as assistant foremen, will be reduced or even eliminated. The jobs of those remaining will be very substantially changed. Indeed they may well feel that their last remaining vestige of status and responsibility has been stripped from them.

Industrial change has brought about a progressive impoverishment of the job of the first-line supervisor. The development of specialist functions has meant that more and more of his traditional job has been whittled away until all that is often left is the day-to-day policing of the workers under his command. And now along comes job enrichment to divest him of this last remaining function. It is not enough to assume that being freed from the demands of detailed, direct and close supervision of the work and workforce will enable him for the first time to become an effective member of the management team and to contribute to a higher level of management planning and decision-making. This is not a job that he has been trained to do and the new competence will not come spontaneously or automatically. Yet it is something that management has to ensure does come about through its reorganization of the management structure over the more autonomous work group, for nothing is more likely to jeopardize the results of the change than disgruntled supervisors reluctant to operate the new system of working even if they are capable of doing so. What is clearly required is that as much attention is paid to the jobs of supervisors, their interests, their responsibilities and job descriptions, and the training they will need to fulfil these, as is paid to the reorganization of shop-floor jobs.

Job enlargement and job rotation

In terms of improving the quality of jobs we have mainly focused on ways of increasing the levels of skill, ability, discretion and responsibility exercised by workers. We have recognized, however, that there are very many jobs where the scope for this is strictly limited. There remains the possibility that even within such jobs there may be some scope for injecting greater interest through job enlargement or rotation. It may be impossible to enrich jobs vertically, but possible to extend them to include a greater variety of tasks, although each task may not require greater skill or ability. Alternatively it may be possible to engender variety and renewed interest by moving workers around from one task to another. These are feasible, if palliative, alternatives. There are, however, two major considerations to be taken into account when considering their desirability.

The first of these is the danger of again regarding job content in isolation and not taking into account the impact that changes in job content have upon social relationships on the job and other sources of gratification or compensation. There is a tendency to assume that the relationship between task complexity or variety, job interest and job satisfaction represents a straight line: the more complex or varied a set of tasks are, the more interesting the job will be and the more satisfied the worker will be with the result. In practice this has been found not to be the case for, as far as very simple assembly jobs are concerned, the tasks are such that they allow the operator to perform them unthinkingly, automatically, even unconsciously. This frees the mind to day-dream or think about something distinct from the task being done, or alternatively to chat, gossip, joke and interact socially with other members of the work group – if noise, distance and rela-tionship make this possible. There tends to come a point when the complexity of the tasks requires full attention, making both fantasy and social interaction impossible, while the tasks themselves are still not sufficiently interesting or rewarding to compensate for the loss of social contact or day-dreams.

Similarly job rotation and enlargement may break up established work-group relationships, without substantially increasing the interest of the job. Indeed it may well be that management attempts to impose rotation or enlargement on the work group will achieve exactly the opposite of what management is setting out to do. Workers may see the attempts as moves towards closer supervision and more control over activity and task distribution. One essential component of increased worker discretion in the job is less supervision. In practice, work groups and their members will if given the opportunity, tend spontaneously in their informal social and task organization to make the work as interesting and palatable as they can. They adopt informal practices of job sharing and rotation among themselves and vary both pattern and pace of work within groups, to suit individual preferences and abilities to the extent that they are permitted to do so by supervision and the physical organization of the plant. What the work group cannot control unilaterally, of course, is the style and degree of supervision, the level of manning and the technical and physical layout of the plant. Management has to make the changes in these areas.

Thus, as far as job rotation and enlargement are concerned, management must create the conditions where this can naturally come about, through the style of supervision, the level of manning and the physical layout of the work area, rather than by imposing preconceived systems of rotation and enlargement on the work group. Though the intention may be to increase the workers' job interest and autonomy the effect is likely to reduce them because of closer supervision and loss of social satisfactions through the break-up of established group relationships. This again underlines the fact that work structuring is not an established technique which can be applied without consideration of the ideas and interests of the group members. While management may have ideas about desirable changes from previous experience and research, the details have to be worked out with the work group involved, and their ideas incorporated, if the results are to be effective.

Richer Jobs for Workers?

John Hughes and Denis Gregory

Reprinted with permission from *New Society*, 14 February 1974, pp. 386–7.

On the face of it, the current interest in 'job enrichment' ought to be welcome. But trade unionists criticize it, for divorcing the concept of the quality of working life from important aspects of the work situation. Here we would like to distinguish a trade union view of job enrichment from the narrower abstractions emanating from government and management. First we would like to define what we mean by the term: an increase in the satisfaction and responsibility attached to a job – either by reducing the degree of supervision over it, or by giving a worker a unit of work, with which he has the freedom to choose his method and sequence of operations. We do not mean 'job enlargement' – where a worker is required to increase his number of operations. Nor do we mean 'job rotation' – the practice of rotating a worker around a variety of simple, usually automated tasks.

A critical look at the government's statement on job enrichment *On the Quality of Working Life*, illustrates the way in which job enrichment is being abstracted from the totality of the work situation. The report comments on how '. . . the basic circumstances of workers' lives have improved over the last century'. It claims that, 'the contemporary unemployment rate – though agreed by everyone to be too high – is in fact much lower than it was on average from the turn of the century to World War II': that 'work has become a less dangerous activity: fatal accidents in industry have been cut by three quarters although the working population is half as large again'; that 'despite intense concern over recent price increases, the increase in retail prices has consistently lagged behind the increase in weekly wage rate'; and that 'food prices have become less volatile'. The paper deliberately omits discussion of specific topics like safety, or workloads, or shiftwork.

Here then, are two crucial assumptions: first, that the lot of the working man has improved so much, that the only real problem remaining is the need to humanize the bleaker elements of industrial life. Secondly, that where the more mundane problems of shiftwork, safety and workload still exist, these can be dealt with separately and in any case do not directly affect the worker and his tasks at the workplace! Unfortunately these assumptions are optimistic. Shiftworking is a prime example. Despite the disruptive impact of shiftworking on family and social life, it has at least doubled in the last twenty years. For manual workers in manufacturing industries, the incidence of shiftworking increased from $12\frac{1}{2}$ per cent in 1954, to 25 per cent in 1968. Available data indicate that this rise has levelled off since 1968. Data from the New Earnings Survey of 1968 give the table below:

Table 1: Percentage of full-time male manual workers getting shift bonuses September 1968

	%
skilled manual	14.9
semi-skilled	33.4
unskilled	18.9

It is significant that the very workers who are most often the objects of attention in job enrichment schemes, the semi-skilled are also those most affected by shiftworking. In the light of this, to state that shiftworking does not directly affect the worker and his tasks at the workplace, is to ignore the high and increasing incidence of shiftwork: to deny that it is socially disruptive is to be blind to a vital area, where changes could result in job enrichment.

The claim that 'work has become less dangerous' is also seriously misleading. If we examine accidents recorded in the Factory Inspectorate's classification of 'all factory processes', which account for over 80 per cent of all accidents recorded by industry as a whole, the following disturbing trends emerge:

Table 2: Accident trends

	fatal	all
1964	344	217,950
1972	261	216,495
1973 (estimated)	290 to 300	225,000 to 230,000

Source: Department of Employment Gazette.

Whilst fatal accidents show a decline, the trend in all accidents between 1964 and 1972 has remained remarkably constant. Using all of the currently available accident data for 1973 – i.e. three of the four quarterly analyses, our estimates indicate rising trends in both fatal and all accident rates. Fatal accidents in 1973 are likely to be 13 per cent up on 1972. Whereas the all accident rate is likely to show an increase over the 1964 level of over 5 per cent. At the same time it is important to remember that the number of workers 'at risk' in these industries has been declining over this period. In hourly terms, the total hours worked by operatives in manufacturing industries declined over the period by approximately 20 per cent.

Table 3 demonstrates how the balance between manual and non-manual jobs in manufacturing has been changing over the decade 1964–73. Clearly the diminishing proportion of manual workers – those most 'at risk' – taken with the accident trends, leaves no room for either complacency or optimism.

Table 3: Administrative, technical and clerical
workers' employment in all manufacturing
industries

	total employees (000's)	white collar as % of total employees
1964	8,695	23.1
1972	8,091	27.4
1973	8,048	27.0

Source: Department of Employment Gazette.

The report's statement that 'the increase in retail prices has consistently lagged behind the increase in weekly wage rates' is understandable, but naïve. The New Earnings Survey has long since established that basic wage rates account for only two thirds of take-home pay, the other third being built up from various payments and premiums paid to the worker in respect of overtime, shiftworking and so on. Measuring increases in the index of retail prices against increases in basic weekly wage rates produces an unrealistic picture. In the last decade, too, a sharp increase in the incidence of direct taxation on working-class income has to be taken into account. Nor is this significant decline in retention of original income erased when benefits as well as taxes are taken into account. Moreover, we do not have to look far to be reminded that low pay is still a problem in Britain, as this table shows:

Table 4: Percentage of full-time adult workers
with gross earnings under £25 per week

	men 21 and over	women 18 and over
manual	10.8	83.5
non-manual	7.4	61.7

Source: New Earnings Survey – April 1973.

Consequently, we do not think that trade unions will share the government's view of the area of industrial life which might be affected by job enrichment. They cannot forget *other* aspects of industrial life, including the social impoverishment and physical damage associated with low pay and excessive hours of work: with shiftworking: with industrial accidents, unemployment and job insecurity. Hence unions are unlikely to treat job enrichment as a separate issue.

Managerial attitudes on job enrichment display an even more obviously utilitarian concern. Despite the 'humanistic' trappings, it is readily apparent, from accounts of various job enrichment schemes throughout the industrialized west, that management is primarily interested in the concept as a means of achieving savings in labour costs, without a loss of productivity. In management terms a good job enrichment scheme should aim at cutting down labour turnover, reducing absenteeism, increasing work force flexibility, easing the induction and training of new workers, increasing the quality of output, cutting down on fault rectification, reducing plant stoppages, and reducing manning levels.

What the worker may gain from a 'good' job enrichment scheme of this sort remains open to speculation. Management, in return for what may be a considerable change in work load and working practice, is seeking to pay the compliant worker in units of 'satisfaction' rather than cash. Moreover, if the enrichment scheme contains elements of job enlargement, then the worker is liable to find him or herself working harder for intangible rewards and extra sweat.

That savings in labour costs can be achieved from job enrichment schemes, is well documented. At the Saab-Scania truck factory, at Sodertalje in Sweden, a job enrichment experiment produced considerable results over the period 1969–72: production targets were achieved and overall productivity increased. Actual assembly costs in the latter stages of the experiment ran at 5 per cent below budgeted costs. Adjustments to trucks after leaving the line required less time in 1972, than in 1970. Labour turnover declined for the company as a whole in 1969–72, but declined even more sharply in the experimental chassis section. In addition to this, *On the Quality of Working Life* cites the example of American Telephone and Telegraph. In an experiment concerning nine jobs in ten plants involving over 3,000 workers, this firm achieved a drop in turnover of 27 per cent with the first 18 months of the scheme's operation. Significantly, 'there were also substantial savings due to elimination of jobs and sections, and the total costed savings were estimated at 15 times the expenditure on directing staffing and monitoring the profits'.

The effect on the employees in such cases is harder to ascertain. In all the reports, comments on worker reactions and attitudes appear very limited. Of the seven experiments quoted in the department's report, only one records that there was unequivocal acceptance and liking of the new system of working. Job enrichment schemes only pay lip service to the questions of control at the workplace. For instance, great play has been made of the fact that workers at the Saab-Scania engine plant in Sweden can, within their work groups, 'control' and choose for themselves how they divide up their tasks, and their sequence of operations. However, the pace of the line is still set by management, the operatives still have to complete their tasks in a set time allotted by management, and the 'pace of work is still hectic'. Wider possible aspects of workplace control seem conspicuously absent.

Clearly, management operating in a tight labour market supply situation can gain a great deal from a successful job enrichment scheme. It is frequently overlooked by the pundits, that it was precisely this situation which sparked off the Saab-Scania scheme and the more recent Volvo experiment. The Swedish motor industry, whilst already one of the highest wages cost industries in Europe, encountered severe labour shortage in the late 1960s and early 1970s. This coincided with an upswing in the international demand for their products. The problem could not be solved simply by increasing productive capacity with new plants, since the supply of Finnish and Yugoslavian workers, crucial to the industry, was already stretched to the limit. Moreover, increased reliance on immigrant labour guarantees a whole series of new problems and tensions. Hence job enrichment, under the cover of humanization of the work process, was a heaven-sent strategy for squeezing more work out of the current labour force without adding to the existing cost pressures.

There are some indications that the Swedish adherence to a socio-technical approach in a total work context – as a means of achieving both job enrichment and productive efficiency – may be influencing sections of British management. Careful and participatory pre-planning of two major plant developments in British Leyland are witness to this. Equally, we find 'enlightened' British firms which steadfastly shun the broader approach. For example, one large firm, which boasts of its adherence to job enrichment, last year attempted to ignore a trade union claim for the joint development of a 'rolling' manpower plan.

Clearly, British unions should not allow themselves to be trapped by their recognition that attempts to improve the quality of working life are of great importance. Neither should they tolerate job enrichment being advanced separately, either as a bargaining subject or as an innovatory managerial practice. Unions should insist that the quality of working life can only be improved by a comprehensive and coordinated concern with improvements in the total work situation, and in the total remuneration package. For these two concepts are interlocking. There is a clear need to bargain about the *whole sequence* of managerial decisions which really control job content, security and prospects. These *start* with the prior planning of the human aspects and labour requirements of new investment programmes.

The experience in the 1960s of 'productivity bargaining' suggests some scepticism about managerial interest in job enrichment. Some, at least, of such bargaining pursued job enlargement, often in ways that reduced the social mixing that might make working hours tolerable. It did not noticeably contribute to job security and employment prospects in the subsequent recession (1970–72) and in many cases shop-floor controls built around

earlier pay systems were lost, and managerial controls strengthened.

Besides, the bargaining objectives of the 1970s must create new
areas of suspicion over the objectives of 'enrichment'. Trade
unions are striving harder for a shorter actual working week,
and working year. Inevitably the suspicion will be there that
'enrichment' of the job, improving the 'quality of working life',
is being emphasized to divert attention from the enrichment of
life through increased leisure. As job opportunities for manual
workers, especially in manufacturing, are on a trend of absolute
decline, why not aspire to spread the reduced labour input
requirement over more workers through less work and more
leisure for each?

A final doubt remains. The work of Elton Mayo, and his
consequent discovery of the 'Hawthorne effect', appears largely
to have been overlooked. Mayo in a series of experiments found
that by varying working conditions – even by making them worse
– the productive efficiency of a particular group of workers under
scrutiny could be improved. The key to this odd behaviour lay
in the fact that the particular group of workers *were* 'under
scrutiny'. This led to enhanced group and individual feelings of
importance, which were translated into greater work effort. As
yet, none of the experiments in job enrichment seem to have been
tested to ascertain how much enrichment of a job is, in fact,
attributable to this short-term 'Hawthorne effect'.

Beyond Contract: Work, Power and Trust Relations

Alan Fox

Reprinted with permission from *Beyond Contract: Work, Power and Trust Relations*, Faber & Faber, 1974, pp. 362–9.

The high-trust relationship has been characterized as one in
which the participants share certain ends or values; bear towards
each other a diffuse sense of long-term obligations; offer each

other spontaneous support without narrowly calculating the cost or anticipating any equivalent short-term reciprocation; communicate freely and honestly; are ready to repose their fortunes in each other's hands; and give each other the benefit of any doubt that may arise with respect to goodwill or motivation. Conversely, in a low-trust relationship the participants have divergent ends or values; entertain specific expectations which have to be reciprocated through a precisely balanced exchange in the short term; calculate carefully the costs and anticipated benefits of any concession; restrict and screen communications in their own separate interests; seek to minimize dependence on each other's discretion; and are quick to suspect, and invoke sanctions against, illwill or default on obligations.

It is clear that the low-trust syndrome as we have defined it imposes limitations on human collaboration. Their severity varies with the task, technology, and aspirations of the participants, but no system of interdependence can be other than impeded in some measure by these wary arm's-length relations between superordinates and subordinates. The relevant power-holders in industrializing countries over the past two centuries have considered, however, that the costs of such limitations as they were aware of were outweighed by the benefits of the extreme division of labour from which the limitations sprang. So long as they could rely on holding a supervisory, planning, and managerial superstructure within a high-trust fraternity of shared values, status, and kindred expectations, they could see the system as viable. Hence the uneasiness as low-trust responses show signs of creeping up the hierarchy, and the strong rearguard action against 'breakaway' symptoms among supervisors and other white-collar staffs.

We have noted forces making for the intensification and universalization of low-trust responses, and saw that the projection of these tendencies towards their extreme form implies conflict of a more fundamental and radical kind than pluralistic interpretations of society are happy to accept. But we also note certain counter-tendencies. Advanced technology may not necessarily reknit lower ranks into a somewhat higher-trust fabric than we know at present, but there are some signs in this direction. Technology may in some cases, therefore, marginally help power-holders by mitigating their difficulties in this respect, though it appears unlikely to eliminate them. What is evident, however, is that such conscious efforts as we are now witnessing towards reversing or modifying the scientific management approach are inspired by the same motivations as led to its adoption – namely economic efficiency, growth, or profit. High-trust relations are pursued, not for their own sake, but because they are thought to evoke commitment to managerial ends, improve performance, promote adaptability and receptivity to change, stabilize the labour force. On present showing we may expect a few of the more progressive and sophisticated power-holders to be increasingly alert to possibilities of changing technology or organization in a high-trust direction, provided the benefits seem likely to outweigh the costs over the long period. In describing their motives as those of economic expediency we are not arguing that particular operational managers who may initiate and carry out such changes are necessarily acting under these motives. They may believe the changes to be desirable for their own sake, quite apart from the expected economic consequences. But whether they are allowed by power-holders above them to introduce the changes will depend on whether these can be justified in terms of economic or financial rationality. When, therefore, a manager who is carrying out change speaks and acts with obvious moral conviction he is likely to be doing so only under sanction from others who ultimately control his behaviour and perceive his policies to be congruent with their own goals. The fact that prudence normally deters them from making their position explicit causes the observer's attention to remain focused on the initiating manager and his moral convictions; a situation which may mislead those seeking insight into managerial goals in modern business. The crucial goals and criteria are those which inform the limits within which decision-makers are constrained to act.

Such considerations support the judgement that high-trust relations in work are at present a byproduct of decisions directed towards very different ends. They will remain so in any system, whether privately or communally owned, where prime importance is attached to maximizing the economic return on resources. Under the private profit system the pressures in this direction are of course very strong. The significance of public ownership is that, after removing this structurally induced disposition

common to the controllers of resources, politically effective
groups in society are free to make different choices. They may
of course make the same ones. The ideology of Western-style
economic growth now sweeping the world presents those who
would have them choose differently with an uphill task. Public
ownership is the necessary but certainly not the sufficient
condition for any change in the primary objectives and methods
of work organizations.

We are faced, then, with two different possible motives for
moving away from organizational patterns which generate
low-trust relations. The first springs from the argument that in a
context of accelerating change where personal involvement and
a willing creative approach to problem solving are at a premium,
the promotion of high-trust relations through structural change
offers long-term benefits outweighing any short-term costs. The
argument may meet practical disagreement, and usually does,
but at least the criteria being used are widely understood. The
other motive has hitherto been the concern of a tiny minority.
This is the conviction that high-trust relations are qualitatively
superior and desirable for their own sake. As applied to work, this
conviction takes the form of criticizing the extreme division of
labour and its impoverishing effect upon men's personalities and
the relationships between them. From the individual's subjective
consciousness of work to groups and class relations, the critic of
extreme division of labour can argue that it produces experiences
and relations which fall far short, in qualitative terms, of the best
within human reach. Implicit in many judgements of this sort is
a conception of the individual as an autonomous moral agent,
developing himself by making and accepting the responsibility
for, and consequences of, significant choices, and in the process
maintaining relationships of mutual trust and cooperation with
others.

Measured by these standards, industrial society clearly pays a
price for its mastery of nature. The price has to be paid, of course,
not merely in the context of work. We have sought to identify
dynamics within the job situation which also operate within all
trading, commercial, and business relations in industrial society
and lead to the same kind and quality of interaction. We see
pervading every aspect of human existence an ever extending
network of commercialized relations – the offering of specific

services in exchange for specific sums of money; the carefully calculated and jealously guarded reciprocation; the draining from the transaction of all expressive or other extraneous considerations; the quick suspicion of fraud or default; the ever increasing battery of State-initiated protections and penalties designed to control and punish the bad faith that otherwise increasingly accompanies the impersonal, specific contract. The arguments have been that these dynamics apply in exactly the same way to work relations and spring from the same basic thrust of the industrial and commercial order – the thrust towards extreme differentiation and specialization of function. This is the movement which, in rendering the relevant social relations ever more narrowly specific, squeezes out the reciprocal diffuseness of obligations which is the necessary condition of high-trust relations. It is the movement from social to economic exchange. There is no concern here, however, to mount a simplistic lament for 'the world we have lost'. Quite apart from other considerations, any implication that the profit and loss account of industrialization could be presented in those limited terms would of course be absurdly facile. Unquestionably the choices by power-holders of certain patterns of work organization as against other possible patterns have involved their own and subsequent generations in paying a price, but the gains for which the price was paid have to be seen in terms not only of cars, washing machines, and television sets, but also of the elimination of much poverty, material suffering, disease, and early death, not to mention the vast expansion of individual freedom, with its potentiality for creativity and happiness as well as for boredom and misery.

These truisms are mentioned only to lead up to the points that, except in so far as high-trust relations serve economic values, men are faced with a choice, and that rational choice implies some knowledge of the costs and benefits of alternatives. It has already been suggested that unless power-holders perceive high-trust relations as offering economic benefits which exceed costs they will prefer traditional patterns and policies. But events show increasingly that rank and file employees are not powerless and do not necessarily have to accept the choices of their masters. As yet, however, their preferences show no marked rejection of those choices. They demonstrate marginal disagreement about the distribution of the product and about the precise nature of some aspects of the productive process, but none about its essential characteristics of hierarchy and extreme differentiation of function. These are accepted as necessary conditions for the production of abundance. How far this represents a rational choice is debatable. Many are conscious of material need but have little or no experience of the intrinsic satisfactions of high-discretion work; they are increasingly socialized to raise their material aspirations but never to examine critically the quality of their work life and relationships. In these circumstances they are hardly likely to opt for lower material standards in exchange for intrinsic rewards of whose nature they are aware, if at all, only by repute. It is sometimes argued that with growing affluence diminishing returns will set in; that the pleasure derived at the margin of a rising material standard of life will decline relatively to the consciousness of being deprived of intrinsic satisfaction in work. The behaviour of middle and upper classes throughout the world are no help here, for they comprise those fortunate strata whose members receive ever larger financial rewards as they move ever upward in the high-trust fraternity of work. It would be prudent to bear in mind, however, that given the ingenuity of man in devising new mechanical delights, personal possessions, and status objects, the appropriate reference here may be not to the diminishing marginal rate of substitution but to the appetite which grows by what it feeds upon.

In sum, then, it is clear that there are many questions to ask when we try to assess the likelihood of those low-discretion employees who are relatively comfortably placed becoming prepared to sacrifice some material well-being in order to gain certain intrinsic rewards from work. Should their aspirations move in this direction, there seems no obvious reason to suppose that our present industrial system would be unable to adapt appropriately provided the adjustments sought were relatively marginal, though it is likely that even these would generate stresses of no small order. But marginal changes in job structure could be expected to produce only marginal changes in trust relations and it is conceivable that in time men might seek more than this.

In pursuing the implications of a more fundamental shift of preferences we have to enlarge our view to include the other dimension of trust relations – the lateral dimension which covers those in similar job situations within the organization. There emerged a typology of four different combinations of vertical and lateral trust. First, at one extreme are the favoured who enjoy high-trust relations along both dimensions; second, at the other the deprived who enjoy them along neither. Third, in between are those in high-discretion roles who find themselves in low-trust rivalry with their fellows; and fourth, those who, though deprived of the intrinsic satisfactions of high-discretion work, derive the support, security, and fellowship of high-trust relations with fellow employees.

Which of these patterns would men be likely to choose, given knowledge of the alternatives? Some would opt for the third pattern; men specially confident of their own powers not infrequently relish competititon, for fairly obvious reasons. It is difficult to conceive reasons why persons of average mental health should choose the second, and why prefer the fourth if the first is available? Lack of ambition; fear of responsibility; and the absence of talent are usually offered as possible reasons but these beg questions rather than answer them. Within a society and a culture where ambition is apt to be an individualistic thrust towards personal achievement, recognition, and success; where 'acceptance of responsibility' is often no more than the upward reach of the confident man who knows that his particular abilities can supply a particular demand; and where 'talent' refers to whatever abilities and aptitudes happen to be marketable within the currently prevailing economic arrangements, there need be no surprise that many fail to clear these definitional and practical hurdles, especially when to them are added the inequalities of life chances which so patently inhibit or frustrate aspirations. Social structures and work arrangements are, however, theoretically conceivable which would invite and promote high-discretion contributions in a setting where no premium was placed on individualistic ambition and self-assertion; where men ready to offer their involvement, judgement, and discretion were not deterred from so doing by the prospect of being drawn out to a fine point of 'success' or 'failure'.

Pursuit of this line of thought suggests that the reasons why some might choose the fourth pattern include not only those features of the existing social order which depress and inhibit aspirations but also those which render many high-discretion roles unattractive because they are perceived as being accompanied by characteristics collectively designated 'the rat race' – individualistic rivalry, jealousy, disproportionate valuation placed on personal success and recognition, the competitive tricks of one-upmanship, the jockeying for position, the dread of failure. To the extent that this argument is valid, we can say that those who would choose to forgo high-discretion work in order to enjoy high lateral trust relations would not have to make this sacrifice if offered the choice of work which offered high-trust relations in both directions. We thus arrive at the first pattern, the choice of many socialists down the ages. The arguments here have sought to suggest certain of the logical implications of their vision; implications with which, of course, they would not necessarily have agreed. These implications bear upon the nature of work; the values by which it is designed; the types of experience and relationship which it generates; and the ideologies which encourage men to seek from it rewards of one kind rather than another. To attempt to explore such further implications as what type of economy, society, and polity would be required to contain and express this vision would of course be a venture in its own right. All that can be said is that it would be profoundly different from the one we know now.

This alone will be enough to convince many that such theorizing is mere self-indulgence. Yet it may serve at least two useful purposes. First, it contributes, however imperfectly, to that process of social questioning by which we can convince ourselves that 'what is' need not mean 'what must be'; that there are alternative social patterns towards which we could move given the resolve. Second, it can help us to set up standards by which not only to judge what we have already created, but also to decide what to avoid in the acts of social creation which lie ahead. Most of these will be, not *macro* choices shaping whole social structures, but *micro* choices which though small in themselves can nevertheless between them affect the quality of society and its predominant culture – perhaps reinforcing the quality which currently prevails or on the other hand challenging it with different values. This illuminates the sense in which every act of choice can be important. Unless we have some insight into the probable consequences of different alternatives and are encouraged to evaluate them, choices will be made either in ignorance or in the light of evaluations made by others with whom we may or may not be in agreement.

Union Attitudes to Job Satisfaction

Kenneth Graham

This paper was specially written for this volume, based on a lecture titled 'Union Attitudes to Job Satisfaction and Technology' given at a seminar on 'Job Satisfaction and Design in a Technological World' at Manchester Business School, 13 June 1973.

The attitudes of trade unionists to current or anticipated developments in the field of employment are shaped by trade union objectives and by the means and methods that unions use to pursue those objectives. An understanding of the aims of trade unions and of how they go about their job is essential if their attitudes to job satisfaction and technology are to be understood.

Trade Union Objectives

Thirty years ago the TUC formulated the broad objectives of the trade union movement. After improving wages and conditions, the TUC saw these objectives as:

1. Increased real national income and an increased Share for workers and their families
2. Full employment: this meant a suitable job for every worker
3. The extension of work people's influence over the purposes and policies of industry.

More recently in its evidence to the Royal Commission on Trade Unions and Employers Associations (the Donovan Commission), the TUC elaborated its objectives, some of which are directly relevant to job satisfaction and technology. These are listed below although not in any order of priority (and they are not exhaustive).

1. Improved terms and conditions of employment
2. Improved physical environment at work
3. Job and income security
4. Industrial democracy or greater participation in the administration of the enterprise
5. Availability of employment opportunities.

Trade Union Methods

British trade unions use a great diversity of methods relevant to job satisfaction and technology, particularly collective bargaining which is the process of negotiation with employers. This is the most important trade union method and a central feature of trade unionism. A second method is influencing government decisions in the interests of work people and their families. A further method is participating in the administration of legislation, and in the work of public bodies and agencies.

Trade unions have long recognized that the lives of working people are not only influenced by conditions within workplaces, but that external factors – in particular government action or the lack of it – are important, and have become increasingly so in recent years as successive governments have intervened more and more in industry.

Collective Bargaining

In parallel with an increased awareness of the importance of influencing factors external to the workplace, there have been changes in collective bargaining. Today, particularly over many sectors of private industry, there is greater emphasis on bargaining at the level of the plant or firm rather than at the level of the industry. There have also been changes in the scope of collective bargaining as unions have sought to bring under joint control certain aspects of a firm's operations on which decisions were formerly taken solely by the management. Issues affected by this widening of collective bargaining include manpower questions such as redundancy, redevelopment and training, and organization and methods of work.

Job Satisfaction

The question of job satisfaction is a topical one. Much of the recent increases in interest in this issue stem from positive initiatives by some managements to increase job satisfaction for certain groups of workers by altering the size and shape of individuals' jobs. These initiatives have largely been inspired by labour shortages, high labour turnover and a high rate of absenteeism, and the hope is that action to make jobs more satisfying will help to overcome these problems. In other words, the motivation for improvements in this field has largely come from managements faced with serious personnel problems caused by boredom and alienation among groups of workers. At present the Department of Employment estimate that 'several score' schemes are in operation in the UK, and there are many other schemes operating in Europe, especially in Sweden and Norway.

The fact that the existing schemes have been initiated by managements does not mean that trade unions have little or no interest in job satisfaction. Indeed, unions have been concerned with job satisfaction from their very inception. The reward that a job yields in pay is a primary objective of unions and is an important factor in determining the degree of satisfaction a worker has with his job. Another important aspect of job satisfaction has been the part unions have played in promoting better working conditions – for example, better ventilation, lighting, noise reduction and safety. Improvements in these 'hygiene' factors have at the very least removed some important causes of dissatisfaction. Side by side with this has been the reduction in the time that people actually spend at work, through a shorter working week and longer holidays. All these factors have helped to make the less intrinsically satisfying jobs, (i.e. in terms of lack of individual discretion and responsibility) more tolerable for some individuals. All these steps can be regarded as the removal of causes of dissatisfaction rather than the positive promotion of satisfaction. It must be remembered that any scheme for improving job satisfaction by changes in work organization must not be regarded as a substitute for the kind of improvements in the working environment and the terms and conditions of employment referred to above.

With regard to work organization, that is the size and shape of jobs, unions have been concerned with this throughout their history. The very title 'trade' union reflects the interest of the earliest unions in a particular job. For the most part these unions were composed of workers in a specific craft or trade and since their inception, these have strongly resisted attempts by employers to break down their jobs into lesser skilled tasks. Other unions, representing the lesser skilled, have sought to influence working arrangements and the pace of work. They have also sought promotion for their members to craft status which has led to some demarcation difficulties. These problems have been substantially eased in recent years by a number of factors, for example, by amalgamations which have reduced the number of unions; by improved procedures developed by the TUC and unions themselves for dealing with inter-union difficulties; by productivity bargains under which unions have agreed to end traditional work practices, and by unions representing skilled workers accepting a relaxation in the entry requirements to their trade. Many workers have benefited from these arrangements both in terms of pay and conditions, and in respect of job satisfaction, but it must be remembered that other workers may have lost a part of their job in the changeover and their scope for exercising their skills and initiative may have been reduced.

Change in work organization

From time to time, most managements have sought (and continue to seek) to change existing work practices which often means changing the patterns of work of particular work groups. Too frequently they have succeeded in changing these working arrangements without a proper examination of what the repercussions would be in terms of the effects on the individual worker. For example, introduction of assembly lines may perhaps be viewed in retrospect as the single greatest factor in making many jobs less satisfying. If this factor was considered by managements at all, it was very much subordinated to the economic advantages of installing this production system, and in most instances little serious consultation occurred with the workers affected.

A lesson from that experience is that any proposed change in existing methods, even when prompted by a desire to increase job satisfaction, needs to be worked out carefully in conjunction with the people directly affected in order to ensure that workers' interests are properly taken into account. Where management is motivated to change methods primarily to increase job satisfaction, it will be essential for its plans to be worked out carefully in conjunction with the people directly affected and their representatives, in order to ensure as far as possible that the changes meet their objectives, because if this is not done, any proposed changes are likely to cause considerable apprehension among workers. Of course if it is done, managements are likely to be faced with new demands: for example, the workers concerned may wish to see changes in the payment system and in training and retraining methods and opportunities.

Managements (and also trade unions) also have to bear in mind that an increase in the satisfaction of some workers may only be achieved at the expense of reducing satisfaction for others. Some of the recent experiments in job enrichment have come sadly adrift because of the active or passive opposition of supervisors who have felt threatened by the management's desire to give greater responsibilities to individual workers. It is clear that any changes in work organization must take account of the interests of all the workers concerned, and not just a section of them. Where job enrichment schemes appear to be working successfully, a new role has been developed for supervisors whereby they spend much more time on planning work and on training and other matters linked to the development of skills of workers, rather than on detailed supervision. It is essential therefore that appropriate action is taken in respect of all workers who will be affected.

The other lesson is that when a production unit is being newly established, more thought should be given to shaping the work organization and the production system to the needs of the worker. This is not only desirable in itself, it can of course be imperative for an employer in the circumstances of a particular labour market. In a full-employment, high-pay area with a high general level of education, it may be the only way he can attract and retain the requisite numbers and quality of labour.

Scope of jobs

The extent to which jobs can be made more satisfying by changes in work organization must vary considerably. At one end of the spectrum, there are jobs which clearly already provide a high degree of satisfaction – not only by the nature of the job itself but also by the prospects it provides. In such jobs, the emphasis for trade unionists must be to examine closely any projected changes which could reduce these sources of satisfaction.

At the other end of the spectrum, there are undoubtedly some jobs where the scope for increasing satisfaction by changes in work organization is marginal. The trade union emphasis there must be on providing compensations by way of pay and increased opportunities for leisure activities. It is interesting to note that the United Auto Workers of the USA has not yet been convinced of the validity of experiments at Volvo and Saab and is giving priority to seeking a substantial reduction in the length of the working week, and also a retirement age of forty for motor assembly workers. This view is probably based on the UAW's opinion that although it may be possible to build 'quality' (and expensive) cars without using assembly lines, it may not be economically possible for motor firms to do this as far as family and cheaper cars are concerned. Alternatively, the approach may simply be a traditional view of trade unions, which have long represented workers who perform unsatisfying tasks, that work is an unavoidable nuisance which must be curtailed as far as possible.

It is often said that one day technological advance will make it possible to eliminate human beings from certain production systems, in which at present they perform boring and unsatisfying tasks. This is undoubtedly true of some occupations, and the trade unions will be anxious to ensure that alternative employment with good pay and conditions, and with interesting work is available for the workers affected. However, there will be other occupations in which the main effect of technological advance will be to 'de-skill' tasks and increase the division of labour. Here, trade unions will aim to protect the interests of their members both in respect of pay and conditions and the content of jobs.

Motives

If management's motive is to implement such schemes in the hope that this will lead to workers being less concerned with pay or less attached to their union, they will be disillusioned. Similarly, they will be disappointed if their aim is to secure increased flexibility from the workforce without giving monetary rewards.

Role of the TUC

At present, the TUC is represented with the CBI and the Department of Employment on a Tripartite Steering Group on Job Satisfaction which is investigating the possibility of introducing research into this subject, and considering what steps are needed to stimulate action by industry generally, in introducing programmes designed to increase job satisfaction at the work place. The aims of the Group are:

1. Improving the content of individual jobs so as to make fuller use of workers' capacities; give scope for individual discretion and decision and more responsibility; provide variety and a more meaningful sequence of operations for the worker to carry out; and
2. Improving the organization of work so that work groups are given wider discretion for planning and organizing work among themselves providing variety by job rotation.

The Group propose to publish an explanatory booklet and, if possible, case studies; to organize conferences and seminars; to initiate experiments in industry; and to develop facilities for training in the necessary skills; and to keep themselves informed on relevant research. The TUC General Council have also supported research by the Imperial College of Science and Technology into the ICI Weekly Staff Agreement, part of which was concerned with job enrichment. The investigation covered the reasons why ICI had introduced the programme of changes covered by the agreement; the roles and attitudes of the trade union organizations involved; the issues that arose during the discussion and during the implementation of the agreement; the effects of the agreement on manning levels, redundancy, wages structures and promotion opportunities; and the response of trade unions during the implementation of the agreement.

We believe that the investigation was useful in assessing the problems for trade unions which could arise as the result of changes in work organization of the type which had taken place at ICI Ltd and we are preparing for circulation to affiliated unions in due course, a set of guidelines based on the results of the investigation, for negotiators who find themselves in similar situations. It can be expected that these guidelines will indicate firmly that three essential components of job satisfaction are job income, job security, and job status, and on these questions the issues must be faced that there are conflicting interests between employers on the one hand and workers and their trade unions on the other. These questions cannot merely be surmounted by changes in the size and shape of jobs.

Conclusion

These diverse, yet related developments reflect a large part of the response of trade unions to technological changes and to the growing aspirations of their members. Unions' attitudes to new developments are cautious; they look, and look hard, before they leap. They test new approaches in the light of the experiences of their members. Managements who ignore these essential characteristics of the British trade union movement are unlikely to be able to count on the maintenance of good industrial relations.

Humanizing Work

John Marsh

Reprinted with permission from *Journal of the Royal Society of Arts*, March 1974, pp. 209–10.

The study of man's thinking and behaviour is obviously fascinating, and in recent years we have seen the contagious expansion of research into more work situations and in society generally. A large number of case studies have emerged and the derivative techniques have often been proselytized with an almost religious fanaticism. High priests and gurus in this field have built international reputations and fortunes almost overnight. In most cases their fortunes are the only tangible result. A guru is someone who rediscovers a piece of fundamental truth about human hopes or predictable behaviour; he smothers it with expansive and expensive jargon; then he and his acolytes elevate it into a cult; he may well end up by being the missionary who went to do good and has done well for himself. A harsh comment perhaps, but we can profitably study the ephemeral effect of religious cults of the past century.

A little social science goes a long way . . . I think it is too early to employ social science experts to advise all and sundry in the workplace, as if it were a laboratory.

I have no doubt that we must continue research into human behaviour; at centres of learning there are vast armies of researchers, teachers and students concerned with relationships at work and in the community. I think one important test must be in the extent to which the behavioural sciences are needed or can be understood and applied by the healthy and robust layman in his everyday situation.

Further, some of these sciences can be of enormous help to those who are genuine casualties in their mental capacity for working and living. But who indeed is to judge whether one is a casualty requiring such specialist help in the work situation?

There is even an ethical question about my right as an employer to instruct or persuade my employee to go on behavioural science courses which may alter their attitudes and their personalities to some degree. Just as an employer I have no right to send my employees on political or religious indoctrination courses, I believe that the same principle applies as far as behavioural science techniques are concerned.

In the British scene I would think most employees resent being manipulated at work by these techniques, but I believe that they do wish to be involved in matters which concern them, which is a very different thing.

Finally on this subject, I realize that my remarks will cause annoyance to some very sincere practitioners; I would aver that the answers to many questions about human behaviour at work are more to be found in the philosophy of the ages. Man with all his virtues and weaknesses remains much the same; in spite of our much vaunted twentieth-century discoveries and our uneven but substantial material progress, it has proved so far to be the most violent century of all. We know more of the nature of physical things, but we are still searching for eternal truths based on compassion for our fellow men, and I hope we shall retain belief in forces beyond our present understanding. Where religions and ideologies have not yet succeeded will social sciences *per se* be other than a means of knowing a little more of ourselves? In what humility of perspective can we use them? The solution for individual fulfilment is likely to come from within the spirit of man, and his capacity for developing a personal philosophy.

The Nature and Context of Job Restructuring in the Engineering Industries of Europe

Ray Wild

Reprinted with permission from the paper given at the IPM National Conference, Harrogate, 1973.

The need for change in the UK

One objective of this study was to examine the significance of developments in engineering mass production systems in respect of the future situation in the UK. The availability of labour, the nature of markets and demand, emphasis on industrial democracy, government policies and possible EEC legislation are all important in this respect. In addition two other issues appear to be not only relevant but also potentially misleading.

Much of the current discussion of mass production work has been prompted by reports of exercises undertaken in other European countries. However in some respects countries such as Sweden and Norway differ substantially from the UK, hence it might be inappropriate simply to attempt to copy the type of exercise undertaken there. Examination of some of the factors which distinguish the UK from Scandinavian countries suggests that both the creation or emergence of production problems, and the manner of their solution, are possibly influenced by similar factors, the following specific cultural factors being seen as prerequisites for effective change, as well as dimensions distinguishing the UK from the Scandinavian countries:

1. A positive and cooperative attitude on the part of the workers to change
2. Workers have a strong desire for participation and accept its legitimacy
3. Absence of an instrumental orientation to work
4. 'Human', forward thinking management, having a belief in the legitimacy of worker participation
5. Industrial relations mechanisms conducive to negotiation and consultation
6. Organismic or flexible organizational structures in industry

7. High educational and living standards.

The argument that 'what is now happening in Scandinavia, will shortly happen in the UK' is not necessarily invalidated by such observations, since conditions in the UK may change, especially with the development of closer links with Europe. These observations do nevertheless suggest that change in another country is not *in itself* sufficient justification for similar changes in the UK.

Despite substantial research, it is not generally proven that highly rationalized and constrained manual work itself necessarily gives rise to worker dissatisfaction or alienation, that self-actualization is a dominating motive amongst workers, or that job dissatisfaction is necessarily dysfunctional for the organization. We must, however, dismiss this last point since it is surely no longer acceptable to argue that productivity alone is a reason for a company to seek change. Furthermore the establishment of a rationale for job restructuring provides no proof of the needs for such action. Fundamentally such proof rests with the examination of the nature of the job needs and attitudes of workers.

There are two apparent paradoxical situations. Firstly the fact that in attitude surveys amongst workers engaged on flow-line type work it is rarely found that more than 25 per cent express dissatisfaction with their jobs. Secondly it is noticeable that even when, as in the present situation, there is considerable public attention on the effects of rationalized work, UK workers – even those currently involved in industrial disputes – tend not to criticize the nature of their jobs except in terms of pay, hours, conditions etc. Thus we see that although workers may benefit from job restructuring, not only may they not necessarily seek such changes, but they may even initially resist them in order to gain other benefits. One is therefore led to the conclusion that the present absence of pressures for work changes from UK workers does not imply that such changes would not prove beneficial. Whilst dysfunctional and counter-productive worker behaviour, such as high absenteeism and turnover, low quality and high grievance activity might be seen as an indication of the need for changes, the absence of these 'indicators' cannot be taken as proof of the inappropriateness of these same changes.

Whilst the publication of a government report and the views of the EEC can only accelerate changes in the UK – if changes are seen to be required, there is a danger that the wide publicity has helped establish certain misconceptions which may in effect promote resistance to change. Such misapprehensions appear to be prevalent in respect of group-working and the nature of flow-line work. Group-working, it seems, is often mistakenly seen as an alternative production system; thus the real possibility of providing enriched and motivating work together with the use of flow-line production systems is often overlooked. Widespread reference to the work undertaken at Volvo and Saab appears to have given the impression that these companies have abandoned flow-line work, whereas in fact the real significance of their work is not their abolition of the assembly line, nor simply the enrichment of assembly work, but the provision for job enrichment within the context of flow-line work through the adoption of certain work organizational changes. The focus on the supposed need to abolish flow-line work, which stems perhaps from fundamental misinterpretations of certain well publicized exercises together with a misunderstanding of the nature of group-working and a failure to distinguish between individual job and organizational change may have the effect of exaggerating the difficulty of the solution of the problems which have been discussed. This in turn may discourage companies from either recognizing such problems, should they exist, or in looking to their solution.

The Future?

The fact that workers and unions in the UK currently appear to exhibit somewhat different orientations to their work than their colleagues in other countries cannot surely be taken as an indication of the absence of a need to consider job restructuring and work reorganization. Certainly the UK is not currently subject to the same 'pressures for such changes' as for example Sweden or Italy, nor would it be quite so easy to introduce these changes in the UK. Furthermore, the current interest in 'behaviourally oriented' changes in the UK, if based on somewhat distorted views of the nature of the changes introduced in other countries, may be seen as a reaction rather than an expression of a need. However the situation will surely change, and the need for job restructuring and work reorganization will increase.

Concern with the restructuring of an individual's work will surely be overshadowed – as evident in developments in other countries – by efforts to create autonomous, responsible work groups, within the context of worker participation and the democratization of the shop floor. Work groups pervade the industrial scene, emphasis however will be on formal functional groupings, which are of particular relevance in respect of assembly system design. The creation of formal work groups provides increased opportunity for the provision of those job attributes which are commonly considered to be desirable, by providing a vehicle for job restructuring. Further, unlike the restructuring of individual jobs, the creation of such groups permits the accommodation of workers who do not require restructured jobs.

A significant degree of group autonomy is unlikely to be achieved without consideration of the production process. For this reason it is likely that in certain circumstances rationalized and paced flow-line systems may be replaced by systems which permit responsible autonomous group-working. Equally, however, it is clear that some of the benefits of group-working will be achieved in situations which necessitate intensive material flow, low work in progress and division of operation, e.g. in the assembly of large items such as motor vehicles. It is likely, therefore, that increased attention will be given to the formation of formal functional work groups within flow-line systems. In fact, it is probable that in such situations the creation of formal functional work groups will be found to offer greater benefits than simple job changes through increases in cycle time, or formal job rotation. The use of comparatively highly mechanized and integrated assembly systems, e.g. automated assembly systems reduces the potential for added work responsibilities. However, in such cases the creation of vertical work groups integrating manual workers, supervision, technical and service workers, provides scope for increased autonomy.

Finally it will surely become more widely recognized that successful work organization, and job and work changes are both difficult to achieve, and necessarily give rise to quite widespread effects throughout various levels of an organization. The nature of such changes and the manner in which they are pursued must always be determined by local factors and thus simple supposedly 'universal' techniques must always be suspect.

This does not mean that certain broad principles or even a general policy might not be identified, but simply suggests that in the final event changes of this type must be approached on a pragmatic basis.

Further Reading: Job Satisfaction in Context

TONY BANKS, 'Autonomous Work Groups', *Industrial Society*, July/August 1974. pp. 10–11.

K. COATES, *Can the Workers Run Industry?* London, Sphere, 1968.

W. W. DANIELS, *Beyond the Wage Work Bargain*, London, P.E.P. 1970.

T. H. FITZGERALD, 'Why Motivation Theory doesn't Work', *Harvard Business Review*, July/August 1971.

H. A. TURNER, G. CLACK AND G. ROBERTS, *Labour Relations in the Motor Industry*, London, Allen and Unwin, 1967.

H. J. J. VAN BEINUM, *Morale of the Dublin Busmen*, London, Tavistock Institute, 1966, Chapter 7.

R. WILD AND D. BIRCHALL, 'Means and Ends in Job Restructuring', *Personnel Review*, Vol. 2, No. 4, Autumn 1973, pp. 18–24.

Bibliography

T. BURNS (Ed.) *Industrial Man*, London, Penguin, 1969.

M. BUTTERISS, *Job Enrichment and Employment Participation – a Study*, London, Institute of Personnel Management, 1971.

B. CARROLL, *Job Satisfaction*, New York, New York State School of Industrial and Labour Relations, Key Issues No. 3.

R. COOPER, *Job Motivation and Job Design*, London, Institute of Personnel Management, 1974.

R. FORD, *Motivation through the Work Itself*, American Management Association, 1970.

R. M. GAGNÉ (Ed.) *Psychological Principles in Systems Development*, Holt, Rinehart & Winston, 1965.

C. GREENE, 'The Satisfaction – Performance Controversy', *Business Horizons*, October 1972, pp. 31–41.

R. J. HOUSE AND L. A. WIGDOR, 'Herzberg's dual-factor Theory of Job Satisfaction and Motivation: A Review of the Evidence and a Criticism', *Personnel Psychology*, Vol. 20, Winter 1967. pp. 369–89.

M. LIU, 'Putting the Job Satisfaction Debate in Perspective', *Management International Review*, 4–5, 1973, pp. 27–36.

J. R. MAHER (Ed.) *New Perspectives in Job Enrichment*, New York, Van Nostrand Reinhold, 1971.

E. J. MILLER AND A. K. RICE, *Systems of Organisation*, London, Tavistock, 1970.

H. M. F. RUSH, *Job Design for Motivation*, Conference Board, 1971.

P. P. SCHODERBEK AND W. E. REIF, *Job Enlargement: Key to Improved Performance*, Ann Arbor, University of Michigan, Bureau of Industrial Relations, 1969.

M. SCOTT MYERS, *Every Employee a Manager*, New York, McGraw-Hill, 1970.

W. T. SINGLETON, *Man-Machine Systems*, London, Penguin, 1970.

SOCIAL POLICY RESEARCH LTD, 'Worker Participation in Britain', *Financial Times*, Business Study, 1974.

G. THOMASON, *Experiments in Participation*, London, Institute of Personnel Management, 1971.

G. THOMASON, *Improving the Quality of Organisation*, London, Institute of Personnel Management, 1973.

H. C. VAN BEEK, 'The Influence of Assembly Line Organisation on

Output, Quality and Morale', *Occupational Psychology*, Vol. 38, 1964, pp. 161–72.

V. H. VROOM AND E. L. DECI (Eds.) *Management and Motivation*, London, Penguin, 1970.

P. B. WARR (Ed.) *Psychology at Work*, London, Penguin, 1971.

Index